EMPIRICAL ANTHROPOLOGY

The Editors

Georg Pfeffer is a Professor emeritus of Social and Cultural Anthropology at the Free University of Berlin, Germany.

Nibedita Nath is a Lecturer in the Department of Anthropology, Government Women's College, Sambalpur, Odisha, India.

Empirical Anthropology

Issues of Academic Friends and Friends in the Field

Felicitation volume in the honour of Prof. Deepak Kumar Behera

Edited by
Georg Pfeffer
Nibedita Nath

CONCEPT PUBLISHING COMPANY PVT. LTD.
NEW DELHI-110059

ISBN-13: 978-93-86682-36-9

First Published 2018

Published and Printed by

Since 1974

Concept Publishing Company Pvt. Ltd.
A/15-16, Commercial Block, Mohan Garden,
New Delhi-110059 (India)
T : 91 11 25351460, 91 11 25351794
E : publishing@conceptpub.com, *W*: www.conceptpub.com

Cataloging in Publication Data--Courtesy: D.K. Agencies (P) Ltd. <docinfo@dkagencies.com>

Empirical anthropology : issues of academic friends and friends in the field / edited by Georg Pfeffer, Nibedita Nath.

pages cm

"The present volume has been written in honour of Professor Deepak Kumar Behera by his friends and colleagues of the past decades"—Preface.

Includes bibliographical references and index.

ISBN 9789386682369

1. Tribes—India—Social conditions. 2. Tribes—Health and hygiene—India. 3. Anthropology—Fieldwork—India. I. Behera, Deepak Kumar, honouree. II. Pfeffer, Georg, 1943- editor. III. Nath, Nibedita, editor.

LCC GN635.I4E47 2018 DDC 305.800954 23

PREFACE

The present volume has been written in honour of Professor Deepak Kumar Behera by his friends and colleagues of the past decades. He is felicitated as a meticulous teacher who was always full of understanding for his students, as an untiring researcher, and as an administrator full of energy and integrity. Moreover, he has represented Indian anthropology for ten years on the governing board of the *International Union of Anthropological and Ethnological Sciences* and as such, has obtained the unconditional respect and the lasting friendship of innumerable anthropologists of all continents.

Professor Behera came to study anthropology in the 1970s and the early 1980s, when he was the research assistant of his academic mentor, Professor S.N. Ratha. His Ph.D. preparation implied extended empirical research within the multi-faceted Christian community of Odisha which made him conceive and report on the various congregations containing members of different castes and tribal units, and according to certain criteria, the latter was distributed across a number of denominations. Later research concentrated upon the *Scheduled Tribe* of the Kisan in the Sambalpur District, before a project on *Ashram* Schools and others in the tribal area provided the major theme of our scholar for the rest of his life. Children and their conditions and rights made-up the subject which he studied and taught. Children were also the cause for which he fought relentlessly facing national and international decision-makers. The basic content of his message was to remove the dominant authoritarian and patronizing attitude towards children and *demand* what is their due in a democratic society. Children have a right to live and grow-up without fear and poverty, ignorance and exploitation, but neither the authorities responsible, nor the general ethical standards of adults are sufficiently activated to safeguard this right. The publications of Professor Behera's research have shown how children continue to be injured and insulted, neglected and bullied simply because they are physically weaker. On conferences and in specific committees he has introduced children to personally voice their anger over the malpractices and their demand to be taken seriously.

International communication among anthropologists is another strong point of Dr. Behera. He has been a visiting Professor at German Universities and he has, among others, provided German, French and Australian anthropologists with selfless help and the most reliable support one can imagine. In the course of these endeavours, he has also provided the younger anthropologists of Sambalpur University with many opportunities to collaborate with the foreigners in these complicated and strenuous efforts of ethnographic research and subsequently complete their dissertations on the results of their extended fieldwork. This volume will introduce such research efforts of his anthropological friends in India and it will demonstrate how the international guests in Odisha were supported by Professor Behera to find new friends in the field.

ACKNOWLEDGEMENTS

We take this opportunity to thank all the contributors to this volume who have joined us in felicitating Professor Deepak Kumar Behera, Vice Chancellor, Sambalpur University and Professor, Department of Anthropology, Sambalpur University, Odisha, India. Their academic generosity has enabled us to complete this project successfully. This volume **"Empirical Anthropology: Issues of Academic Friends and Friends in the Field"** is the result of their scholarship and hard work. However, we remain responsible for the shortcomings, if any in this volume. We are also thankful to our colleagues, friends and family members who encouraged us time and again to move forward to complete the project. Last but not the least; we are thankful to Concept Publishing Company Pvt. Ltd., New Delhi for showing interest in publication of the felicitation volume.

Georg Pfeffer
Nibedita Nath

CONTENTS

BIO-NOTES OF THE CONTRIBUTORS

Atal, Yogesh began his career as Assistant Professor of Social Anthropology at the University of Saugar in the year 1959. He was the Director of Research at ICSSR, New Delhi and Secretary-General AASSREC. He has also worked as Regional Adviser, Principal Director, UNESCO. Prof. Atal is author of a number of books and has edited nearly 40 books and monographs for UNESCO. Besides being an internationally acclaimed social Scientist, Prof. Atal is a poet and a littérateur. After retiring from UNESCO, Professor Atal functioned as Director-General of the Indian Institute of Education. He also taught for a while at the Birla Institute of Management Technology, New Delhi. He was Chairman of the Programmes Committee of the Indian Association of Social Science Institutions (IASSI) and served as a Member of the ICSSR. He was also a Member of the Governing Board of the G. B. Pant Social Science Institute, Allahabad and the Governing Board of the National Institute of Health and Family Welfare, Government of India. He was editor of the Hindi Research Journal *Manav* brought out by the Ethnographic and Folk Culture Society, Lucknow. He now serves as a Member of the Administrative Reform Group of the Planning Board of Rajasthan. Besides, he is Editor-in-Chief of the IASSI Quarterly: *Contributions to Indian Social Sciences.* He is also Professor Emeritus at the Madhya Pradesh Institute of Social Science Research, Ujjain. He is a Member of the Indian National Commission for Co-operation with UNESCO, Ministry of Human Resource Development, Government of India.

Email: *yogatal@gmail.com*

Berger, Peter obtained his Ph.D. from Berlin in the year 2004. He is Associate Professor of Indian Religions and the Anthropology of religion at the Faculty of Theology and Religious Studies of the University of Groningen. His ethnographic research since 1996 focuses on the Adivasi communities of South Odisha. His books include his ethnography of the Gadaba, *Feeding, Sharing and Devouring: Ritual and Society in Highland Odisha* (De Gruyter, 2015) and he co-edited *Ultimate Ambiguities: Investigating Death and Liminality* (Berghahn, 2016), *The Modern Anthropology of India* (Routledge, 2013), *The Anthropology of Values* (Pearson, 2010) and *Fieldwork: Social Realities in Anthropological Perspective* (Weissensee, 2009).

Email: *p.berger@rug.nl*

Bhattacharya, Kumkum Professor, Department of Social Work, Visva-Bharati has been teaching since 1979. She has wide experience of research among tribes of eastern India, especially the Santals and other minority communities. One of her areas of interest is culture-personality studies and the various ways in which minorities and marginalized communities constitute the plurality of Indian civilization. She is also interested in understanding the ways in which minorities and marginalized communities adjust and adapt to plural situations. The other abiding area of academic interest is revisiting Tagore's ideas of Rural Reconstruction and the role of a university in extension activities. She has recently published *Rabindranath Tagore: Adventure of Ideas and Innovative Practices in Education,* Springer International (2014).

Email: *kmkm.bh@gmail.com*

Bhattacharya, R.K., Ph.D. and M.Sc. in Anthropology, the University of Calcutta, served as Director, Anthropological Survey of India from 1993 to 2002. He held dual charge of the Raja Ram Mohun Roy Library Foundation for a year and subsequently of the Eastern Zonal Cultural Centre for about four years. He joined Indira Gandhi Centre for the Arts, New Delhi as Professor, Janapada Sampada in 2002. His research interests are study of the Muslims and the communities of various tribes of our country. He has worked in and steered the all-India *People of India* project. He has published many articles in books; he has edited volumes and has published his Ph.D. dissertation as a book, *Moslems of Rural Bengal* (1993).

Bhoola, Sheetal is a lecturer and a post-doctoral student at the University of Kwa-Zulu Natal, South Africa. She teaches Sociology and Anthropology at under-graduate level and her Ph.D. focused on Culinary Tourism initiatives in Durban, Kwa-Zulu Natal, South Africa. She has also studies on The Indian Diaspora, Food, Anthropology and Tourism. Her current research focuses on Passenger Migrant Indians in South Africa and their progression to social mobility. She has published many papers in both local and international academic journals.

Email: *sheetalbhoola@elkomsa.net*

Bhowmick, Pradip K. is Associate Professor in Rural Development Centre, IIT, Kharagpur since 1990. He has done his Post-doctoral from Ranchi University (Jharkhand). He obtained his Ph.D. degree from Indian Institute of Technology, Kharagpur (West Bengal). A total number of twelve scholars have completed Ph.D. under him. He has published more than 30 papers in different peer reviewed, national and international journals and edited books. He has published more than 15 books. Prof. Bhowmick is the Evaluator-*Cum*-Facilitator of CAPART (Eastern Region) under Ministry of Rural Development, Government of India. He is the editor of the journal Man and Life.

Email: *pradipb@hijli.iitkgp.ernet.in*

Goswami, Sebanti was formerly attached to the Calcutta Medical College, Kolkata. Recently, she is an Associate Professor of the Department of Obstetrics and Gynaecology, Malda Medical College and Hospital.

Kakoty, Sangeeta is an Associate Professor and HoD, Department of History, Arya Vidyapeeth College, Guwahati-16, Assam. She has qualified UGC-NET. She has 17 years of teaching experience. Besides this, she is a News Presenter (Casual) in English (N.E. News) for Doordarshan (since 2000, B "High" Drama artist with All India Radio, Guwahati (since 2003), Anchor for various Stage and Television programmes (since 1994) and Voice-over artist for several documentaries and advertisements (since 1995).

Email: *sksk301@gmail.com*

Luithle-Hardenberg, Andrea is a lecturer in the Department of Cultural Anthropology at the Goethe University, Frankfurt/ Main. *Luithle-Hardenberg has taught in the Department of Cultural and Social Anthropology at the Asia-Orient-Institute, University of Tuebingen from 2011-2016*. She has conducted extensive fieldwork in India (Gujarat and Orissa) and in Kyrgyzstan. She received her Ph.D. in Cultural Anthropology from the Free University, Berlin. Her Ph.D. thesis (2006/11) "Die Reise zum Ursprung" ("The Journey to the Origins") establishes the importance of the pilgrimage to Shatrunjaya for the collective memory and the identity of the Shvetambara Jains in Gujarat. Her first post-doctoral project focused on Alexander Walker's historical accounts of the Shvetambara community in early 19th century Gujarat. It has led to the international joint volume Cooperation, Contribution and Contestation: The Jain Community, Colonialism and Jainological Scholarship. Her current habilitation research project, "Sacral Resources in Secular India" deals with Shvetambara child ascetics (bal munis and bal sadhvis).

Email: *a.luithle@gmx.net*

Marak, Queenbala is at present working as an Assistant Professor in the Department of Anthropology at North-Eastern Hill University, Shillong, India. She has received her BA, MA, and Ph.D. degree in Anthropology. Her research interests mainly lie in the anthropology of food, tribal enthnography, material culture, and prehistoric anthropology.

Email: *qmarak@gmail.com*

Medhi, Biranchi Kumar was the HoD of the Department of Anthropology, Gauhati University, Assam. Presently, he is working as a Guest Professor in ACE, Research and Training Centre, Guwahati. He has published around 85 papers in different national and international journals and edited books. He has guided a total number of 22 Ph.D. scholars. He has attended a good number of seminars. He is the member of different bodies. Such as founder member of Indian National Confederation and Academy of Anthropologists (INCAA). He is life member of North East Council for Social Science Research and Anthropological Society of North East India. His areas of specialization are material culture, social relations, Health, religion, arts and crafts, social structure, urban problems, ethnicity etc.

Email: *birinchimedhi@rediffmail.com*

Nath, Nibedita is a Lecturer in the Department of Anthropology, Government Women's College, Sambalpur since 2014. She completed her Ph.D. in the year 2007 under Sambalpur University availing Doctoral Fellowship from ICSSR, New Delhi. She has secured first class first position at B.A., M.A. and M. Phil. levels under Sambalpur University. She was the recipient of OSANY AWARD for being the best graduate of humanities. She received gold medal for being first class first in Post-Graduation in Anthropology and also qualified UGC-NET in 2001. She began her career as a part-time lecturer in the Department of Anthropology, Sambalpur University in 2003. Then she worked in RMRC, Bhubaneswar and NAWO, Odisha Chapter in projects funded by Win Rock International India, Ford Foundation, WHO/UNDP/World Bank, SWISS AID and Trocaire. In between she has also worked as a guest faculty in JISSAR, Bhubaneswar and in Department of Anthropology and MSW Programme in Sambalpur University. She was a lecturer at KIIT school of Social Sciences, KIIT University from 2011-2014. She has to her credit visited Europe for the international conference *Childhoods* held at University of Oslo, Norway. She was the member of International Union of Anthropological and Ethnological Sciences (IUAES). He has published more than 25 papers in different national, international journals and edited volumes. Dr. Nath has authored one book and is the associate editor of two volumes and editor of two books. Her current areas of interest are children and childhood, women and tribal studies.

Email: *nibedita_nath@rediffmail.com; drnibedita.nath@gmail.com*

Otten, Tina (Ph.D.) teaches at the Institute of Ethnology of Westphalia-Wilhelms-University of Muenster, Germany. Earlier, she has held appointments at Free University of Berlin and Ruhr-University Bochum. Research focuses on ways in which people conceptualize social identity, experience change and in the different modes in which new ideas are absorbed and influence ritual and political structure, medicine, gender- and kinship relations. Her Ph.D. dealt with concepts of illness, focusing on healing rituals and social change among Rona people of Odisha and was obtained at the Free University of Berlin, Germany. Recent post-doc research, granted by ESRC and basedat the School of Oriental and African Studies, University of London, investigated social and political relations in Phulbani, Odisha. Earlier research, conducted with grants of the German Research Foundation, focused on new emerging rituals and oral epics, and its relation to historical royal and recent political structure in southern Odisha, India.

Email: *tina.otten@gmx.de*

Pfeffer, George (born in 1943) completed his Ph.D. in the subject of Ethnology at Freiburg University in 1970. The title of his dissertation is "Paria Groups of the Punjab". After fieldwork in coastal Odisha, he completed his post-doctoral degree at Heidelberg University on the Sasana Brahmins of Puri in Odisha. Since 1980, Pfeffer has conducted research on tribal societies in Western Odisha. He was a Professor of Social and Cultural Anthropology at the Free University of Berlin between 1985 and 2008.

Email: *gpfeffer@gmx.com*

Rath, S. N. was Former Professor of Sociology and Social Anthropology, Sambalpur University, Orissa. He is presently working as Dean of Humanities Social Sciences-*cum*-Director, Alluri Seetharama Raju Centre for Tribal Studies, Mahatma Gandhi National Institute of Research and Social Action, Hyderabad. He has awarded Ph.D. from Guhati. He has been trained under the fostering care of Late Professor A. Aiyappan at the Utkal University, and Professor Cora Du Bois of Harvard University. He has been active in the field of teaching and research for more than half a century, beginning as a Research Scholar from 1961-63 and then as a lecturer at the university of Gauhati in 1963 followed as the founding Professor and Head of the department of Anthropology and Sociology, Sambalpur University, Orissa, from 1976-1996. He has successfully guided 16 Ph.D. scholars. Professor Ratha's research output includes three books, two edited volumes and more than a hundred papers. Professor Ratha, now in his 21st year of retirement from formal service, has been as active as ever in teaching and research. He is in the executive committees of many National and the International Academic bodies including the 'International Union of Anthropological and Ethnological Sciences'. He was awarded the Professor D. N Majumdar Memorial Medal 2003 for Field Work and empirical data based publications by the Indian Social Science Association.

Email: *snratha@rediffmail.com*

Ray, Subha is the Professor in Anthropology, University of Calcutta.

Email: *srayanth@gmail.com*

Reddy, Sunita is an Assistant Professor at the Centre of Social Medicine and Community Health, School of Social Sciences, Jawaharlal Nehru University, New Delhi, India. She has taught briefly at Indian Institute of Technology, New Delhi and Department of Sociology, Delhi School of Economics, Delhi University before joining JNU in 2004. She has worked on issues of women and child health; breast-feeding practices, tribal women's health, childbirth and child rearing practices among the tribes. Her current area of research is "Medical Tourism and Reproductive Tourism", "Surrogacy" issues. She has published many articles in peer reviewed journals, contributed papers for edited volumes. She delivers lectures for Indian Foreign Service probationers. She is a core group member in formulation of various guidelines on disasters at National Disaster Management Authority, New Delhi. She is a founder member of "Anthropos India Foundation" a trust which promotes visual and action anthropology. She is also an honorary president of an organization called 'SATAT' which works for empowering women and children.

Email: *sunitareddyjnu@gmail.com*

Reichel, Eva worked as a senior lecturer at the Institute of Social and Cultural Anthropology at the Free University of Berlin/Germany. He has authored the book *Notions of Life in Death and Dying.* The other book *'The Dead in Tribal Middle India'* was published in 2009 by Manohar/ New Delhi. It is based on long term fieldwork among the Ho, a tribal community in Jharkhand and Odisha.

Email: *eva_reichel2002@yahoo.de*

Roy, Chaitali Dutta is an Associate Professor of the Department of Obstetrics and Gynaecology, IPGME&R and SSKM, Kolkata, West Bengal.

Sen Gupta, Debarupa completed her post-graduation in Anthropology. She has recently joined as the Assistant District Coordinator in the Institutional Strengthening of Gram Panchayats (ISGP) Programme-II of Panchayats and Rural Development Department, Government of West Bengal.

Singh, Anand is Proffessor of Anthropology, UKZN. He is teaching since 31 years. His areas of interest are Indian Diaspora, migration, children and youth studies, sustainable development. He has wide publications in national and international journals and books. Anand Singh has researched and published extensively on children and youth in the transformation of education in post-apartheid South Africa. He is currently the Convener of the IUAES Commission for Migration Studies, an area that he has worked extensively on since the year 2001. His current teaching includes introduction to anthropology, qualitative research methods, thoeries in anthropology and the anthropology of development.

Email: *singhan@ukzn.ac.za*

Som, Nivedita completed her Ph.D. in Anthropology. She is the Assistant Professor in the Department of Anthropology of Vivekananda College for Women, Barisha, Kolkata, West Bengal.

Email: *nivsom.som@gmail.com*

Subedi, Bamdev is a Ph.D. Scholar at the Centre of Social Medicine and Community Health in Jawaharlal Nehru University, New Delhi. Mr. Subedi received his Master's degree in Anthropology in 1998 from Tribhuvan University, Kathmandu and his M. Phil. in Social Science in Health in 2013 from JNU, New Delhi. His areas of interest are ethno-medicine, local health traditions, medical pluralism and political economy of health. Currently, Mr. Subedi is pursuing his Ph.D. on "Medical Pluralism: Perceptions, Practices and Patterns of Resort in Dang, Nepal." He has a decade-long working experience with rural communities on the issues of community health in Nepal. He has a few publications in journals and edited books.

Email: *bamdevsubedi@gmail.com*

Srivastava, Vinaya Kumar is currently serving as the head of the Department of Anthropology. He has been trained in anthropology and sociology at Department of Anthropology and Delhi School of Economics, University of Delhi. He earned his doctorate in social anthropology from University of Cambridge. Prior to joining the Department as a lecturer in 1985, he taught sociology in Hindu College and had also acted in the capacity of Teacher-in-charge of the Department of Sociology there. He has also acted as Principal of Hindu College from March 2010-2012 while on lien from Department of Anthropology. He teaches courses on anthropological theory and methods, urban anthropology, medical anthropology, tribal and peasant societies in the Department. He was awarded numerous honors and fellowships like Science Merit

Award, University Gold Medal for being the highest rank holder in Anthropology, All India Post-Graduate Scholarship from 1972-1974, National Scholarship from 1974-1976, Smt. Kunda Datar Gold Medal for being the best candidate in M.A. Sociology, R.D. Sanwal Memorial Prize for getting the highest marks in M.A. examination in Sociology, Fellowship under the Faculty Improvement Programme, 1979, National Scholarship to Study Abroad, Government of India, 1980, Commonwealth Scholarship to study Social Anthropology at Cambridge (U.K.) in 1988, Rashtriya Shiromani Award, 2006, by Delhi Telegu Society for distinguished work in anthropology, Post-Graduate Research Award, University Grants Commission, 2006.

Email: *vinaykumarsrivastav@gmail.com*

Subramanyam, V. is U.G.C. Emeritus Professor (Fellow) at Department of Anthropology, Andhra University. He has served the same department as Assistant Professor, Associate Professor and Professor since 1986 to 2010. His doctorate was earned from Andhra University in 1985 and was based on field work among Rural Muslims of Andhra Pradesh, India. He established Centre for Study of Social Exclusion and Inclusive Policy at Andhra University in 2007 with the financial support of UGC, New Delhi. He conducted several major and minor research project studies throughout his academic career. He has received grants from U.G.C, I.C.S.S.R, Ministry of Tribal Affairs, D.S.T., T.C.R. and T.I., S.S.A. and A.P. Tribal Welfare Department. He has published sixty two research articles and four books. He was appointed recently as Member with the designation of Social scientist in Backward Class Commission of Andhra Pradesh State by the Government of Andhra Pradesh.

Email: *vsubramanyam23@rediffmail.com*

Suna, Sunita is the Regional Executive for the World Student Christian Federation (WSCF) Asia Pacific Region. Presently, she is based in Hong Kong, where the regional office of WSCF is located. She received a Master's degree in MSW (Master of Social Works). Ms. Suna is from Odisha, India. She worked with Dr. Tina Otten as an interpreter while they lived in the field in Koraput district, Odisha for research work.

Wolff, Juergen taught mathematics and physics at a grammar school in Berlin/Germany. He is interested in anthropological issues all his life. He accompanied his wife on her way to 'the field' in Jharkhand and Odisha and stayed on for some months in the course of a sabbatical. He has revisited the area several times.

E-mail: *wolff-reichel@web.de*

EXPERIENCES OF FIELD-WORKING ANTHROPOLOGISTS

Issues of Academic Friends and Friends in the Field

GEORG PFEFFER AND NIBEDITA NATH

Despite various transformations, fieldwork remains at the heart of anthropological research and continues to be "the rite of passage" for aspiring anthropologists. Indeed, an immersion in "the field" and gaining knowledge through experience and interaction continue to be the predominant methods of anthropologists. What this immersion entails and how it is being transformed into knowledge has been a central topic in anthropology since the inception of the discipline. The way we think about anthropology has undergone a series of intellectual leaps through the years; yet key intricacies of anthropological fieldwork experience remain to be uncovered in order to demonstrate anthropology's potential, strengths and rigor (Spencer, 2010). The writings of Begley (2009) and Watson (1999) provide important suggestions on the issues of academic friends and friends in the field, a topic that is further elaborated in this volume. It was selected, because Professor Deepak Kumar Behera is an academic friend of all contributors and without his untiring support, the German anthropologists would not have been able to conduct field-research in the province of Odisha.

Experiencing emotions as part of anthropological research can be explored as "emotional labour" when anthropologists believe they have to "manage" their emotions to elicit knowledge. While many anthropologists have followed suit with the "confessional" literature about the "ethnographic self", which places limits on the possibility of knowing the "Other", others have made important contributions to understanding how the ethnographer's subjectivity, lived experience and relatedness in the process of fieldwork may lead to valuable insights and valid ethnographic knowledge. But despite the accumulation of self-reflective experience in anthropology, in the mid-nineties, it was still far from clear how fieldwork experience makes knowledge. The main reasons for this uncertainty included the difficulty of putting experience into writing; and the tension between two poles of framing knowledge: on the one hand, rationality and objectivity — sometimes taken to extremes in the hope of a "scientific" method — and on the other, subjectivity and intuition — sometimes taken to extremes in the postmodernist denial of realism.

Our feelings and personalities enacted through our engagements in relation to our fieldwork — whether acknowledged as part of our professional activity or not — continue to define, rather than undermine the strength of anthropological knowledge-production. Our individual trajectories in making sense of fieldwork experience sometimes mirror those of our discipline. It is not unusual to encounter young anthropologists who arrive at their first fieldwork site under the spell of romanticism, scientific idealism and the promises of "traditional empiricism," only to uncover both personal and professional challenges in becoming a participant observer.

Most anthropologists in the field will experience feelings of isolation and loneliness. However, the current conditions of the field situation add another dimension. This has contributed to further feelings of isolation, frustration, fear, distrust, insecurity, and with no clear way to seek support for both the informants and the anthropologist.

As students of anthropology, we spend most of our academic lives learning about the "field" as one of the most crucial aspects of anthropology. As anthropology is concerned with the interactions and relationships of people, we undertake fieldwork to understand the complexity of social life. This focus on long-term fieldwork is what separates anthropology from other disciplines. It is a major factor to establish a scholar as an anthropologist. She or he plays an important part in the narratives of the construct. Thus, anthropologists have chosen to embed themselves within the realities of those they study rather than distancing themselves from them (Begley, 2009).

If, very broadly speaking, we think of anthropology as the discipline of explaining the behaviour and thoughts of people bounded within a culture in terms that are intelligible to people outside that culture, then fieldwork is that part of the process which takes place when the anthropologist is dwelling among the people she or he hopes to describe. This is not to say that the anthropologist only begins to acquire knowledge in the field; we are all aware how significant the pre-fieldwork period is for establishing concepts, understandings and notions of the people and their culture.

Much recent debate on the nature of ethnography centres on the question of experience: what goes into it, what can be extracted from it, how far it determines or merely frames knowledge, its specificity and privacy *versus* its generality and availability? The debate is never far from polemic. There are those for whom subjectivism is a term of abuse – as the Freeman *versus* Margaret Mead debate seems to suggest– and those for whom it is almost a principle, the sin being the unawareness of what is methodologically unavoidable.

Against this backdrop, the volume brings into focus the anthropologists themselves and their experiences of fieldwork. It addresses the challenges and the ways that they impact on the research process itself, as well as the effects they have on the field-working anthropologists. Emotions in the field are often buried in individual memories and personal diaries, in confidential accounts to friends and family, colleagues and students. And yet, despite "scientific" efforts to exclude, tame, or redress our own feelings and personalities, subjectivity leaves its mark upon all facets of research: from the topics we select and the methods we employ, to the tone and hidden messages of our ethnographies. How do our emotional experiences, attachments and detachments affect us as both persons and researchers? How do we cope with them, integrate them, and employ them as methods for deeper understanding? How do emotions influence our participant observation? How do we reconcile the emotional and the subjective with our scientific goals, and what are the consequences of such integrations for anthropology? Are all of the above issues relevant to the training of anthropologists? The chapters in this volume engage with these questions and provide valuable insights. We portray the uneven trajectory of knowing and bear witness to the forces affecting the anthropologists and their fieldwork relations. Some of the usual difficulties surrounding the reflection upon lived experiences during fieldwork have been presented by the contributors to this volume.

The book is divided into two sections, namely, **"Issues of Academic Friends"** and **"Friends in the Field"**. The first section contains variety of articles of different taste by Indian Anthropologists. The eleven papers of the first section of the volume are placed under five sub-sections, namely **(A) Tribes, Governance and Administration, (B) Health and Food, (C) Language and Lyrics, (D) Youth** and **(E) Miscellaneous.** This section contains a number of interesting articles raising various issues by academic friends (mostly by anthropologists). The different papers of the first section of the book "Issues of Academic Friends" are as follows: State and Governance Issues in the Tribal Context, Some Ideas in the Context of Tribes of India, Ethnographic Methodological Approach for Indigenous People's Development in Cultural Perspective: A Case Study of Vulnerable Tribes in Vishakha Agency of Andhra Pradesh, India, Health and Disease among Indigenous People: Epidemiology and Ethno-Medicine, Health-Related Quality of Life of a Group of Women with PCOS: A Study in West Bengal, India; Food and Gender: A Case Study of the Matrilineal Garos, Language of the Santals: It's Lyrical Expression, Youth, Achievement and Mutual Responsibility: It's Time to Theorise on Positive. Social Inclusion among the Lodhas a VTG: An NGO Initiative, Universe of Women in the Mobile Theatre of Assam, Matrilateral Cross-cousin Marriage among the Komiti – A Telugu Speaking Caste. These chapters are extremely important as these address many contemporary anthropological issues.

The second section is a unique section which narrates field work traditions. It narrates the field work experiences of the German Anthropologists in India. The second section titled, **"Friends in the Field"** is consisting of seven papers. The section "Friends in the Field". includes the following papers: Public Vegitarianism and Public Menstruation: Staging Chastity in a Jain Pilgrim City in Gujurat, Scholarly Commitment: John Deeney and the Ho of Kolhan, Narrations of Commitment: Friends in the Field, The Field, the Anthropologist, and the Researcher, Researcher and Assistant Entering the Field: On Becoming Friends and Kin, Closeness and Disjuncture: On Friendship in the Field, Getting Bye with a Little Help of a Friend.

The second section is a unique one depicting the rich fieldwork traditions through the experience shared by a good number of German field-working anthropologists in India. Their narrations of fieldwork experiences and field data make this section a rather unusual contribution to the long list of fieldwork literature. A total number of twenty-seven scholars (mostly Indian and German anthropologists) have contributed papers to this multidimensional volume. The rich fieldwork experiences shared by the authors of the volume show the challenges and opportunities for young anthropologists who search for ways to think and talk about fieldwork, and the methodological lessons that follows:

Yogesh Atal in his article discusses thc concept of State and Governance in the tribal context. He writes that earlier studies on tribal cultures had hardly focused on the political dimension encapsulating the concepts of State and Governance. Tribal societies no longer remain the exclusive preserve of the anthropologist. He opines that today tribes are seen in a multi-disciplinary perspective; of course, the trans-disciplinary orientation provided by anthropology is still valid. Unfortunately, anthropologists are increasingly moving in other directions and becoming indifferent to tribal studies. In fact, today's tribes do not match with their earlier descriptions. He concludes by stating that we need a new approach to study State and Governance in tribal context.

Vinay Kumar Srivastava critically examines the usage of the word *adivasi* for tribal communities. He submits that we continue to use this word not realizing its implications for the psychic and social profiles of people for whom it is used. Srivastava is also concerned with the concept of "mainstream", treating it not as an empirical entity, but as an ideational one. Finally, he compares and contrasts the ideas of development and protection in the context of Indian tribes.

V. Subramanyam focusses on the newly carved state of Andhra Pradesh consisting of 27 tribes with 5.3 per cent of tribal population. He confines his analysis to the six *Particularly Vulnerable Tribal Groups* (PVTG), namely—Chenchu, Gadaba, Khond, Konda Reddy, Konda Savara, and Porja, discussing developmental issues of the PVTGs inhabiting in Vishakha Agency of Andhra Pradesh. He explains the significance of the ecological and cultural background in the context of the development of the PVTGs. Mostly descriptive by nature; his paper advocates a cultural perspective to the development of the sample PVTGs.

Reddy and **Subei** provide an epidemiological and ethno-medicinal account of health and disease among indigenous people. Some of the important questions addressed by these authors are how to define 'health', 'illness' and 'disease', and they also ponder over the difference between healing and curing as well as the illness aetiology. Health conditions of the indigenous people of India are examined in the context of globalization. The paper presents a general conceptual framework for understanding various health issues in the context of tribal India. The authors highlight some of the central categories related to health, illness, disease, aetiology, epidemiology and the contribution of medical anthropologists to the study of indigenous people.

Debarupa Sengupta *et al.* deal with the health related quality of life of a group of women with the Polycystic Ovary Syndrome (PCOS) living in West Bengal, India. The study is concerned with 80 women aged 14-38 years from the outpatient department of two medical hospitals in Kolkata and the results reveal that the health-related quality of life among the PCOS participants differs significantly with respect to their actual weight status and their perceived health status. The authors conclude that the perceived health status and actual weight status of PCOS women are likely to determine the health-related quality of life. Therapeutic intervention alone would not help much to improve the PCOS health related quality of life which will rather depend upon the awareness and a change of lifestyle.

Queenbala Marak is discussing food and gender among the matrilineal Garos. She highlights the significance of food in a community. Besides being a key component of culture, it reveals layers of identity and differences. She is of the opinion that when food choices and reasons behind the choices are studied, a divide is noticed between the sexes. In some food-getting tasks, men and women work together often completing the same tasks. On the other hand, many clearly gendered aspects reflect differential control. The divide extends to the public and private domains with the former being assigned to men while the latter is that of women.

Bhattacharya and **Bhattacharya** write on the language of the Santals and its lyrical expression. They strongly feel that decay, decadence and extinction of languages and dialects have followed intrusions of dominant people among the marginalized ones. Communication opened up when market economy was ushered in and as a consequence, communities that existed as socio-cultural entities in relative isolation or seclusion could not remain so any longer. In most cases, the changed economic system and practices sharpened and redefined the differences between the marginalized and the relatively dominant communities. Those living in relative isolation had no other option, but to develop strategies for encountering the intruders as well as negotiating over their situation. Language is and becomes a significant identity marker and communities have a strong impetus to use this marker to distinguish themselves from others.

Singh and **Bhoola** in their paper highlight the achievements of the youth and their mutual responsibility. They refer to the works of many early ethnographers who collectively emphasised on youth as a luminal transitional stage, i.e. "no longer a child but not yet adult". The paper focuses upon the positive issues in the lives of youth and their steadfastness in turning challenges into goals and outcomes. The authors not only emphasize the anthropological focus on micro-level studies, but also believe in the added value of the case study method to convey the meaning of "mutual responsibility" among youth regarding responsibilities of the entire family.

P.K. Bhowmick is reporting on the initiative of an NGO in matters of social Inclusion among the Lodha, a *Particularly Vulnerable Tribal Group* (PVTG) in West Bengal. As our society speeds forward to new technological and economic heights, it elevates some people and leaves others behind. Social exclusion can encompass life and livelihood as a whole and can severely restrict participation in social services, welfare, security networks, consumer culture, and political choice, bases of popular solidarity and also in the understanding of the circumstances surrounding the people at large. In the Indian context, exclusion revolve around institutions that discriminate, isolate, shame and deprive subordinate groups on the bases of identities like caste, religion and gender. The paper analyses various inclusive welfare measures initiated for the overall socio-economic transformation of Lodha by an organisation, namely Samaj Sevak Sangha and the Institute of Social Research and Applied Anthropology located under Narayangarh Development Block, Bidisa, Paschim Medinipur District in the State of West Bengal.

Medhi and **Kakoty**, focussing, on theatre try to depict the universe of women in the mobile theatre of Assam. The arena of performing arts is a broad one that encompasses music, dance and drama. The authors investigate the space allocated to women in the scenario of the Assam theatre. The authors raise some critical questions as a prelude to their analysis as to the space allocated to women in the arena of the performing arts and the various forms of interference by the patriarchal society and the severe discrimination of women who dared to break the shackles of convention. The authors introduce the current changes in the scenario and try to answer all of these questions by presenting empirical evidence. The paper concludes that women are still in the back seat of the project driving the Mobile Theatre of Assam.

S.N. Ratha subsequently argues that the role of kinship in regulating sex and marriage is a universal socio-cultural phenomenon. The regulations may be obligatory, permissive or prohibitory. The Komiti, a Telugu speaking South Indian trading caste, marry three categories of close relatives: the mother's brother's daughter: the father's sister's daughter and the elder sister's daughter. The first option, called *mēnārikam,* is prescriptive and resembling the Kachin type. The second one is called *ēduru* (alternative) *mēnārikam* and preferential, as is the third one, if one adopts Needham's categories for this case. The refusal of a marriage is found to be linked to the dowry, which is a deciding factor in a Komiti marriage. The demand for dowry is weighed against the economic solvency of the groom's family. Kinship terms and marriage types are interrelated. The associated kinship terminology is a function of the respective marriage type. Ratha concludes that a marriage type not so much influences the kinship terminology, because it applies to all or most marriages within the society; but rather because of the weight of the social prescription and the value attached to such marriages.

Andrea Luthle-Hardenberg article on the vital role played by ascetic values in the ethics and religious practice of the Jain religion and its community of Western India offers a personal account. She discusses some of her vivid field experiences and observations in her paper and argues that the essential conditions for a successful pilgrimage are not only the temporary wandering but also the strict observance of a vegetarian diet, as well as the equally strict observance of sexual abstinence. The basic principle of this penance is transformation: the sacrifice of physical well-being, including sexuality, is considered as the fundamental condition for attaining spiritual progress. In Jainism the fundamental restrictions of pilgrimage, namely vegetarianism and celibacy, are closely interconnected. According to this concept, eating meat corresponds with sexual aggression and demand. In contrast, sexual desires can be kept in check by means of a vegetarian way of life. Rules of gender segregation, which apply for all of northern India in general, are considered by the Jain pilgrims with a special emphasis. The paper also exemplifies the practical consequences of the strict observances of chastity and the central impact of vegetarianism.

Eva Reichel thereafter sheds light on a few crucial and sensitive moments when she was in search of a suitable field site to do fieldwork among the Ho, a tribal community in Central Eastern India. The focus was on some of those who, due to their commitment and local knowledge, contributed to implement the project of fieldwork in the early stage. They paved the way to spot "the field", to enter it and eventually settle down in a concrete house. Her collaboration was such that she thought them as "friends in the field". As a consequence, the narrations written in the paper are from a more personal angle and she has not attempted to hide a certain subjective bias.

Jurgen Wolf's contribution offers an entirely new subject by discussing the field, the anthropologist, and the researcher in the perspective of the accompanying spouse. He presents his lively experiences during a number of field-research excursions to tribal middle India, narrating the highs and lows that "the field" presented for him in the form of the difficulties he encountered while struggling to define his role adequately and the arguments and conflicts that unfolded when the perspectives informed by his training as a natural scientist collided with those of his wife, a trained anthropologist.

Otten and **Suna** vividly present the way the researcher and his or her assistant enter the Field to become friends and kin. Following the earlier analysis presented by ethnographers, they have ordered fieldwork into three phases, "preparations", "the time in the field", and "the post-fieldwork period". The entry into the field is unique and very special for each researcher, though the structure of the fieldwork process is similar in every research. Memories of the entry and friendship in the field constitute the central theme of their paper. Every community has specific normative ideas on friendship which may only partially coincide with the researcher's concepts. In the tribal villages an incorporation into the given kinship system is the general method of assigning a social position. It is required to construct formal as well as informal forms of friendship. Anthropological research in the "field" involves different levels of relationships between the actors, thus influencing directly or indirectly immediate and subsequent commitments. The entry is a unique experience for any researcher and for the local counterparts. This initial duration was emphasized by the authors along with the importance of learning the language and being part of a group. In order to be accepted, time was required. Gender roles also apply to the researcher, though perhaps not as strictly as to others.

Peter Berger is discussing the ambiguities of "friendship" in the ethnographic field. On the one hand, it is argued, making friends is a necessary corollary of the ethnographic quest of *understanding through difference* and is especially so in the initial situation many ethnographers find themselves in. Hence, relationships of closeness develop that entail many different components, for example mutual learning, commensality and conviviality, shared experiences and emotions during significant events and the establishment of trust. On the other hand, it is again the nature of the ethnographic situation — as encountered and described by this author — and the locations of the researcher in relation to her or his hosts that lead to disjunctions. Asymmetry, muteness and different temporalities are discussed in this regard. Friendship is thus a crucial, but also a highly ambivalent, volatile and problematic aspect of ethnographic fieldwork. Moreover, as a cultural category friendship cannot be taken for granted but has to be understood in a comparative perspective.

Georg Pfeffer in his paper discusses the ethnographer's dependence on a few key consultants. His article describes an anthropological field situation that these very personal relationships. Such proximity may be responsible for particular privileges which, in fact, may turn into severe or even fatal hardships of a "friends in the field". As a general message, the account denies that a formal or predictable relationship with consultants, informants or interpreters can ever be achieved in the course of ethnographic fieldwork. Such an endeavor remains a very personal effort that is bound to produce some far-reaching consequences.

The volume is an important addition to the "Fieldwork Tradition in Anthropology". It will help all those scholars who are about to enter the adventure of long-term fieldwork. The rich ethnographic experiences shared by Indian and overseas contributors to the volume will go a long way to help researchers to sort out some of the issues they are likely to face in the field.

References

Begley, Larissa R., 2009. "The Other Side of Fieldwork: Experiences and Challenges of Conducting Research in the Border Area of Rwanda/Eastern Congo," *Anthropology Matters*, 11 (2).

Spencer, Dimitrina. 2010. "Emotional Labour and Relational Observation in Anthropological Fieldwork," *In:* Dimitrina Spencer and James Davies (eds.), *Anthropological Fieldwork: A Relational Process*. UK: Cambridge Scholar Publishing.

Watson, C.W., 1999. "Introduction: The Quality of Being There," (pp.1-14) *In:* C.W. Watson (ed.), *Being There: Fieldwork in Anthropology*. London: Pluto Press.

SHORT BIOGRAPHY

Professor Deepak Kumar Behera
Vice-Chancellor, Sambalpur University, Odisha
Former Vice-Chancellor, Berhampur University, Odisha
Fulbright Visiting Fellow (USA) (2007-08)
DAAD Fellow (Germany) (2013)
Carlos Chagas National Foundation Research Fellow, Brazil (2004)
National Research Foundation Fellow, Republic of South Africa (2001)
CISCA Fellow, European Union (2011)
Indo-French Academic Exchange Fellow, ICSSR, India (2006)
Indo-Israel Cultural and Educational Fellow, UGC, New Delhi (1995)

Dr. Deepak Kumar Behera is the youngest recipient of prestigious "**Sarat Chandra Roy Award**" conferred by Asiatic Society, India. He was the **Vice-Chancellor of Berhampur University,** India for three years. He obtained both his Master's degree (Gold Medalist) and Ph.D. from Sambalpur University, India. He has been in the teaching profession for more than 30 years. Professor Behera was a **Fulbright Visiting Scholar at California State University** at Long Beach during the Fall semester 2007-08. As a Fulbright Professor, he independently taught a course on "Childhood in a Changing Context (With Special Reference to South Asia)" to the students of Department of Human Development of the University. Professor Behera went as **DAAD Guest Professor to Tubeingen University, Germany** for the period April-July 2013. He was also a **Visiting Professor in the Dept. of History and Area Studies, Aarhus University, Denmark** (2011), Department of Anthropology, **University of Free State, Bloemfontein, South Africa** (2001, 2003), Department of Anthropology, University of Durban-Westville, Durban, South Africa (2001), **Institute of Psychology, Federal University of Rio de Janeiro, Brazil** (2004) and **Maison des Sciences de L'Homme, Paris and CNRS-EHESS, Toulouse** (2006). He has to his credit more than 100 research publications in reputed journals and edited volumes. Most of his publications are in the fields of tribal studies, social exclusion, gender studies and children and childhood. Professor Behera has in total **authored/edited twenty-two volumes**. Of those, ten published volumes of *Contemporary Society: Tribal Studies* [Concept Publishing Company (P.) Ltd., New Delhi] are jointly with Professor Georg Pfeffer of Institute of Ethnology of Free University of Berlin, Germany. Some of the books published by Professor Behera in the field of children and childhood are: *Contemporary Society: Childhood and Complex Order* (Manak Publication, New Delhi, 1996), *Children and Childhood in Contemporary Societies* (Kamla-Raj Enterprise, New Delhi, 1998), *Public Images of Children* (Guest Editor, Special Issue of *Journal of Social Sciences,* New Delhi, 1999) and *Children and Youth in the Metropolitan Cultures* (Guest Editor, Special Issue of the *International Journal of Anthropology,* Florence, June 2001, jointly with Professor Margaret Trawick of Massey University of New Zealand), *Childhoods in South Asia* (Pearson Education, New Delhi, 2007), *Extending Ethnographic Research with Children in the Asia Pacific Region* (Guest Editor, Special Issue of *The Asia Pacific Journal of Anthropology*, 12 (5), November 2011, jointly with Professor Roxana Waterson of the Department of Sociology, National University of

Singapore). He has successfully completed **more than a dozen research projects funded by UGC, ICSSR, Ministry of Welfare, National Literacy Mission Authorities, Winrock International, Shastri Foundation, WHO, German Research Council** etc. Professor Behera has **participated in more than 25 different international conferences held in Mexico, Germany, Belgium, Sweden, Israel, Denmark, USA, South Africa, China, Japan, Italy, Norway, France, UK, Bangladesh, Brazil, France, Egypt, Singapore, Australia, Ireland, Scotland, Korea etc.** He has delivered several invited lecture in different overseas universities and research institutes (like Hebrew University of Jerusalem, Israel, Tel Aviv University, Israel, University of Orange Free State, South Africa University of Durban West-Ville, South Africa, University of California at Santa Cruz, University of Illinois at Chicago, University of Utah, Logan etc.) He was the Editor of the *Journal of Social Sciences* during 1997-2002. Professor Behera was elected as a **member of the Executive Board of International Union of Anthropological and Ethnological Sciences (IUAES)**, the apex anthropological body at the international level, in the year 1997 and served in that position for two consecutive terms, i.e. for the period 1998-2009. He is also a member of Permanent Council of IUAES and in that capacity he represents India in all IUAES platforms. He has been a member of the Governing Council of Association of Indian University since August 2013. He is the **founding Chairman of the IUAES Commission on Children, Youth and Childhood.** Professor Behera was a member of the Advisory Board of the Centre for India Study at Aarhus University, Denmark. He is presently also a member of the Advisory Committee of the ICSSR-ERC, Kolkata. He is the Vice-President of the Institute for Social Research and Applied Anthropology, India. **Eighteen scholars have already received their Ph.D. degree and one Scholar received D. Litt. Degree under the supervision of Professor Behera.**

SECTION I

ISSUES OF ACADEMIC FRIENDS

A. TRIBES, GOVERNANCE AND ADMINISTRATION

ONE

STATE AND GOVERNANCE ISSUES IN THE TRIBAL CONTEXT[1]

YOGESH ATAL

I

Let me begin with a statement: earlier studies carried out in the various tribal contexts had hardly focused on the political dimension encapsulating the concepts of state and governance. The reason is easy to imagine. There was virtual absence of state-like institutions in many tribal societies, particularly the small ones. That is why tribal societies were generally treated as *acephalic*—societies without a stately apparatus and a governing head. In Anthropology, terms such as *Society* and *Culture,* were used as broad categories encompassing all aspects of social organization.

It is interesting to note that the British anthropologists used the term social anthropology for the specific branch dealing with 'social structure' and 'culture'. The American anthropologists used the term cultural anthropology for virtually the same subject matter as is found in British social anthropology.[2] That must be the reason that British social anthropology appears much closer to sociology although the latter has not paid much attention to structures related to kinship and marriage. Political sociology is comparatively a recent arrival both in sociology and in social anthropology/cultural anthropology.[3] For the discipline of anthropology, culture and society were all-inclusive concepts following the holistic perspective. What distinguished the discipline of sociology from anthropology—British or American—is the total absence in sociology of the physical aspects of man, and lack of concern for prehistory and archaeology.

The dimension of government was encompassed in the broader concepts of culture and society. Tribal groups living in the milieu of a complex culture, such as India, were covered by the regional regimes in which they were located and were treated as part of the regional social system—governed by the regional political culture and the indigenous practices relative to governance.

India has the unique cultural configuration where the boundaries of religion and regional regimes were *not* coterminous. People belonging to a given religion resided in several regional regimes. Boundary disputes separated the regional regimes despite the religious unity that covered the supra-regional entity of the empire. That entity was tried to be created by the Mauryas, the Mughals, and the British colonialists. The residents of the so-called *Bharat Bhumi* lived under different political regimes, be they princely States, or the epigenetic empires, and yet they practiced religion of their heritage.

That is why when the British left the country there were around 600 princely States that had coexisted with the Raj; upon the attainment of independence from the British Raj each one of them individually joined the newly found Indian Union that combined several traits of a Federation. Most individual tribes did not have state-like structure. They were parts of the monarchical supra-tribal states in which they were located. Of course, living in remote and generally inaccessible areas their interactions with the rest of the regional society were minimal. With the development of the terrain such interactions grew in number and gave rise to cultural reciprocity. Tribes became subsystems of such regional systems. Many tribal families moved to villages to live in company of other Hindu castes and were also treated part of the village system as a 'caste unit'.

Needless to stress the point that Anthropology and Sociology had their origin in the West which regarded itself superior—biologically as a 'white' race asserting that it was eugenetically *nully secundus,* and civilizationally as a modern paramount colonial power. Sociology willy-nilly became the study of the civilized societies, and anthropology of the so-called 'un-civilized', 'jungle' societies lacking in several traits of the modern, Western society and civilization. Sociology and Social Anthropology, thus, focused on the 'social', but charted different territories. Thus, Physical and Prehistoric anthropology found proximity with biological and geological sciences, and Sociology and Social Anthropology remained dedicated to the social sphere—the civilized and the primitive. Rather than emphasizing on the key question of theoretical orientation, the practitioners of the two disciplines unsuccessfully used technique of data gathering as their differential characteristic. I regard it ridiculous to differentiate the twin disciplines of sociology and social anthropology in terms of techniques of investigation.

Survey method today is no longer the monopoly of the sociologist, and no one stops an anthropologist to use tools other than participant observation. Just as different types of tools are used to chop off different vegetables and meat, but the outcome is the same—i.e. preparation of the meal—so is the study of societies. You classify the meal in terms of whether it is vegetarian or non-vegetarian, and not on how the meat or vegetables were cut.

Since anthropology researched the unlettered people speaking an esoteric language, the outside researcher had no option but to get inducted into the culture of society first by observation through participation. With growing literacy and education among the tribal segment of our society, as of others, it is possible to interview the tribal respondents with the help of a questionnaire or a schedule. In tribal Africa one finds several examples of tribal statehoods and large nations which yield for macrocosmic studies. The people in these societies have been exposed to the culture and society of their colonizer, and most of them have become proficient in the language of the colonizing country. In such societies, it is possible to use other techniques of data collection. This changing pattern also alerts us to the fact that tribe is *a transitional* category—such as youth—and people from the tribe move towards the other end of the continuum marked by civilization and 'modernity'.

The existence of the two academic disciplines—anthropology and sociology—in many of the universities throughout the world has, however, occasioned time and again the fruitless boundary question. Since anthropology covered both the biological and social aspects of man and had focused mainly on the primitive and the past—thus also sharing interest with archaeologists, particularly pre-historians—it was easily separated from sociology which only obliquely touched human biology and focused more on the modern and the historical antecedents.

Both the disciplines—sociology and anthropology—had time dimension and cultural phenomena as key concerns, and yet both had operated in differently marked academic territories. Sociology became the study of 'own' society and anthropology was defined as the study of 'other' societies.[4]

The term 'other' was employed only for the tribal societies/ communities living in the hinterland, with difficulty of access. These were small microcosms with simple life. While there were violent clashes between tribes living in the same vicinage, these tribes had simple political organization. As such, these were called 'apolitical' or even 'acephalic' societies. Only some very large tribal groups, particularly in the African continent, had somewhat elaborate political organization mainly to protect their society from outside intervention, but very little of policing was carried out within the community. That is the reason that anthropological studies of these societies had little to offer on the political dimension, much less on the statecraft. The situation in India was rather different. Even as part of the British Raj, the tribal societies were distinct but part of the same political regime and, despite several protective measures, the tribes came in contact with other tribes and the people of the wider society. The spread of Christianity among them opened that door widely.

Regarding 'state' as the domain of study for political science (earlier called 'government' and 'politics') sociology also did not offer much in this terrain. It is the electoral politics in democratic countries that created space for the study of 'political behaviour'. Tribal societies no longer remained the exclusive preserve of the anthropologist. People from other disciplines, such as political science, public administration, linguistics, economics and social work also extended their sphere of study by including the tribal terrain. Tribes are today seen in a multidisciplinary perspective; of course the transdisciplinary orientation provided by anthropology is still valid. It is a pity that while scholars from other disciplines have expanded their scope to include the tribes, anthropologists are increasingly moving in other directions and becoming indifferent to tribal studies. One is struck by the absence of any dependable restudies of several of our tribes. The students are fed by the material generated in the late nineteenth and first half of the twentieth century about the so-called 'Tribal India'. Today's tribes do not match with their earlier descriptions. We need a new approach.

To recap, while social anthropology and sociology covered the same social sphere, the division of labour between the two led one to focus on the tribes and the other on the so-called civilized society. Interestingly enough, it is the students of tribal societies who polished the concept of *Culture*, and the students of advanced and cultured civilized societies talked of *Society*. Political science treated tribal societies as acephalic and thus as stateless.

II

For long, the term '*state*' was used as an umbrella concept for the political dimension of the social system. The need is now arising to distinguish between *government* and *governance*. The latter is seen as a phenomenon confined not only to the state but to all forms of secondary groups. It led people to distinguish between *nation-state* and the *civil society*, and also between a state and a nation. Marxian theory described tribes as classless society, and in evolutionary terms it talked about Ancient Society, Feudal Society, and Class society (that exists in a Capitalist frame). This theory regarded tribal-hunters as representatives of classless primitive communism. It was anthropologist Bronislaw Malinowski who tore this myth through his classic work *Crime and Custom in Savage Society* (1926)[5] finding the concept of private property in operation among the Trobriand Islanders.

When scholars started studying colonial societies of other indigenous civilizations—such as that of India—the question of assimilation of several cultures, including tribal communities, came to the fore. Thus, with the spread of colonization, the tribal societies came under the umbrella of the colonial rule. In this process, several tribal groups were brought under a common flag and became subsystems of the newly created wider political system—the state. However, the colonial administrators were keen to prevent the tribal communities from the so-called 'outside' influence with a view to manifestly safeguarding their cultures and traditions. For them, tribal communities were like 'anthropological zoos', and their protection from the outside onslaught was necessary to save their unique cultures. Critics found in such an approach a malicious design to keep them backward and deprive them from the fruits of development and civilization.

Apart from the stated philanthropic view the hidden agenda was, thus, to create a 'distance' between the tribal and the other advanced members of the indigenous civilization so that the colonial rulers could practice 'divide and rule' politics to continue their hold and thwart any attempts to dislodge them.

However, the tribals also joined the struggle for independence. The national leadership, largely drawn from the non-tribal sections of the society, worked to bring the tribals out of their narrow shells and join the freedom movement. Some scholars, such as G.S. Ghurye, never considered the tribals any different from people of Hindu India. Even J.H. Hutton—the Census Commissioner for 1931 Indian Census, felt that the "...tribal religions ...represent, as it were, surplus material not yet built into the temple of Hinduism".

It must be noted that both the colonial administration and the social reformers worked to change the living profile of the tribals. The colonizers—the government and the Christian missionaries—played their role in spreading education and in converting the tribals into the fold of Christianity. Other social activists brought in elements of Hindu religion and culture in them. In the tribes of Central India, there are several ritual practices and deities that exhibit Hindu connection. Some people are of the view that these tribal groups represent those who have been pushed back into isolated and inaccessible forests by the invaders who came to capture this vast land and enslave the regional regimes.

With the attainment of independence from the colonial rule in the post-Second World War era the tribal communities—particularly their leadership—became aware of their civil rights. Many of the tribal groups accepted the new arrangement, but the more advanced among the tribal groups were instigated by the colonial rulers and religious missionaries to resist their integration into the so-called mainstream. Tribes of the north-east India offer good example of such a variegated response.

As part of their "divide and rule" policy, or the hidden agenda behind keeping the tribals protected from 'cultural invasion' by neighbouring non-tribal Indians, the British instigated the Nagas way back in 1937 to keep away from the purview of the Government of British Act, 1935, and to agree to remain under the British Crown as a separate entity. Thus, when the country attained its independence in 15 August, 1947 the so-called Naga National Council declared independence from the new India. This situation continued until July 1960 when Naga People's Convention signed a 16-point Agreement with Government of India. As a result, in December 1963, Nagaland formally became an Indian state with special constitutional rights—a subsystem of the Indian political system. This arrangement received a further jolt when in 1980, the disgruntled Naga leaders set-up a National Socialist Council of Nagaland (NSCN). That Council also suffered a split eight years later. But this period was a period of continuous disturbance and physical violence until 1997 when a ceasefire accord was signed with the Government of India. This ceasefire was again broken and conflicts arose in March 2015. The present day Indian Government, however, successfully intervened and a new Naga peace accord was signed on 3 August, 2015.

It must be said that all the states of our north-east are living in constant military supervision, and the situation is very abnormal. There are efforts to bring a climate of harmony, but not much success has been achieved. A lady activist, Irom Chanu Sharmila (born: 14 March, 1972), is on *hunger strike* since 5 November, 2000. Her primary demand to the Indian Government is to repeal the Armed Forces (Special Powers) Act (AFSPA). While beginning her fast she vowed not to eat, drink, comb her hair or look in a mirror until AFSPA was repealed. But nothing positive is still in sight.

Questions related to statehood in this segment of our society need to be anthropologically investigated; for this, a new orientation is required. It is hazardous that anthropologists continue to recite even today the idiom of "saving the tribal cultures" as if they were ignorant of massive change that has occurred in our tribal population because of several steps taken to integrate them into the mainstream of Indian society which is multi-cultural, like a cultural grid, and not an ocean that usurps whatever approaches it.

The situation has somewhat improved now with the adoption of a common agreement by the Nagas. However, the fact remains that some sections of the various tribal groups on our Eastern borders exhibit ambivalence towards the integration with the rest of the Indian society. They live in the midst of confusion and confrontation, with heavy military presence. This is the case notwithstanding the fact that Hindi is fast spreading in these areas and the people are getting exposed to the Indian mass media, particularly the Hindi films and songs. Similarly, The Naxalite movement that was started in West Bengal by the peasants has somehow succeeded in endorsing support of many tribal groups of the Central Indian region to challenge the Indian state. Technically, when actions are oriented towards the system concerned they tend to cement the societal base even when these are confrontationist. It is only such actions that are *not* oriented to the system concerned—that is, when they are outwardly oriented, and thus secessionist. Such activities are dysfunctional for the society and need a different type of action. North-east is hit by such tendencies and is viewed as troubled area having people with different orientations—some treating the rest of India as the positive reference group, others oriented towards anti-national group of people. It is to curb such a tendency that military presence is considered necessary to seal the *apertures* or to create *insulators* with a view to protecting the integrity of the system. Recent instance of military action, when the Indian forces successfully carried out their mission by entering into the territory of Myanmar, was one such step in this direction.

But where is the answer to the continuous ambivalence prevalent in our north-east? Have we, as anthropologists, ever thought of studying this ghastly phenomenon? Here I see the challenge, and the invitation for the anthropologist of the new era. Today's anthropology is not expected to be the handmaiden of the colonial power. I am afraid, such change of orientation is still lacking in the anthropology we practice.

Happenings in Tribal India, particularly the north-east and the central India need to be studied in an anthropological perspective with scientific objectivity as a dimension of social change that clearly indicates orientation towards the Indian nation-state. Factors that are creating disillusion among them and feeding seeds of sedition need to be carefully and objectively analyzed.

III

Let me now turn to the issue of 'governance'. The word '*governance*' has come in vogue towards the end of the twentieth century when the World Community organized a Summit for Social Development (WSSD)[6] in Copenhagen in 1995 and underlined the need for good governance. Governance is an interdisciplinary concept, although the science of public administration regards it as its defining characteristic. With focus on development, all social science disciplines are becoming futuristic in their orientation and looking for fresh approaches. The origins of social sciences—including anthropology as well—were in their initial phases oriented towards the past. The post-Second World War era brought the present in the prime focus where developing societies of the non-west began treating the west (which now is called the 'north') as the positive reference group for emulation. As we approached the conclusion of the twentieth century we have begun worrying about the humanity's multifarious Future. The new perspective leads to a search for 'good practices' that can be emulated irrespective of their origin—the developed north or the developing south—or to innovate the new practices. The world community has come to realize that while the various societies face common problems there cannot be a common solution. The solutions will have to be culture-specific. This marks the return of anthropology. Culture has again found a berth in the centre stage.

The World Summit for Social Development (WSSD), held in

Copenhagen, Denmark in 1995 was, thus, the first major attempt by the international community to address the issue of 'Social Development'. It underlined the fact that while in the post-Second World War era a good deal of economic development has occurred there was great deficit on the social front. Problem of poverty is a universal phenomenon, so are unemployment and the increasing tendencies towards social disorganization. For the resolution of these problems, the World Summit recommended culture-specific solutions. I see in it an invitation, and a challenge, for anthropology.

The failure of many programmes of social development was earlier attributed to culture. Tradition was treated as the main stumbling block and a key culprit. Now, the international community acknowledges bad governance as the main cause for the recurrent deficit on our social front. It is now accepted that good and well-meaning programmes have suffered because of their poor implementation, attributable to bad Governance characterized by rule-ridden bureaucracy and corruption in high places. Corruption can be seen in the ill-treatment of the common man as well as in the stealth of government resources. The common man is hurt by the growing culture of *Sifarish* (recommendation) and demand for facilitating money (now well-known as *Suvidha Shulka)*—nothing moves until you pay under the table. For the middle class, this may be easy way of expediting decision-making, but for the poor it is great harassment. While such corruption does not cheat the treasury, it causes bureaucratic delays and makes small statured *babus* rich with black money. Big corporations from the private sector give such lollipops to the senior bureaucrats to ensure favourable decisions and, in return, they also secure offers for re-employment after their retirement from public office. Political parties likewise benefit from such offerings. Similarly, people in high places steal from government exchequer by taking wrong decisions in (i) allotment of quotas; (ii) auction of public property at ridiculously low rates compared to their market value; and (iii) purchase of goods and military equipment from international dealers.[7] The amount of black money stacked in foreign banks is so huge that if brought back and distributed to public at large every single citizen of this 1.20 billion population would get around 1.7 million rupees, so says the spokespersons of the present government. Some regard it as an over-estimation; others believe that there is much more than this figure. One thing is clear: corruption is rampant and needs to be studied to seek guidelines for good governance. Unfortunately, we have hardly any empirical research that could unveil the dynamics of such transactions. What we have are figures or stories of individual cases of fraud that have gained publicity.

Can anthropology enter this terrain? Using the techniques of observation—that it claims to own—can it produce a new set of good case studies? This is as difficult a field as the tribes were in earlier times. Overcoming difficulty of access and living away with strange people in jungles entrepreneurial anthropologists carried out their empirical studies and produced good monographs. Why can not we prepare case studies of corruption in a similar manner? In this regard, one finds increasing use of 'sting operations' began by the magazine *Tehelka.*

In view of lack of perspective to comprehend the phenomenon of corruption I have done a book, entitled *Combating Corruption: The Indian Case.*[8] I invite colleagues to carefully review the book and evolve suitable methodology for the investigation of the different facets of corruption.

Governance is, of course, a broader concept than corruption. It refers to "all processes of governing, whether undertaken by a government, market or network, whether over a family, tribe, formal or informal organization or territory and whether through laws, norms, power or language". It relates to "the processes of interaction and decision-making among the actors involved in a collective problem that lead to the creation, reinforcement, or reproduction of social norms and institutions". In other words, governance is a process related to the implementation of plans and projects decided by the government. Its emphasis is on performance, and the designing of appropriate strategies to achieve the target efficiently—in lesser time and in correspondence with the intention of the programme.

The term *governance* ought to be differentiated from government. The governance process includes all the actors involved in influencing the decision-making process (such as Planning Commission or NITI, interest groups, parties, media etc.). In other words, Governance "is the way the rules, norms, and actions are produced, sustained, and regulated". However, these rules and norms are only facilitators and are, and should be, subject to revision and constant review. Rules relate to ways of doing things in the most efficient manner. Should they turn out to be the hurdles, they ought to be changed in the interest of good governance. Rule worship goes against good governance. Weber told it long ago, but have we paid heed to it?

Governance is now being defined as the rules of the political system to solve conflicts between actors (legality). It has also been used to describe the "proper functioning of institutions and their acceptance by the public" (legitimacy). And it has been used to invoke the efficacy of government and the achievement of consensus by democratic means (participation). Thus, Governance has three facets namely, legality, legitimacy, and participation. It is a concept designed to help identify states in terms of their performance.

Associated with governance is the concept of 'best practices'. As a follow up to the World Summit for Social Development, the United Nations system set-up several specialist groups one of which was on 'good governance'. Led by the World Bank, the group had representatives from other UN agencies. I had the honour to represent UNESCO in that group which worked to develop outline for preparing case studies of good governance from various countries of the world.[9]

Scanning through UN generated literature one finds that Good governance has eight major characteristics. It is participatory, consensus oriented, accountable, transparent, responsive, effective and efficient, equitable and inclusive, and follows the rule of law. Good Governance implies minimization of corruption. It also demands that the views of minorities should be taken into account and that the voices of the most vulnerable in society be heard in decision-making. Good governance ought to be responsive to the present and future needs of society.

Figure 2.1 shows this clearly.

Fig. 2.1: Characteristics of good governance.

The all-inclusiveness mentioned in this paradigm has provided a space for the so-called 'indigenous people' which is a synonym of the tribal people. Indigenous peoples are peoples defined in international or national legislation as having a set of specific rights based on their historical ties to a particular territory, and their cultural or historical distinctiveness from other populations that are often politically dominant. The concept of indigenous peoples defines these groups as particularly vulnerable to exploitation, marginalization, and oppression by nation states that may still be formed from the colonising populations, or by politically dominant ethnic groups. As a result, a special set of political rights, in accordance with international law, have been set forth by international organizations. UN has issued a Declaration on the Rights of Indigenous Peoples to guide member-states in the preparation of national policies to collective rights of indigenous peoples.

This step by the international community has somewhat served the purpose of reuniting the indigenous populations that have been overwhelmed by the colonial regimes, and is more appropriate to countries such as USA, Canada, Australia, and New Zealand. But it has also put breaks to the assimilative trends of various tribal communities in countries such as India that have been in constant interaction with other cohabitants of the same soil, causing a new set of problems for governance. Indigenous people's approach, to my mind, is continuation of the old anthropological perspective. Earlier they were kept separated to facilitate their governance in a multi-cultural society, now the integrating groups are being encouraged to return to their isolation—an uphill task in view of the increasing informational proximity. It must be said that the term *peoples,* in association with the 'indigenous', is derived from the nineteenth century anthropological and ethnographic literature which defined them as "a body of persons that are united by a common culture, tradition, or sense of kinship, which typically have common language, institutions, and beliefs, and often constitute a politically organized group". Such definition is no longer applicable to all the tribes, much less to the Indian tribes. While I would support all our effort to alleviate poverty from all the sections of the Indian populace, I would hesitate, despite my calling as an anthropologist, to reintroduce the divisive concept of Indigenity to keep tribals deprived of the fruits of development. We cannot lead them back to the corridors of past, nor many of the leaders would prefer such an isolationist policy. Sociologists and anthropologists pleading for such an isolationist policy are hurting the cause of national integration.

A good example of such an approach, is Oommen's book of essays titled *Pluralism, Equality and Identity: Comparative Studies.*[10] I view this book not only as a theoretical contribution but also as an elaboration of Oommen's ideological agenda. It emerges that Oommen is opposed to, what he calls, 'hegemonic' national culture. Discarding Furnivall's concept of 'plural society', he talks of pluralism in the sense that a country—like India—consists of several societies or nations. Describing India as a *multinational* nation—as against a *multicultural* society—the author distinguishes between nations and *ethnies*. Reading the text gives the impression that he has viewed Indian social structure from the vantage point of a minority and found faults of dominance and hegemony in the majority community against whom he parenthetically recommends greater solidarity amongst the 'nation-groups' (read minorities). Oommen considers all minorities as 'out-groups'. He also distinguishes between the native religions and the alien religions to stress the point that it is the alien religions that are discriminated against. In doing so, he fails to take note of the phenomenon of conversion which accounts for the majority population of so-called alien religions, such as Christianity and Islam.

Oommen offers his own definition of pluralism to contrast it with Plural society. For him, pluralism means attitude of the in-group (that is Hindus) towards the out groups. Interestingly enough, he calls natives as out-groups constituting 40 per cent of India's population and contrasts them with 83 per cent Hindus—a strange statistics where the two figures add up to 123 and not 100!!! One is also surprised to hear from the author that rapid spread of English as the *lingua franca* is a sure invitation to cultural hegemonization—a danger that he would like to be avoided at all costs. Coming from a person who has, in one of his earlier essays, complained of Indian Sociology being dominated by Hindus and *Hindiwallahs*, such a remark on English—the only language of his professional writings—is worthy of note. The book is likely to invite debate on the concept of *Nation* as used by the author.

In the wake of colonization, and the creation of 'plural societies' when people revolted against alien regimes their freedom fights were used for generating nationalist feelings amongst different groups of the plurality regime, and the independence from the colonial era engaged all the newly independent countries in the massive exercise of 'nation-building'. *Having* a nation and *building* a nation are two different realities. Oommen's rigid stance suggests that nations only exist, you cannot build a nation. To deny the process of nation building, a space in the conceptual framework is to close the eyes from reality. It gives the wrong message that a nation cannot be built as an epigenetic reality at the supra-regional level. Uncharitable critics may also read in between the lines a plea for the further partition of the country.

IV

I must say that Indian sociology or social anthropology has been good at description, but largely poor at theoretical formulation. Much of what goes by the term theoretical is indeed rhetoric, and assertion of personal point of view. This must change.

When you look at Indian sociology people just name Srinivas for his widely and blindly used concepts of *Sanskritization* and of *Dominant Caste*. Of course, disciplinary politics has prevented some other concepts introduced by Indian scholars from gaining popularity. I must admit that of late the concept of Sanskritization is being critically reviewed but the debate has become more political than intellectual. Those criticizing Sanskritization are equally guilty of not examining the candidacy of other concepts such as *Sandwich Cultures, Insulators,* and *Apertures*—that I proposed and that are now used internationally. In my Sociology textbook I have attempted to give due acknowledgement to Indian scholarship for their theoretical and conceptual contribution.

I strongly feel that adding more definitions to the existing concepts is a futile exercise. The function of the definition is to outline the territory of each concept and provide an orientation to the student so that the dialogue becomes meaningful. Loose usage of the words leads to wrong conclusions. A word becomes a concept when its meaning or usage is conceived properly. One word with different meanings, and several words for the same meaning, causes confusion.

This is happening with the words like *Tribe and Caste.* A good deal of damage has been done by their misuse even by practitioners of sociology and social anthropology. In a way, such confusion may be functional for the Indian political system where caste is dying in the sociological sense but is continuously being revived at a supra-caste level by the ill-informed politicians, and journalistic social scientists. The concept of tribe, which also suffers from lack of consensus regarding its definition, is to be seen as a stage in human development rather than as a fixed social category. While no new tribes are emerging, the existing tribes are at different stages of movement towards the non-tribal civilizational milieu. To continue to treat them as tribals is to pursue the hidden agenda of keeping them deprived or deny them the privilege of getting out of the secluded milieu. Indian tribes are increasingly getting assimilated in the wider Indian social system that is pluricultural. It is reflected both in their geographical and psychological mobility. The sphere of their empathy is continually enlarging.

Ethnographers are generally regarded as less theoretical, and indifferent to concept formulation. This must be the reason that while most of social anthropology, particularly in its formative period, was based on fieldwork conducted in the groups designated as tribes; we do not find any satisfactory definition of the term. The British officials who wrote about Indian society while working for the colonial administration used the word caste and tribe as interchangeable—such as the Rajput Tribe, or the Brahman Caste—which is a caste cluster. Elsewhere in the world independence made single tribe societies as a nation state. Multi-tribal states bound by single colonial administration raised queries about the definition of such new entity as multi-ethnic or society with different nationalities.

When we look at our north-east, we find the creation of several new states by fracturing the original Assam. Even its original capital—Shillong—became capital of another newly formed state of Meghalaya[11] and Assam had to build Guwahati as the new capital. Now, Bodos are claiming for a new state. In the pre-colonial era, the small groups lived an isolated life and had a limited *Weltanshauung*. But the British brought them into a single administration which transformed these tribal structures into subsystems of a broader nationhood. The interlinkages between tribal communities, who continue to live mostly in their original habitats, have become subsystems of the wider national system namely the Union State of India, and have become interacting units of the wider social system. It was, I submit, part of the policy of "Divide and Rule" that the tribes were tried to be kept aloof—as anthropological zoos—and their changing character was undermined. Anthropologists fell prey to this strategy and continue to consider those groups as tribes that are listed in the so-called schedule. If a new group is added to it, such as the Muslim Gujjars of Jammu & Kashmir, it becomes valid subject matter for anthropological research. Dictates of the state guide the choice of a people for study.

Anthropologists should seriously take the challenge of defining a tribe. I hold the view that the group called *Tribe* is a transitional category and its study should be appropriately reoriented. Today anthropologists are no longer confined to the study of the tribes; and the tribes are being studied by people coming from other social science disciplines. It is intriguing to find that even in the north-eastern universities we have separate departments of anthropology and of tribal studies. No longer are the two synonyms. Tribes in a multicultural society such as India must be studied as subsystems that are gradually moving towards assimilation with other neighbouring groups. Tribes are part of Indian society and the Indian state. Treating them as separate entities as in the past is an invitation to create conditions for disintegration of the wider society. The tendency is fissiparous.

Notes

1. This is a revised and much improved version of the paper presented as a keynote speech at the INCAA conference held in Bhubaneswar in February 2015. INCAA has kindly allowed me to have it published in this volume.
2. In the writings of British Anthropologist, Bronislaw Malinowski, one finds a move toward the over-arching concept of 'Culture'; Radcliffe-Brown—on the other hand—focused on 'Social Structure'. In later works the two concepts reigned over all types of anthropology. In prehistory and archeology, the focus was on material culture; in social anthropology culture became the key handle for the philosophical— i.e. supernatural—precepts of the local community.
3. My book titled *Local Communities and National Politics* (published by National Publishing House, Delhi in 1971) is the first monograph by an Indian social anthropologist on the 1967 General Elections. The study was based in three interlinked communities in the State of Uttar Pradesh, and it combined survey research, observation, and computerized data analysis, and is regarded as a work in the area of Psephology.
4. See John Beattie's *Other Cultures* (Free Press, London, 1968). The book provides a lucid introduction to social anthropology. The first part of the book tells what social anthropology is and seeks to do, what areas it covers, and the methods of investigation employed by social anthropologists. The second part discusses the major categories of research through which social anthropologies have advanced our knowledge of other cultures. These include marriage, kinship, political organization, law, economic and property relations, magic, religion, and social change.
5. Bronislaw Malinowski, *Crime and Custom in Savage Society*, 1926, London, Kegan Paul.
6. For this Summit, UNESCO appointed me to co-ordinate the contributions from the Organization. I was also seconded for some time to participate in the preparation of the Draft Report for WSSD.
7. Bofors was the first major revelation. But compared to recent embezzlements, the sum involved in the Bofors deal seems ridiculously small. See Atal and Choudhary, *Combating Corruption: the Indian Case*, Orient Blackswan, New Delhi, 2014.

8. The book, done in collaboration with Sunil K. Choudhary, is published by Orient Blackswan, 2014.
9. Governance and anti-corruption initiatives of the World Bank focus on internal organizational integrity, minimizing corruption on World Bank-funded projects, and assisting countries in improving governance and controlling corruption. Combining participatory action-oriented learning, capacity-building tools, and the power of data, the World Bank Institute (WBI) supports countries in improving governance and controlling corruption. Using a strategic and multidisciplinary approach, WBI applies action-learning methods to link empirical diagnostic surveys, their practical application, collective action, and prevention. The WBI also periodically releases Worldwide Governance Indicators (WGI) and country diagnostics.
10. T.K. Oommen, 2002. *Pluralism, Equality and Identity: Comparative Studies*. New Delhi: Oxford University Press, pp.189-90.
11. The names of the new states in the North-East are Sanskrit based such as Meghalaya and Arunachal Pradesh. The acceptance of such nomenclature is a good indicator of their lineage. In Arunachal people fluently speak Hindi though the school has not taught them the script. They speak but they cannot write.

TWO

SOME IDEAS IN THE CONTEXT OF TRIBES OF INDIA

VINAY KUMAR SRIVASTAVA

Introduction

Allow me to begin this article, written in honour of Professor Deepak Kumar Behera, with a submission. It is that we should study, examine, analyze, and interpret our society and its relationship with other societies, as well as the subjects that deal with a systematic and comparative study of societies, social anthropology being one of them, with a critical perspective. Usually what happens is that even when we want to change we do not succeed in changing the concepts with the help of which we endeavour to understand the ensemble of social relations and cultural practices. We may not either have viable options or may not want to think about a battery of alternative concepts which may seem to have larger explanatory power. Perhaps the psyche of 'no-change' or even 'anti-change' may grip us to the core.

Why does it fetter us may be because it gives us some sort of 'intellectual security'; we may think that by subscribing to the dominant thoughts we would guard ourselves against a volley of negative criticisms, since invariably new ways of thinking and analysis are quite vulnerable to ridicule and rejection, and also in this way we may subscribe to the line of those who vouchsafe our academic (and financial) interests. The outcome is that the same intellectual practice, the same paradigm, as it has been enduring for years, keeps on thriving. Little changes, here and there, do occur, which are rather loudly described as our accomplishments.

Against this backdrop, if there is anything cardinal to social anthropology, it is a critical understanding of our knowledge, our ways of living, our policies and politics, the inertia of our thought and the fears on our part in this regard. We feel secure in the existing repository of our concepts and arguments, and attempts to step out of the 'snug chambers' in which we are 'cozily' suspended are invariably postponed, for such attempts may single us out, exposing us to a series of intellectual uncertainties and in some cases, even to the episodes of career jeopardy. A complex of factors instills in us scholarly conservatism. In spite of our dissatisfaction with the type of scholarship we practice, the spirit to reject it in favour of a new and more relevant paradigm is enfeebled; so continuity conquers change, as it has done in the past. This goes against the spirit of social anthropology, which is a critical enterprise, and the knowledge it generates can play a seminal role in initiating desirable and just changes in society, in helping people to have the benefits of inclusive development.

It may however be noted here that the word 'critical' does not carry the image of a 'negative' and an 'iconoclastic' attempt; if we think so it is our short-sightedness. In fact, by critical we understand a 'balanced appraisal' of the state of knowledge. Those of its aspects which stand the test of time need to be supported and carried forward, and contrarily, those which have not, need to be replaced with more operational alternatives. In my opinion, criticism is the process of constantly (and ruthlessly) reviewing our knowledge; we should be circumspect of any kind of commitment that we may have for our creation. Needless to say, knowledge advances in this process of an endless dialogue, negotiation, and dialectics.

Ideas and Discourse

In April 2016, I got an opportunity to attend a seminar that the Department of Anthropology of Mahatma Gandhi International Hindi University at Wardha (Maharashtra) had organized. The theme of the seminar was: "Rehabilitation, Environment and the Adivasi Society: In the Context of the Human Rights." It was a timely topic and discussion on this was important considering the fact that a myriad of schemes and strategies have been in operation for the welfare of tribal communities for several decades, and it is high time that we study and discourse their impact on ameliorating the life-chances of people, region-wise. Moreover, it is well known that forty per cent of the displaced persons happen to be tribal and the number of the project-affected people from this group would be much higher, a category on which authentic figures are not available (Mathur, 2013).

The case studies of the displaced tribal families that anthropologists and social workers have amply documented tell sordid and heart-rending tales of people being ousted from their homes, reluctantly and forcibly. Over time they sink into the quandary of 'involuntary nomadism', the 'homeless people'. In many contexts, their land (agricultural as well for residence) has been sacrificed at the altar of the 'modern temples of development', or they have been the victims of the 'land-sharks', the illegal mafias that oust people from their resources and also tacitly enjoy the patronage of the politically powerful people. Often done in connivance with the local power structures, the 'victims' are often unable to raise their voices against the injustice criminally meted out to them (Padel, 2010). The slender hope they have is from the legal machinery and the non-governmental organizations, where the process of getting justice and the wherewithal for decent survival is painfully lethargic (Dhagamwar, 2006).

The feeling of 'cipher-ness' descends on them as they are forced to flee from their ancestral homes, the places they have been occupying for decades. Just look at the faces of the involuntary migrants, sullen and morose, staring at future with resignation. With their meagre personal belonging, they are often seen sitting listlessly, anxiously awaiting human and divine interventions to rescue them from the misery of life. Not only are they the 'sufferers of development' but also of a system that has a class character, which either does not aid the destitute or comes into action after much damage has already been inflicted on the people (Xaxa, 2008). The image of tribes, as 'happy-and-satisfied' people, who freely and wholly enjoy their lives in the lap of the unpolluted and salubrious environ, as one gets from the monographs that Verrier Elwin, D.N. Majumdar, and Christoph von Furer-Haimendorf wrote after spending years and years with small communities, is crushed when we look at these people on the margins of the already overpopulated cities.

I thought it was important that these issues were taken up for another round of discussion. I remembered Michel Foucault's idea (1990) that when we talk about a subject, a discourse is created, which would over a period of time engage, sometimes contagiously, a wider public, and may later become a harbinger of change. I also thought that the discussions that happen in confines of the university should find a place in newspapers and the other media bodies so that people at large are informed of the ideas and the problems that are engrossing the academic world. Let the academic discussions not remain cloistered to its ivory towers, so to say.

Although the theme of the seminar was good, what captured my attention was the use of the word *adivasi* in its title, and I decided to begin my key-note address to this seminar with a comment on it. Let me recapitulate some of those ideas here.

The Meaning of the Term *Adivasi*

When we use the word *adivasi*, without trying to intellectually explode it and examine its relevance, it is likely to be interpreted as an approval of its appropriateness. And this also implies that we tacitly think that none, including the people for whom this term is used, has any objection to its use, although at no juncture have we tried to find out as to what the people who are called '*adivasi*' think about it. Do they have any reservation about its use for them? Here, we should not forget that the words carry images, stereotypes, and notions that fuel people's imagination about communities. Ask people about the pictures that float in their minds when they hear words such as 'tribal', '*adivasi*', 'rural', 'urban', and 'modern'. If these images are incorrect, exaggerated or underplayed, satirically or fun-arousingly constructed, just envision the damage they wreak on the morale of the community for which they are devised and uncritically used!

Or, although the people called *adivasi* do not like the use of this term for them, they keep their lips sealed about it, for they think that any protest, howsoever mild, would annoy the dominant groups, who could unleash a reign of terror jeopardizing their bare minimal survival. Any defiance of the way in which the politically and economically powerful sections think and speak about the groups at lower rungs of the hierarchy would amount to asserting their might, which they would not like and obviously retaliate harshly. If the lowly-placed groups do not react to the caricatures in which the dominant people construct them, it does not imply that they like it. The silence of the subdued is an unfortunate outcome of the structure of dominance; they become the 'tongue-less and muted groups'. It is also likely that they may not mind its usage since it is used to identify them, as a 'marker of their identity'. They may think as do the others that notwithstanding the appropriateness or inappropriateness of this term or its value-judgement, we have to continue with its usage, since terms are imperative for classifying communities so that one could be distinguished from the other.

Moreover, in spite of their innate problems, certain terms continue to be used for they become an ineluctable part of the social taxonomy of the state. Perhaps this could be said about the term *adivasi*; what intrigued me was why the Wardha seminar did not use the words such as 'tribal', 'Scheduled Tribes', or the Hindi word *janjati*, preferring *adivasi* over these words. Was it done inadvertently, thoughtlessly, or just casually? In the sense that one may use any word, it does not really matter till the time it identifies the group of the communities about which we want to talk [*see* Sundar, (ed.) 2016].

Creating *Adivasi* Identity: The Case of *Karma* Dance

I am reminded of an incident. Some years ago, one of the English newspapers printed a picture. It was of a scene of the *karma* festival which the tribal communities of Central India celebrate and still do with great involvement. On the occasion of this festival, a dance is organized, known after the name of the festival. The picture printed in the newspaper was of the *karma* dance.

Earlier this dance used to take place in the settlements of the tribal people. In those days, the permanent residents of the village who used to be away to towns and the other villages in connection with work and employment would return to their native places to observe the festival. However, in recent years, the number of migrants from these villages to cities has increased; but also the migrants have moved to far-off cities from where it becomes difficult for them to travel to their natal villages. Not only that it is a journey of some days, during which they would have to be without wages, but also it would be an expensive proposition, from the cost of the journey ticket to buying gifts for kin and affine.

Back in the villages, the scenario is dull. Because of large-scale migration, the ancestral habitations of these people have almost been depopulated. Some of them have paved way for the installation of the programmes of development. Some of them have become so slim and impoverished that neither is the festival celebrated there nor do people wait impatiently for its arrival. So engrossed are they in the everyday struggle of survival—getting food, fuel, and fodder—that they have sadly become distanced from the cycle of fairs and festivals. However, those of their kin who have migrated have shifted the fulcrum of these festivals to the cities where now they are almost permanently shifted. Now *karma* is celebrated with intense enthusiasm and far more elaborately in cities, thus adding to the cultural diversity in the towns they inhabit. Moreover in towns and cities, some of the migrants have done well and thus are able to set apart some of their savings for these ritual celebrations.

The picture printed in the newspaper was of the celebration of *karma* dance in a neighbourhood of Delhi; and when I had a closer look at the picture, I noted that one of the dancers was a female research scholar from my department. The caption below the picture was: "The *karma* dance of the *adivasi* of Bihar and Jharkhand." At no place was mentioned that the tribespersons in the picture were from Delhi; name of the venue, the Delhi neighbourhood, or any other, was also stated nowhere. It was my guess that the dance might have been performed in Delhi since one of the dancers was from my department, and later my conjecture received confirmation.

A couple of days later I met this researcher in the department. I reminded her of the picture on *karma* dance, and the fact that I was able to recognize her in the dancer's attire. She told me that the Munda migrants to Delhi have constituted their own association, and each year they organize a set of cultural programmes on the occasion of *karma*, one of which is the dance. For this, every year a number of accomplished dancers are invited from Hazari Bagh to train the amateur dancers of Delhi. One of the major objectives of the Munda association is to keep the tradition of their society alive and to familiarize the posterity with it, and instill in them love for their tribespersons. Such associations working for arousing the sense of social unity and cultural awakening have emerged among other communities as well—she substantiated this point citing examples of the associations of tribal people from Bihar and Jharkhand in Delhi. The urban world is unmistakeably a mosaic of cultures.

Tribes as Markers of Differentness

Once again drawing her attention to the picture, I asked: "Whilst introducing the content of the picture, the newspaper called the dancers *adivasi*. Do you agree with the usage of this word for your community?" I still remember her reply, a mix of emotion and agitation. She said:

"None of us ever likes the use of the word *adivasi*. Do you think we are '*adivasi*'? Do we appear to be '*adivasi*'? Do we look 'primitive'? In fact, we are far more educated than the reporters who came to interview us and take our photographs. When they were told that *karma* is a 'tribal' dance, they became interested in us, and might have thought that this is the dance of the simple, non-literate, rustic folks, and a report on it would make an interesting reading for the readers. Not only they, but also all others call us '*adivasi*' as if we are small, insignificant, downtrodden, and subdued creatures, and an exhibition of our culture, our exhibits, would greatly entertain the civilized, educated, urban people."

Although she did not use the word 'exotic', central to her reply was the idea that in spite of the changes that have occurred in them, the tribespersons have not been able to free them from the images of 'cultural strangeness and exoticism'. Newspapers intending to fill their pages with the photographs of tribes in their traditional costumes and the descriptions of their traditional practices lend ample support to the notion of 'tribal exoticism'.

Listening to her reaction, which was in Hindi, I was reminded of what anthropologists usually say: "Strange and peculiar objects sell, for they take away the boredom of city dwellers." Cities aim towards uniformity and routine, which overtime produce a general environment of 'disinterestedness and unexcitedness'. People crave for change; they look for agencies that break this routine. And that is the 'ethnic colour'. People flock to shops that market 'tribal products', proudly displaying them in their living rooms. Unsurprisingly a shop may be named 'Tribe', stocking objects supposed to be from different tribes of India. Ethnic products decorate people's homes, which add to its diversity.

However, it may be noted that many products sold in these shops which are believed to be the handiwork of tribal persons are in fact not theirs, not manufactured by them, but have been made in big factories, to cater to the market. It is well known to anthropologists that tribal families make these objects for their own subsistence—for use and gifting—and certainly not for commercial activities. Obviously, the number of such items they make would be limited, for they are for personal consumption. When the urban demand for these objects is high, the tribal families with their limited technology and the domestic mode of production are unable to cope up with it. Against this backdrop emerge the big manufacturing units, sometimes having the patronage of multinational organizations, which produce these objects on a mass scale, better in quality, shine and finish. The beauty of tribal objects rests in its roughness, ruggedness, a sort of natural finish, which is a crucial mark of their being hand-finished. Look at the irony: tribal exhibits sell, but the profits instead of going to the people, the original creators of the ideas of these objects, go to the capitalists, their mass-scale manufacturers. A student from Nagaland once told me that the shawls—famously known as the 'Naga shawls'—sold all-over urban India are in fact manufactured in industrial units located in Dimapur and the parts of Assam. Many workers in these enterprises are Naga themselves, employed on wages and are not the co-sharers of the profit. In recent years, many non-Naga have learned the art of making these shawls and are employed in these units or have themselves started their own manufacturing centres.

An important idea to examine here is the separation of the technology from the community. In a traditional context, the technology of producing artifacts and the community that produces them are inseparable; for instance, the 'Naga shawls' are made by the Naga, and they are called so for that reason. Once the entrepreneurs, who hail from different communities, come to know that these artifacts have the potential marketability, they start appropriating the technology. The traditional technology which has an inalienable relationship with the people, its creators and preservers, on being separated, is developed, and modified to increase its efficiency and productive robustness. No more does it remain 'traditional', a part of the subsistence economy. It now moves into the commercial system—it has to cope with the demands of production on a mass level. Bearing little resemblance with its past, its products are still couched in the 'ethnic name'. The latter is 'commodified', but what sells under its name is qualitatively different from what used to be the traditional product. Thus, the technology, the people who produced and carried it forward, and the name by which it is known are all separated. In the process, the technology is modernized to bear little resemblance with its traditional prototype, those who work on it are from different social moorings, but the original name of the products continues. This process would remind us of the transformation of the little tradition into great tradition. When this happens, the creators of the former are forgotten forever, and the modified and the developed one is supposed to be for the consumption of all.

Incidentally, anyone can appropriate the appellation 'tribal' in the name of his enterprise; to the best of my knowledge there is no rule that prohibits the use of this term, although there should be considering the fact that an outlet titled 'Tribal' may in fact be selling products which resemble 'tribal', but have not been manufactured by tribal people. The appropriation of the word 'tribal' and its goods is a clear way towards commercialization, with the sole aim of enhancing the profit. This is another kind of exploitation to which tribal communities are now being subjected. The 'tribal people' might be critical of the use of the word 'tribal' for them, for they may find it disparaging, but the commercial world wants to extract as much profit out of it as is possible, because the objects connected with it sell. In other words, the pristine tribal material and non-material things have to be kept alive for the urban (and non-tribal) world. The paradox is that the more ethnic the way of living and embellishment of your space, the more modern and urbane you are likely to be classified!

I have also been told that tribal songs and poems, folk tales and puzzles, jokes and wits have been collected by travellers to their areas, some of whom happen to be anthropologists, and instead of publishing these as the 'tribal literature', they have modified these here and there, made them wear the contemporary symbolism, and published these in their own names. These are the other interesting examples of the transformation of little into great tradition; and the appropriation of the tribal cultural capital by the dominant sections of our society.

Another example that can be taken up here is of the local music; many film music composers are well known for picking up tunes (and words) of songs from local tribal and peasant communities, embellishing this and then passing it on as their own composition. This type of plagiarism has remained unstudied and unprotected primarily because tribal literature and music has collective authorship to which more and more ideas and compositions are added and deleted in each generation. Each individual has the right to own it and add to it what he thinks is appropriate. Since, the values of collectivity run through the entire fabric of the tribal communities, there is no scope of an individual claiming his distinct contribution.

Tribes are Open and Democratic

I have also noted in my field visits that tribal and rural people feel happy and gratified when outsiders to their areas make serious attempts to learn their language and songs. In fact, some of them instantly adopt the role of a teacher, trying to facilitate their 'voluntary disciples' in the process of learning. In this way, the local culture spreads. It also came to my knowledge that these people are not closed in their orientations, shutting the doors of their culture to extraneous influences. If something excites them and is not contrarily placed to their own culture, they may unhesitatingly accept it provided the others do not launch objections to it. As they are relatively open, they do not object to the others for being the same. The female members of the Raika of Rajasthan, with whom I had a stint of field experience, would often tape their songs (on my cassette-recorder) they collectively sang on ritual and ceremonial occasions for me to listen and also inspire my women relatives in Delhi to learn. I was impressed with the philanthropy of their culture: If it is good, it must be learned by all; we should not be so mean as to keep a monopoly on things that are good for the entire humankind. I have often heard fieldworkers say that the local people with whom they had worked often displayed reluctance in sharing with them the secrets of their medicine, magical spells, or craftspersonship, for they thought that their learners would start practicing these, eventually standing in an economic competition with them, thus severely thwarting their livelihood.

Whilst I do not doubt the credibility and veracity of these experiences, particularly now against the backdrop of the "commoditization of tribal objects and intellectual artifacts" and the gains ultimately flowing to their appropriators, my experience has been a little different. If the simple communities closely guarded their knowledge, it was because it was thought to be esoteric and sacred. It should not be conveyed to those who would be nonchalant to the mores of holding the knowledge in prestige. The fear that the deities guarding this knowledge would turn awry and displeased was also conveyed to me in some cases, and if it were to happen not only the knowledge would be estranged but those who have transmitted it to unworthy vessels would not go unpunished; on the contrary, a trustworthy disciple, irrespective of his social origin, would not be denied of this knowledge. One may recall here the famous case of Carlos Castaneda (1968), a doctoral student in anthropology, who became a laudable disciple of Don Juan Matus, a shaman from the American Indian community of the Yaqui.

In other words, tribal and rural people would unhesitatingly impart their knowledge to the others, the eager and the inquisitive. The 'ever-givingness', as I would call this practice of sharing knowledge, for which the simple communities are well known, can always lead to a state of alienation, where their acquirers [the 'merchants of astonishment', as

Clifford Geertz (2000) called them] market it for their economic benefits. Thus, unless the notions of collective authorship and tribal rights are legally protected and clearly defined, this kind of plagiarism is bound to continue, whether it is in the sale of ethnic goods or the products of literary activities.

The research student, who was in the *karma* dance party, continued: "We shall have to raise our voice against this kind of media coverage of the tribal communities. In case we do not protest, we would be assumed to be a part of the conspiracy against the tribes. And, we would also be construed as accepting the concepts and images through which tribes are represented." Supporting her ideas, I advised her to place this matter before the association of their community, which should write a strong letter to the editors of the newspaper protesting against their description in its columns so that they come to know that the people of tribal origin do not like the way in which they are described and in future they should refrain from committing an error of this kind.

Media play an important role in changing, shaping and correcting the public opinion. For a sensitive and correct understanding of the tribal situation and its portrayal, the media houses should have on their editorial staff some experts on tribal matters. In a nutshell, my point was that the people should raise their voice against any injustice they think has been done to them; if they do not like something, they should not just confine their protest to private gatherings of their kin and kith, but bring it to the public domain so that people from different walks of life are gradually educated about the tribal issues. This would gradually rectify the mistaken understanding.

Contested Terms

I laid the matter of nomenclature to rest by suggesting that the newspapers should check whether the community about which they are going to write is one of the Scheduled Tribes, and if it is, they should say so, using the term given in the Constitution of India rather than using any other term which may be misleading, ambiguous, or even insulting. I may remind my readers here that during the meetings of the Constituent Assembly, Shri Jaipal Singh Munda (henceforth Jaipal Singh) wanted the word *adivasi* to be included in the Constitution of India for the tribes, a suggestion that Dr. B.R. Ambedkar turned down on the ground that it was a general term, without specific 'legal *de jure* connotation'.

Furthermore, it gave priority to the issue of 'settlement' and not to a 'specific group of people'. Literally meaning 'the people of the pristine times', it became, as the time passed by, a contested term, for it came to imply the 'indigenous people'.

My other submission in this regard is that the term 'tribe' should equally be avoided, for this is anthropological and should be used if the community under discussion has those social and cultural features which are unequivocally 'tribal'; and considering the fact that the changes emanating from extraneous systems are constantly affecting people all-over the country, with the result that the 'hitherto tribes' have already started their journey towards 'de-tribalization', it becomes a formidable task to call communities 'tribal' as the term is understood in anthropological writings. Perhaps, against this backdrop, A.R. Desai (1969) called tribes 'tribes in transition', which incidentally is the title of the recent collection of Yogesh Atal's (2016) essays on tribes he has written over a length of time. My suggestion to the Wardha anthropologists was that when the title of the seminar is in Hindi, we should use the Hindi translation of the term Scheduled Tribe, *anusuchit janjati*.

I have not conducted a full-length survey, but whatever I have learned from my students, friends, and acquaintances who hail from one or the other tribal community that they have reservation about the use of the word *adivasi* for them, notwithstanding Jaipal Singh's emotionally-charged submission before the Constituent Assembly that the "word *adivasi* has grace." Firstly, this word is not in currency among all tribal communities, especially those of the North-Eastern part of India. Some groups in Assam may use the word *adivasi* for them, as has also been reported about the tribes from Kerala, having adopted it from their brethren in Central India. Although it was used in some government publications, the term essentially received its popularity in the writings and speeches of Jaipal Singh and his supporters. Incidentally, in 1938, he also founded the Adivasi Mahasabha. His main submission was that the *adivasi* were the "first settlers in India"; their settlements are at least six thousand years old. It is not clear how he arrived at this conclusion; but more than culling archaeological and historical evidences in support of his assertion, he rested his argument on the fact that the tribespersons were his 'own folks', and being an 'insider' and 'moving about' with them, he knew the truth, which outsiders would perhaps never come to know. As a consequence, the term *adivasi* came to mean, as said earlier, the 'indigenous people'. These ideas were a part of his speech at the Constituent Assembly referred to previously in this chapter.

It was the first meaning, the 'political meaning' of the term *adivasi*, for it tried to define the rights of the people over their colonized land and resources, since they were *believed* to be the first to clear the jungle, make it habitable, and settle down. In fact a robust support to this belief comes from the 'story (or the myth!) of origin' that different tribes hold, according to which after the great deluge or catastrophe, the Almighty created a man and a woman and sent them to earth to live and procreate, and they were the first ancestors of the tribe. So, the members of a tribe believe they were the first to be created in that part of the earth they presently inhabit. However, this myth is irreconcilable with the stories—and also archaeological and historical evidence—of their migration from one territory to the other in search of what is called the green pastures. If the first lends support to their autochthonous status, then the second refutes it, for it conclusively states the difficulties in fixing the status of indigenousness of a population.

The other meaning of the term *adivasi* is given in 'temporal, archaeological, and cultural' terms, which is understood as referring supposedly to the 'people of the past' who are contemporaneously dwelling the not-so-easily-accessible-and-approachable territories of the country. The societies of these people are vital and enduring. They have among their characteristic ways of living what are believed to be the 'traits of their past', and they are nothing but 'non-Western'. In other words, all those aspects that were 'non-Western' came to be called 'primitive'. The term *adivasi* also implied the 'unchanging people', the 'preliterate', the "folks with simple technology, who live hand-to-mouth and are perpetually peregrinating in search of food".

The media, as it has always looked for sensational and attention-gluing items, left no stone unturned in inculcating the images of these people as 'primitive'—the so-called "tattooed people who, being scantily dressed, wore feathers and bead jewellery". Bereft of the tradition of reading and writing, it was believed they gibbered, had no abstract conception of ideas, could count no more than twenty, lived as simply as possible, and the technology they had could easily be learned by the posterity. The stereotypes that the media floated (and is floating) were (and are) diametrically opposed to the writings of the twentieth-century anthropologists who time and again have argued, often emphatically, on the basis of a solid ethnographic evidence that one could learn a lot from these communities about how to deal with nature and preserve it and how to live with amity and interdependence among themselves and with others. The tribes have a lot to teach the world.

But the media runs in its own way. In Hindi films, tribes are often depicted as backward, violent, and non-reflective as well as isolated from the 'enervations of modernity', "as carriers of local artistic and colourful culture, and happy-go-lucky-people"; in both cases, they are shown as a 'timeless humanity' (Taylor, 2002). Just have a look at the debate in reference to the 1972 Hindi film "*Yeh Gulistan Hamara*" and the representation of a tribal community living on the Indo-China border in it in the Proceedings of the Meghalaya Legislative Assembly of 3 April, 1973, and we would be convinced that tribal communities are no more placid, accepting the ways they are portrayed in films. In fact, the members of the Ao Naga community considered a song in the film, *mera nam Ao, mere pas ao*, as offensive; the song was subsequently withdrawn (Hasan, 2011: 32).

Ideas and views on tribes certainly changed in the latter half of the twentieth century, but earlier many anthropologists expressed their deep concern on the vast transformation of tribal people because these changes were evidently detrimental to the survival of local communities; in some cases, however, some anthropologists rued the changes, for they left the tribal people de-tribalized, thus making them uninteresting to the wider public. Two cartoons evocatively summed up these ideas: the first showed two Westerners gifting a laptop to a tribal, saying "Today we are giving you this, tomorrow we will give you the anti-depressants." The second cartoon, a well known strip from the Gary Larson's series called "The Far Side", showed two tribal men removing television sets and lamps from their habitation, shouting "Anthropologists! Anthropologists!" From their window one could see two men in hats moving towards the tribal huts, and they are the anthropologists!

The idea is that the anthropologists want to see the tribal people 'primitive' and in turn, the tribes also want to keep this image of their self 'intact', so all modern amenities they have must be instantly removed otherwise their image as of the 'primitive people' would be tarnished. In this way, they obliged the anthropologists so that they could continue with their study of tribes as the 'unchanging lot'. We all remember that one of the main criticisms of Verrier Elwin's approach towards tribal societies was that it did not want people to change, or help their assimilation with the outside world; it worked towards keeping the people as they were so that they could readily be available for an anthropological study. It was against this allegation that Elwin (1955) wrote his well-known article titled “Do We really want to keep them in a Zoo?”

The Idea of Integration

Having initially espoused the idea of temporarily isolating the tribal communities so that they could be saved from the incessant episodes of exploitation at the hands of the land-grabbers, liquor-vendors, money-lenders, voyeur-seekers, and the state officials of different ranks, Elwin, on seeing the condition of the tribal communities in his field sojourns in the North-Eastern Frontier Agency (NEFA, now Arunachal Pradesh), changed his stand. If ‘isolation’ was perhaps a suitable strategy for the tribes of central India, it was not so for the communities in the NEFA, which were distributed over a vast area, with each community insulated from the other.

Because of being cut-off from the wider world, each of them had virtually remained in the same state as it was in the past. Although, it certainly did not imply that these people were ‘changeless’, what it meant was that the pace of change (which was mostly endogenous) was so slow and imperceptible that it did not mark a qualitative change in the styles of living. Whilst the external world—the ‘connected world’, so to say—was fast changing, trying to bring the institutional benefits to the doors of the people, thus improving upon their lives, the ‘unconnected world’ of the NEFA was continuing with its day-to-day struggles of living, which were multiplying as time rolled by.

Against this backdrop, the strategy of isolation was a misfit. Perhaps it would not have worked effectively even for those areas for which it was initially given, the areas which were rather deleteriously exposed to the situations of asymmetrical cultural contact. Temporary isolation, if stringently enforced, might have saved the local populace from exploitation and ridicule at the hands of the outsiders, but for introducing changes, the outsiders, especially technically-adroit, would be needed to be brought in. Notwithstanding the care taken to regulate the flow of human traffic in tribal areas, the situations of cultural confrontation were not unavoidable. Thus, the policy of isolation had to be rethought, for its advantages were likely to be outweighed by its demerits. Surely, this approach was not applicable to those areas which were already isolated, and desperately needed to be linked with the wider world, as were those of the NEFA.

The process of integration emerged as a viable option to the temporary solution of isolation. Voiced convincingly in Elwin's *A Philosophy for NEFA*, and marvelously summed up as five propositions in his Foreword that Jawaharlal Nehru contributed to the second edition of this book (1959), integration is considered as the 'sheet-anchor' of the tribal policy to which the Indian state has always subscribed (Singh, 1985). Documents after documents, reports of committees and commissions, constituted to look into tribal problems, have unfailingly noted that the final objective of the programmes of development and welfare is to "integrate the tribal communities with the mainstream of Indian society." From the Fifth Five-Year Plan, a lot of attention is being given to poverty-alleviation measures, but the ultimate aim is the "mainstreaming of tribal people". The rationale behind it is that because tribes have always been isolated from that complex of human society where changes keep on occurring fast, where innovations are regularly taking place that are the prime movers of progress, they have not able to make use of any of these. They lagged behind while rest of the society moved from one stride of development to another. The culture of 'non-development' and 'underdevelopment' persisted over generations, leading to a thick precipitation of frustration, disgust, and apathy towards the outsiders; in many parts of the country it culminated into violence, including blood-shed. The panacea to all the problems lay in the integration of tribes with the wider world, for this would lead to their partaking of the gains of development.

Mainstream

Some of the assumptions behind this thinking need to be mooted.

For instance: the idea that the tribes were (and are) an isolated lot. In fact, both historical and ethnographic evidences amply point out that the members of a tribal community were never isolated, although their degree of relationship with the outside world varied from one group of people to the other. Tribes had several economic and social exchange relations with the other communities in and around their neighbourhood. Some of tribal communities carried out long-distance trade relations as well (Singh, 1985). As a result of these interactions enduring for years, the communities were able to *adopt* the cultural traits of the others which they thought were useful, and in course of time, they *adapted* to them or changed them so that they could become synchronous with their culture.

Second, the concept of mainstream has also been fraught with the problems of definition and identification: What and where is the mainstream? In fact, most of the understanding of this concept is at the intuitive level—the assumption that 'we know what it is', so the need for a lengthy discussion on and about it is plainly superfluous.

The government documents conceptualize a singular mainstream, underlying which is the notion of a nation state and its defining and diacritical symbols and institutions. Integration of a community with the mainstream is based on two things: first, it wholeheartedly accepts the battery of symbols and participates in the state's institutions, reposing full faith in each one of them; and second, the state takes all the necessary steps to facilitate the process whereby the 'marginalized' and 'shy' communities participate in the institutions without feeling discriminated. Incidentally, the idea that the tribes are "shy of establishing a contact with the outside world" was one of the criteria that the B.N. Lokur Committee identified in its definition of a tribal society, a definition which is still used for identifying tribal communities for the purpose of scheduling (*see* Srivastava, 2011; *Annual Report*, Ministry of Tribal Affairs, 2015-16).

This is the concept of mainstream from 'above', which may be at variance with and also, exist along, the conceptions that the locally-entrenched communities have. For hill-dwellers, the mainstream is the lifestyle of the plains persons; for lower castes, it is of the upper castes; for the non-Hindu, it is of the Hindu; for rural, it is of the urban. In other words, the local communities think that the mainstream is always decided by the dominant sections in their respective contexts, to which they are expected to submit unchallengeably. Since people have different identities emerging from their differential locations in society, they are expected to succumb to different 'mainstreams'. People find each mainstream 'oppressive'; the more are the demands of the mainstream, the more inwardly and withdrawn the community is likely to become.

Neither is the mainstream space-bound nor just an ensemble of institutions. It is an idea embodying the principle of equality and inclusiveness; a community is said to be a part of the 'mainstream' when it has equal opportunities to participate in the institutions of the society and where its participation on equal terms is not thwarted by any convention, practice, custom, or rule. And in case, there exist some constraints on its participation, it is the duty of the state to remove them at the earliest. The integration of communities to the mainstream is an example of a directed and planned change; for 'mainstreaming' to happen naturally, if at all it occurs, a long time of interaction between communities is the minimal requirement. Furthermore, the natural process involves the existing social dynamics, the inequalities between communities, and therefore, the 'mainstreaming' does not happen on equal lines [*see* Chaudhury and Patnaik, (eds.) 2008]. In other words, communities get linked up, rather than remaining cut-off, but the system of a hierarchical arrangement continues to exist. In other words, becoming a part of the mainstream does not guarantee either equality or the equality of opportunities.

The concept of mainstream dear to me is not at the empirical level. For many writers on this subject, tribes urgently require to be brought into the mainstream, for they are relatively geographically isolated, therefore the gains of progress and development do not reach them as they reach those who are not. Against this backdrop, breaking the isolation of the communities is imperative. In this thinking, the 'mainstream' is the 'wider world', the 'interconnected world', the 'stratified world', the 'world of differences and inequalities', so if the hill tribes start having unremitting interactions with the plains dwellers, then for many, it would be the inauguration of their 'mainstreaming'. In this mode of thinking, mainstream may be defined as "breaking of the isolation of communities and their interaction with the outside world".

It is this empirical meaning that I intend to reject, for as noted earlier, the tribal communities in India were (and are) not truly isolated, and over time their exchanges with the outside world have been fast growing. In other words, they, on their own, courtesy the evolutionary processes, were becoming a part of the outside world, thus, were getting mainstreamed. Such a notion of the mainstream masks the distinction between the two approaches to deal with the predicament of Indian tribes, namely 'assimilation' and 'integration'. In both cases, tribes are being linked to the outside world, but none of them ensures a treatment of equality. Assimilation strips the people of their individual cultural identity, whereas integration does not upset the hierarchical order.

Therefore, the need to look for an alternative concept arises, one where mainstream is seen not in 'empirical' but 'ideational' terms. Mainstream is understood here as 'not a given category', since, if it is conceived in this way, it will be an assemblage of communities, ranked hierarchically, to which more and more groups are gradually attached. The cardinal issue is to create a just and equal society. For achieving this endeavour, it is mandatory that the 'mainstream is built-up' with commitment, consciously, concertedly, and devotedly, on the values of equality and justice. Surely, for realizing this idea, the efforts of the state are of paramountcy; however, they need to be supplemented and strengthened with the conscientious work of the other stakeholders, including the non-governmental organizations, voluntary associations, and the communities themselves.

Development over Protection

Here, one of the conclusions of the Report of the High Level Committee on the Socio-economic, Health and Educational Status of Tribal Communities of India (Ministry of Tribal Affairs, Government of India, May 2014) is of worthy significance. In its Introduction, it observes that although the various committees, commissions, and task forces that the Indian Government constituted in the last sixty years to look into the problems of tribal societies differed in their approaches, they all have dealt with two issues in common—of development and protection.

The first pertains to the progressive and community-wise change of tribes, with the diligent and conscientious efforts of the state, and an equitable distribution of the gains of development to all, especially the most economically and weaker sections of the society. The progress has to be community-oriented (what is known as micro-level planning), for tribes widely differ in terms of their social and economic profiles, and the political power they wield in regional politics, where they succeed in getting their claims and demands met with, which is not the case with demographically smaller communities, mostly engaged in foraging, shifting cultivation, monsoon-dependent farming, or working as labourers in the agricultural sector or unskilled workers in the industrial. The central idea here is that the progress of a country is dependent upon the overall, equitable development of its people. Development has a bigger aim: to empower people so that they are able to execute their own plans of change and sustain them as well. In fact, the lack of development and continuation of social and economic backwardness is supposed to be one of the principal causes of the left-wing extremism in certain parts of India. It is said that the perpetrators of violence in these areas capitalize on the woeful state of local poverty and deprivation, and their exhortations mislead the gullible people who fall prey to their nefarious designs.

With no intention to undermine the place of development in bringing about a qualitative change in the lives of people, of equal importance is the issue of safeguarding the dignity, esteem, and interests of people. The earlier discussion on the appropriateness of the use of the term *adivasi* for tribal people made is richly clear that it is rooted in a system of inequality; the use of this word is not only derogatory but also an attack on the self-esteem of people, who come to be labelled as 'of pristine times'. Many of the so-called 'hate crimes' against the members of tribal societies, especially from the north-eastern part of the country, have their origin in the complex of beliefs perpetuated over time that regards them as quaint and inferior. At this juncture, it may be pointed out that one of the prime duties of the state and all the other agencies that are concerned with the issues of tribal development is to work towards changing the 'mind-set' of the entire society regarding the stereotypes they nurture about tribal people. The media should not paint them as 'bizarre' and like 'museum exhibits'.

Whilst the term 'development' has become a cliché, a phrase often used boisterously for gaining political victory, and a lot of effort is being purportedly paid to it, the state has unequivocally failed with respect to protecting the rights of tribespersons. The Report of the High Level Committee notes (p. 26): "...the protective measures have been violated by the very State which is supposed to ensure the enforcement of these protections." The Report concludes that this is one of the main causes of the marginalization of Indian tribes. It is well known that tribal rights are violated in the episodes of their displacement to make land for development programmes. Sachchidananda, a keen observer of the tribal life in Bihar, once told me that the "state is the greatest alienator of tribal land". The gains of development largely go to the upper classes, for they are the ones who have the infrastructure where these gains could be ploughed back; furthermore, we should not forget that economically and politically powerful classes lose no time in improving the ways of 'pocketing' the positive outcomes of development.

Against this backdrop, in many parts of the country, the tribal communities have opposed the programmes of development—in some cases, tooth-and-nail—not because they are anti-development, but because they know that development would lead to a spoilage of their habitat, their nature, their 'mother earth', from the womb of which they draw the resources they need for their bare, essential survival. And once their habitat is rendered hopeless, they know their survival would be irrevocably paralyzed. They know well, as can easily be inferred from the reports, including of the popular media, from different parts of tribal areas, the sordid stories of those of their brethren who became destitute after the much-acclaimed programmes of change came to their areas. Development, for most of them, is not sort of a curse they have to live with. This would explain the feeling of anti-development that has settled among many of them, and would also explain the rise of their ethnicity and the social movements of revivalism.

Who does not want Good Life?

Who does not want to live with dignity? Who does not want a comfortable living, free from pangs of hunger and rounds of deprivation? Who does not want that his children settle down in good jobs and have security in life? Tribesmen are no exception. They are a witness to the images of affluence that incessantly circulate in the channels of media. Like the deprived people in general, they ask them why they have not been to get the comforts the others have, why are they discriminated in independent India? The answer they reach, sometimes with the help of the activists and social workers traversing their areas, lies in what is popularly known as thc "class character of development", in the hiatus between the rhetoric of development and its ground-level reality, what development has led to—the alienation of land, the despoliation of their habitat, the exploitation of their women and children, and their plunging into the ranks of 'worried community'.

It is true that for improving upon the state of affairs for tribes the state policies and their outcomes need to critiqued. The state officials, tribal experts, and the members of the local communities should establish an interactive platform, setting aside their affectivity for a particular skein of arguments and the intellectual power they think they hold because of a particular vantage point in the discourse and the academic specialization they may hold. The non-establishment of a dialogue between stakeholders has been one of the main causes of the lack of clear understanding on matters on tribal importance. More than that it is extremely important that tribal issues and problems are 'mainstreamed', implying that the wider society comes to have a reliable and empathetic understanding of the tribal people, their culture and the issues that confront them.

References

Annual Report. 2015-16. Government of India: Ministry of Tribal Affairs.

Atal, Yogesh, 2016. *Indian Tribes in Transition*. New Delhi: Routledge Publications.

Castaneda, Carlos, 1968. *The Teachings of Don Juan: A Yaqui Way of Knowledge*. California: University of California Press.

Chaudhury, Sukant K. and Soumendra Mohan Patnaik (eds.), *Indian Tribes and the Mainstream*. Jaipur: Rawat Publications.

Constituent Assembly of India, Volume 1. [parliamentofindia. nic.in/ls/debates/vol1p9.htm]. Accessed on 8 January, 2017.

Desai, A.R., 1969. "Tribes in Transition", (pp. 221-31) in A.R. Desai (ed.) *Rural Sociology in India*. Bombay: Popular Prakashan.

Elwin, Verrier, 1955. Do we really want to keep them in a zoo? In *Adivasi*. Government of India: Ministry of Information and Broadcasting (pp. 9-22).

——. 1959. *A Philosophy for NEFA*. Shillong: North-Eastern Frontier Agency.

Foucault, Michel, 1990. *The History of Sexuality: An Introduction*. Volume 1. New York: Random House.

Geertz, Clifford, 2000. *Available Light: Anthropological Reflections on Philosophical Topics*. Princeton: Princeton University Press.

Hasan, Daisy, 2011. "Talking back to 'Bollywood': Hindi Commercial Cinema in North-Eastern India", (pp. 29-50) in Shakuntala Banaji (ed.), *South Asian Cultures: Audiences, Representations, Contexts*. London: Anthem Press (pp. 29-50).

Mathur, Hari Mohan, 2013. *Displacement and Resettlement in India: The Human Cost of Development*. London: Routledge Publications.

Padel, Felix, 2010. *Out of this Earth. East India Adivasis and the Aluminium Cartel*. Delhi: Orient Blackswan.

Report of the High Level Committee on the Socio-economic, Health and Educational Status of Tribal Communities of India. May 2014. Government of India: Ministry of Tribal Affairs.

Singh, K. Suresh, 1985. *Tribal Society in India: An Anthropo-Historical Perspective*. Delhi: Manohar Publishers.

Srivastava, V.K, 2011. "A critical reading of the Draft of the National Tribal Policy", (pp. 92-132) in Arun Kumar Ghosh and Ram Dayal Munda (eds.), *The Other Side of Development, The Tribal Story*. New Delhi, Seattle: Konark Publishers Pvt. Ltd.

Sundar, Nandini (ed.) 2016. *The Scheduled Tribes and Their India*. New Delhi: Oxford University Press.

Taylor, B., 2002. Public folklore, nation-building, and regional others: Comparing Appalachian USA and North-east India. *Indian Folklore Research Journal*, 1: 1-27.

Xaxa, Virginius, 2008. *State, Society, and Tribes: Issues in Post-Colonial India*. New Delhi: Pearson Education.

THREE

ETHNOGRAPHIC METHODOLOGICAL APPROACH FOR INDIGENOUS PEOPLE'S DEVELOPMENT IN CULTURAL PERSPECTIVE

A Case Study of Vulnerable Tribes in Vishakha Agency of Andhra Pradesh, India

V. SUBRAMANYAM

Introduction

Tribes in India constitute the second largest population, next to Africa, representing 635 tribes with the population of 10,42,81,034 (8.6%) as per 2011 census. A large chunk of tribal population in India is concentrated in high altitude forested zones of Eastern Ghats, Western Ghats, North-Eastern, Central and Himalayan Mountains. Tribal population in India is distributed in almost all the states except Haryana and Punjab. The newly carved Andhra Pradesh state consists of 27 tribes with the tribal population of 26,31,145 (5.3%), distributed in all the 13 districts. The district Visakhapatnam represents 16 tribes with the population of 5,57,572 (14.53%). Out of the total 16 tribes, 3 tribes considered as vulnerable tribes namely Khond, Gadaba, and Porja. These tribes are still at pre-agricultural stage of economy, with low literacy, stagnant or diminishing population and living in isolation of extreme backward condition. More than 60 per cent of these vulnerable tribes population stand at below poverty line and experiencing the severity of social exclusion and denial of equal opportunity to participate actively in the ongoing development process of the state and nation.

Indigenous and Tribal People

The definitions of indigenous communities contained in the ILO convention 107 of 1957 reflect the historical context of North America, South America and Australia. All the three components of the definition have been taken over from the historical situation of those regions. For instance; it is in these areas that the indigenous communities, peoples and nations are those which had a historical continuity with pre-invasion and pre-colonial societies that developed in their territories. Secondly, it is in these areas that the 'indigenous people' consider themselves distinct from other sectors of societies, now prevailing in those territories or parts of them. Thirdly, here the indigenous peoples form at present "non-dominant sectors of society and are determined to preserve, develop and transmit to future generations, their ancestral territories and their ethnic identity as the basis of their continued existence as people in accordance with their own cultural patterns, social institutions and legal system".

These three components in the definition of the indigenous peoples do not exactly fit in with historical situations of the old world. In India, the colonial encounter not only affected tribal communities, but also non-tribal societies. Thus, pre-invasion and pre-colonial situational experiences seem to be critical to the definition of indigenous peoples.

The colonial experience though has been savage and barbarous all-over the world; there was a significant measure of difference in the nature of this historical experience between the new world and India. Colonization in the new world and Australian indigenous people were exterminated and prosecuted in several parts. Their population declined and mixed populations came into existence on large scale. Thus, in the new world and Australia indigenous people were confronted with severe challenges to their productive natural resources and cultures.

In contradistinction to this scenario, the tribal people of India faced different situations. They played a positive historical role in the development of languages and culture of the country. Some of them participated in the anti-colonial struggle and post-colonial transformation and reconstruction.

Concept of Tribe and Policies of Tribal Development

Defining the Scheduled Tribes, Article 366 of the Indian Constitute observes "Scheduled Tribes means such tribes or tribal communities or part of or groups within such tribes or tribal communities as are deemed under Article 342 to the Scheduled Tribe for the purpose of this constitution", the important characteristic features of Tribe are backwardness, illiteracy, geographical isolation and poverty. In Indian Constitution, the main criteria for specifying communities as Scheduled Tribes includes: (1) traditional occupation of a definite geographical area; (2) distinctive culture which includes the whole spectrum of tribal way of life i.e., language, customs, traditions, religions, beliefs, arts, crafts etc., (3) primitive traits depicting occupational pattern, economy etc.; and (4) lack of education and techno-economic development (Verma, 1995: 6). The British government had introduced the nomenclature 'tribe' in India to designate and keep separate the simple little communities from the rest of Indian population. The colonial administration confined to a deliberate policy of segregation and kept the tribals away from rest of Indian population due to rampant tribal exploitation (economic and cultural). The colonial administration adopted the ethnographic methodology to understand the cultural background of all the ethnic groups including tribes of India, with the help of Thurston for their smooth administration and formulation of development policies. The post-independence tribal policy in India was essentially an extension of the paternalistic and protectionist policy adopted by colonial regime and was in a way international in its spirit. With regard to tribal development, there are two schools of thought, one is Gandhain policy of 'assimilation'/ 'integration' and second is the Verrier Elwin's policy "National Park" isolation. The policy of isolation should not workable forever in the era of Globalization. Hence, automatically the tribal's integration into the mainstream population due to the process of acculturation will happen. The fear of losing cultural identity is in the minds of certain tribal leaders, who are opposing Gandhian 'assimilation'/'integration' policy.

Vulnerable Tribes

Particularly Vulnerable Tribal Groups (PVTGs) are tribal communities among Scheduled Tribes, who live in mere isolation in inaccessible habitats. They are characterized by a low rate of growth of population, pre-agricultural level of technology and extremely low levels of literacy. Government of India has identified 75 particularly vulnerable tribal groups (PVTGs), located in fourteen states and union territories including Andaman & Nicobar Islands. The State of Andhra Pradesh has 35 tribes. Out of which 12 group are classified as PVTGs, namely (1) Bodo Gadaba, (2) Gutob Gadaba, (3) Bondo Gadaba, (4) Khond Porja, (5) Parangi Porja, (6) Dongaria Khond, (7) Kutia Khond, (8) Chenchu, (9) Konda Reddy, and (10) Konda Savara. The PVTGs found in Visakha Agency are: (1) Gadaba, (2) Khond, and (3) Porja.

Ecological and Cultural Background of Vulnerable Tribes

The district Visakhapatnam has two distinct regions of contrasting ecological and topographic features, one with plain landscape extending from the sea coast up to the foothills of Eastern Ghats with moderate temperature and the other covered by thick forests, a top elevated Eastern Ghats with cold climate. The total geographical area of the agency area of the district is 11,167 sq. kms. Most of the tribal habitats are found in the agency area of district. Visakha agency is a part of the Eastern Ghats in Andhra Pradesh state. The entire agency area falls under the sub-plan strategy of Paderu I.T.D.A. which consists of eleven tribal mandals, namely: (1) Paderu, (2) Hukumpeta, (3) Chinthapalli, (4) Araku valley, (5) Ananthagiri, (6) Koyyuru, (7) Gangaraju Madugula, (8) Munchingput, (9) Pedabayalu, (10) Dumbriguda, and (11) Gudem Kotha Veedhi. About 16 predominant tribal groups are distributed in the agency tracts of hills and forests.

The entire agency area in Visakhapatnam district is covered with thick forest growth of numerous trees and dales. Trees like *gal nut*, *nalla maddi*, jackfruit, tamarind, teak, mango, *buruga*, eucalyptus, *sampangi*, bamboo etc.; tree creepers like *adda*, *soapnut* are common in the forest. Tropical crops like coffee and pepper are also found in the thick forest area of Paderu, Chinthapalle and Gudem Kotha Veedhi Mandals. A number of wild animals are also present in the forest areas of Eastern Ghat. The most commonly found animals are bison, deer, bear, *cheeta*, tiger, fox, wild pig, hare, wolf etc. Snake, numerous birds, wild fowls and peacocks are also very common in the area. Over the period of time, the tribals have established symbiotic relations with the forests and they largely depend on the flora and fauna for their livelihood. Most of the PVTGs are habituated to inhabit in the interior forests amidst wild animals. Their population is sparsely distributed in all the eleven tribal mandals of sub-plan area. Each PVTG settlement is surrounded by forests, hills, *podu* (shifting) fields and fruit bearing trees. Terrace cultivation is also seen in some of the non-timber forest produce collection. They are struggling hard to eke out their livelihood with the above mentioned subsistence activities with the result of depletion of forest resources day by day in their habitats.

Ethnographic Features

A brief account of ethnographic details of some tribes is given below. Food habitats, dressing pattern, material cultural and ritual practices are almost similar in all the three PVTGs. They have superstitious beliefs and worship animate and inanimate objects.

Porja

Porja is a hill tribe, inhabiting in Visakha agency area and they are spread over the adjoining hilly areas of Odisha. They are shifting cultivators. They raise crops in the *podu* plots on the high level hill slopes. Their mother tongue is '*Parji* dialect' a corrupt form of 'Odia' language and they use 'Telugu' language for inter-group communication. The term 'Porja' seems to have been derived from Odia words '*po*' and '*raja*' which means 'son of king' as described by Thurston (1909). The Porjas say that, they are the brothers of *rajas* (king), but the *Rajas* took riding horses, while Porja's could not get on to the back of the horse, and ultimately put up with all the burden of cultivating the lands. This tribe has several endogamous sub-groups, differing in their language, food habits and customs depending on the locality. Most common sub-groups found among Porja are: (1) Parangi Porja, (2) Jodia Porja, (3) Konda Porja or Bonda Porja, (4) Gadaba Porja, (5) Didayi Porja, and (6) Pengu Poja. Though marital relations do not exist in between the sub-groups, but communal relations exist. Social hierarchy is also found among these groups. Majority of population in Visakhapatnam agency belong to the Parangi Porja group. They belong to Naga and Surya clans. They do not have any title or suffix after the name of individual to identify the tribe. Surnames such as Pangi, Killo, Vanthala, and Korra, are found. Both clan and lineage exogamy are strictly observed. In certain settlements, the Porjas practice village exogamy also.

The Porja women are fond of tattooing. Girls more than five years of age are found with tattoo mark on the faces and hands. Bodily decoration is not the only motive behind this practice. It is a religious belief of the Porjas that after death one will leave everything behind in this world and to please the god of death '*Yama*', one will have nothing but indelible tattoo marks carried with its body. For tattooing, the services of women expert are hired on the basis of payment of remuneration in the form of grains.

The traditional *moitorjibu* (sacred friendship) is also in practice among Porjas. These associations are found irrespective of caste, creed, sex and these associations are continued from generation to generation. The main objective of the friendship is to promote the well-being of each other. Sometimes, the unmarried boys and girls enter into this sacred friendship and they can marry if they belong to marriageable clans. The Porjas especially the Jhodia Porja perform an enchanting folk dance called Jhodia *Nat* or Jelli *Nat* or Nandi *Nat*. In the past traditional youth dormitories have functioned very well among Porjas. But now such institutions are disappearing.

Porjas are physically very strong, stout and hard working. In comparison to other tribal communities, they have distinct cultural practices especially with respect to their settlement pattern, dress, ornaments, economic life, beliefs, worships, manners, customs and folk traditions. To some extent there is venophobia (fear of strangers) among them. They prefer to remain aloof from other communities. They inhabit either in small settlements or in separate hamlets away from the main village, share big settlements with other tribes like Bagata, Valmiki, Kotiya, Kondadora, Nookadora, Gadaba etc.

Khond

According to Macpherson (1863) "'Kanda' in Telugu means 'hill'. As these people live in deep forests and hills, they are called Khondulu". Khonds are also called as Kodulu, Samantha and Jatapu. In Visakha Agency they are called as Kodulu, Samanthulu, whereas in Vizianagaram agency they are known as Jatapu. They call themselves as '*Kuvingi*' in their *Kui* dialect. Khonds speak '*Kui*' language among themselves and only men speak Telugu with other communities. The physical stature of the Khonds indicated that they had a higher percentage of the Caspion blood in them. Majority of the Khonds were bright tawny in complexion with wavy hair and both prominent cheek bones. They were short and below medium in stature. They were mainly dolichocephalic mesorrhine people.

Khonds prefer to stay on the tops of interior forests. The hill and forest environment assures them in isolation and lives in fashion. Living in remote areas, they did not favour outside intrusion. They love to build their houses on the hill slopes of the valley, where they practice shifting cultivation. They stay in separate settlements apart from the other tribes. Most of their houses are thatched. They built their houses on the ground with hewn slabs laid one upon another. All those were plastered inside, thatched, and constructed in two rows. The walls of the houses were made of timber bound together and plastered over with mud. Roofs of their houses are made with bamboo and then thatched them as thickly as possible with grass.

Khonds amuse themselves in various ways such as hunting, dancing and singing. They are passionately fond of hunting. As they are the forest dwellers they pursue it with eagerness and love. During hunting session universal drunkenness and revelry is prevailed. Socio-religious festivals, big events in the community provide them with many fold opportunities for musical performance and dancing. Drums and trumpets are used while dancing on request. Shepherd's pipe is another musical instrument of the Khonds. The most important musical instrument is called the Khond 'Deka' which is used for personal pleasure while singing in the hot season. Peacock dance is very popular among Khonds which is performed by males only. Both men and women participate in the traditional tribal dance *Dhimsa*.

Podu (Shifting cultivation) is the basis of subsistence of Khonds. They are experts in felling of the trees and in preparation of *Podu* fields. Usually, the shifting cultivators raise the mixed crops like millets, pulses and oil seeds in the *Podu* fields during the rainy season. Khonds are experts in the extraction of oil from *niger*, *pungam* (Ganuga) and *Kusimi*. A few of them make wooden furniture and baskets with bamboo.

Gadaba

Gadaba call themselves '*Mogililu*' or '*Modililu*' in their own dialect. In the past they were the Palanquin bearers. Thurston (1909) mentioned that this tribe owes its name to the fact that their ancestors emigrated from the banks of Gadabari (Godavari) river, and settled at Nandapur, the former capital of the *Rajas* of Jeypore. Majumdar (1941) expressed his opinion that the Gadaba proceeded to their present habitat from the banks of the river Godavari. In *Savara* language the word 'go' denotes greatness and 'do' signifies water. Hence, the euphonic combination of word *gada* would be great water, meaning the river Godavari. It is more appropriate that the Gadaba and Savaras are classified as belonging to the same ethnic stock. In Andhra Pradesh Gadaba population is distributed in Visakhapatnam, Vizayanagaram and Srikakulam districts. This tribe is also found in Koraput and Ganjam districts of Odisha.

In Visakha agency area, most of the Gadaba settlements are located in the valleys, adjacent to the hill streams. Gadabas largely subsist on terrace and shifting cultivation. Settled cultivation also found in few Gadaba settlements. They raise the paddy in terrace fields and mixed crops like millets, pulses and oil seeds in *podu* fields during *Kharif* season. Very little land is available to them for cultivation which may not be sufficient to eke out their livelihood without the pangs of hunger. Some of the Gadaba families rear the sheep and goats which substitutes their income from agriculture.

Gadabas have their own dialect. Gadaba language is said to belong to the Mundari group. Majumdar said that the Gadaba belong to Austro-Asiatic linguistic family. They use the regional language Telugu for inter-group communication. Gadaba is divided into five sub-groups, namely: (1) Bodo Gutob, (2) Parenga, (3) Olaro, (4) Katheri, and (5) Kapu. Of these, the last two are settled in plains. The other three sub-groups found to live in the agency tracts. Most of the Gadabas in Visakha agency area belonged to Bodo or Gutob sub-group. The common surnames found in this sub-group are: (1) Korra (sun), Naga (Cobra), Bhag (tiger), Kera (parrot) and Gollori (monkey). People belonging to the same *intiperu* (surname) are considered brothers.

The traditional dress of Gadaba women is a bustle or dress improper, called *ire* or *kilte*. In the past, Gadaba females clothes were manufactured by themselves from cotton thread and the fibre of *Silloluvada* or *ankudi chettu* (hollarrhena anti-dysenterica) and *boda luvada* or *bodda chettu* (*Ficus glomerate*). The fiber is carefully dried and dyed blue or reddish brown. The edges of the cloth are white or blue or stripes of white or blue at regular intervals. Now-a-days, the Gadaba woman is wearing machine made *saree*. The present generation is not wearing their traditional clothes. Generally, Gadaba women have tattoo marks on different parts of their body. The tattoo marks are found on both the hands including upper portion of the palm. Every woman will invariably have a vertical line in the middle of the forehead. Tattooing is locally known as *pachabottu*. The Gadaba girls commonly have tattooing at the age of 10 to 14 years. Women among Gadaba are very fond of wearing silver ornaments.

Gadaba have folk tales, folk songs and dance of their own. They perform *Dhimsa* and *Koppu* dance. They have the belief in evil eye and spirits, they worship the village deities like *Asiramma*, *Jakaramma*, *Nookalamma*. *Jakarama Panduga* is an important festival for them. *Disari* is the religious priest who officiates rituals among them.

Role of I.T.D.A. in Poverty Alleviation among Vulnerable Tribes

The problem of tribal development is a difficult exercise in view of the paradoxical situation of an attempt to preserve the tradition while modernizing it an effort for continuity and change. The Government of India has initiated several initiatives and measures for tribal development under the programmes of planned change since independence. After India's independence both Central and State Governments paying attention to alleviate poverty among the tribals by adopting different developmental strategies and approaches like Multipurpose Tribal Development Blocks, Modified Area Development Approach (MADA), Tribal Development Block, Girijan Development Agencies and Tribal Sub-plan Approach with a focus on Integrated Area Development. In each Five Year Plan certain budget has been allocated for the tribal development. The tribal sub-plan strategy has been adopted for the tribal development from Fifth Five Year Plan period onwards. Till date, the same strategy is in operation for poverty alleviation and development among tribals of India.

The Integrated Tribal Sub-plan Strategy is considered to a land mark in the history of tribal development in India. The salient features of the strategy include an area and group specific approach in a balanced and integrated manner, in a cohesive operational area taking cognizance of the resources and needs of the local populations. Both the tribal concentrated and dispersed areas are covered under this strategy, unlike in the past. The vertical and horizontal integration of the administrative structure was aimed at autonomy facilitating a smooth functioning of the Integrated Tribal Development Agencies. Apart from the common infrastructural development in tribal areas, certain special programmes were initiated by the government through Integrated Tribal Development

Agencies. Special attention was paid to bring the vulnerable tribes on par with the other tribes Seventh Five Year Plan onwards.

Special Programmes for Vulnerable Tribes Development

Certain income generation programmes specifically introduced in the primitive tribal areas in order to reduce the poverty among the PVTGs. Few additional ITDAs were established exclusively for the development of most vulnerable tribes in different states. For instance, the Integrated Tribal Development Agency exclusively for Chenchu Tribe development was started functioning with its headquarters at Srisailam in Kurnool district from 1st August, 1988. The main focus of this ITDA is to improve the socio-economic conditions of Chenchu tribe predominantly inhabiting in Nallamalai forest zones of Andhra Pradesh. Similar kind of programmes were also extended by the ITDA at Paderu to the vulnerable tribes like Gadaba, Khond and Porja inhabiting in Visakha Agency area.

The ITDA at Paderu has initiated the programmes like education, agriculture and animal husbandry, economic betterment schemes, medical and health facilities, housing and self-employment, for poverty alleviation among Gadaba, Khond and Porja tribes. Apart from these, this ITDA has made special efforts on land development, supply of agriculture inputs, irrigation, horticulture, sericulture, distribution of lands in the reserve forest to grow coffee and pepper crops under the shades of big trees.

Economic supporting schemes like labour employment in forest department, petty trade, vocational training and employment were also introduced for the betterment of life of PVTGs. Under ISB Sector, financial support schemes were implemented. In this scheme, 80 per cent subsidy from special central assistance, 20 per cent margin money from TRICOR funds was sanctioned to all the beneficiaries keeping in view the guidelines given by Director of Tribal Welfare.

In addition to the above mentioned economic development schemes, certain infrastructural facilities like transport, communication, electricity, housing and health facilities were extended and strengthened in the predominantly vulnerable tribes habitats. Mobile health clinics were also organized in such areas. Anganvadi programmes under ICDS were strengthened in the primitive tribal areas to enhance the nutritional status among pregnant women, lactating mothers and children aged below 5 years. Still poverty continues due to depletion of forest resources, environmental degradation and low level of PVTGs participation in the ongoing development process in sub-plan area of Paderu.

Strategies for the Sustainable Livelihood and Development of Vulnerable Tribes

Conservation of natural resources, maintenance of balanced biodiversity with indigenous knowledge system and population control are considered to be the appropriate measures for the sustainable livelihood and development of PVTGs. A useful attempt has been made by the World Bank to analyze more closely the goal of sustainable development as shown below in the so-called ESD triangle. This or some variant of it is widely accepted in debates concerning sustainable development as a concise summary of the objective which are subsumed under this concept.

Social Objectives

- Empowerment
- Participation
- Social Cohesion
- Institutional Development and Growth

Ecological Objectives

- Ecosystem integrity
- Carrying Capacity
- Biodiversity
- Global Issues

Economic Objectives

- Equity
- Efficiency

Source: Sarageldin and Steer, 1994.

This issue of sustainable development is more appropriate in tackling this problem with the aboriginals who are considered as most backward. The most widely quoted definition of sustainable development is that "development which meets the needs of the present without compromising the ability of future generations to meet their own needs" (World Commission on Environment and Development, 1987).

People's participation in the development process is one of the means for sustainable livelihood and development. Community driven development sustains forever rather than imposed and enforced development. People involvement and participation are much essential for the success of any development programme. Participation is a crucial issue in development thinking and practices.

Most of the agencies involved in the development activities including non-governmental organizations and multilateral agencies like the World Bank and the International Monetary Fund have all arrived at a near consensus that development cannot be sustainable and long lasting unless people participation is made central to the development process.

Community participation is an active development process by which beneficiary or client groups influence the direction and execution of a development project with a view to change their well-being in terms of income, personal growth, self-reliance or other values they cherish. Most of the earlier Anthropological studies on the issue of tribal development emphasized that tribal participation was requisite and solution for the success of any kind of development programme taken up by either state or Central Government. The participation includes people's involvement in decision-making process, in implementing programmes, sharing benefits of development programmes and their involvement in effort to evaluate such programmes. People's participation in development is now being sought the world over because there has been a consensus on the usefulness of participation in development programmes.

Conclusion

In general, the poverty level among Scheduled Tribes is substantially higher than the national average. Still more than 60 per cent of the PVTGs stand at below poverty line (BPL). They are facing the problems like food insecurity, indebtedness, land alienation, illiteracy, malnutrition and ill-health. Most of these problems have a causal relationship with poverty. Food is the major problem for large majority of PVTGs and they go to bed with hunger and empty stomach. Long starvation for food leads to malnutrition, diseases and early death. They are not able to meet the basic need of food. They are searching and crying for food, but not successful in getting required minimum calories. The poverty of these tribes is primarily linked with the environment. This kind of poverty can be referred as environmental poverty. Enhancement of PVTGs surrounding and environment is the prime requirement for the sustainable livelihood and development of these groups.

The main issues related to the sustainable livelihood and development of PVTGs are lapses in development programmes, rehabilitation, corruption, policies, environmental degradation, deforestation, soil erosion, forest policies. Proper education and motivation are still needed to tackle all these issues. ITDA initiated community mobilization programmes should be intensified more in the PVTGs settlements in order to make them able to participate fully in such programmes.

Indigenous knowledge systems of these tribes should be taken into consideration in order to plan and implement the agricultural development, afforestation, housing, nutrition, health, and family welfare programmes to get fruitful results. Ashram and residential type of school system have already improved the educational standard of tribes in Andhra Pradesh. Such kind of schools still needed in more number especially in the areas where PVTGs are residing to raise the literacy levels among them. ICDS programme need to be strengthened in Khond, Porja and Gadaba settlements to tackle the problem of malnutrition among the high risk groups like pregnant women, lactating mothers and children below five years age. Empowerment of tribal is a good strategy for their active participation in all ongoing development activities and policies of nation.

References

Ramakrishna, P.S., 2001. *Ecology and Sustainable Development.* New Delhi: National Book Trust.

Subramanyam, V., 2003. "Development and Communication in Vishakha Agency of Andhra Pradesh", *Eastern Anthropologist*, 56 (1): 61-73.

Subramanyam, V., 2004. *Strategies for the Sustainable Development of Primitive Tribes in Vishakha Agency area of Andhra Pradesh.* UGC Major Research Project Report, Andhra University, Visakhapatnam, Andhra Pradesh (Unpublished).

Thurston, E., 1909. *Castes and Tribes of Southern India.* Government Press, Madras.

Verma, R.C., 1995. *Indian Tribes through the Ages.* New Delhi: Publication Division, Ministry of Information and Broadcasting, Government of India.

World Commission for Environment and Development (1987), Our Common Future, Bruntland Report, Oxford University Press.

B. HEALTH AND FOOD

FOUR

HEALTH AND DISEASE AMONG INDIGENOUS PEOPLE

Epidemiology and Ethno-Medicine

SUNITA REDDY AND BAMDEV SUBEDI

Introduction

Today, indigenous people around the world have been struggling with rapid socio-economic change and development. In many places, they are being displaced by the development, excluded and marginalized by the nation making process and the most affected by the adverse impact of globalization. This chapter is an introductory chapter for young anthropologists and aspiring medical anthropologists who want to develop conceptual understanding on the health issues, especially on tribal health. The main objective of this chapter is to highlight some of the conceptual terms related to health, illness, disease, etiology, epidemiology, and make a discussion on the health status of the indigenous people in India in the above context and further describe the contribution of medical anthropologists in the study of indigenous people. Some of the questions addressed in this chapter are: how do you define 'health', 'illness' and 'disease'? What is the difference between healing and curing? What is illness etiology? What are the two principal etiologies of non-Western medical systems? What is the health situation of indigenous people of India and the impact of globalization on health?

Anthropology and Qualitative Study of Indigenous People

Anthropological studies are considered to be the best in the study of indigenous people. This is particularly because anthropologists spend an extended period of time living with the indigenous people; identify with them and follow the qualitative methods often relying heavily on participant observation, in-depth interviews, documentation and recording of culture; and produce "rich ethnographic details about their cultural practices, perception and behavioural aspects" (Reddy, 2008: 61). Developed with the study of history and culture of tribal, native, or indigenous people anthropology "tends to provide more holistic account of phenomena and tends to be highly empirical" (Kottak, 2011).

Anthropological methods emphasize on qualitative techniques. The qualitative methods focus more on the meaning than measurements and more on depth than breadth. According to Padgett (2012) qualitative method is like "a mile deep and an inch wide" whereas quantitative method is like "an inch deep and a mile wide". Qualitative method follows (emic) insider rather than (etic) outsider perspective, person centred rather than variable centred approach, holistic rather than particularistic, contextual rather than decontextual" (Padgett, 2012: 2). These methods help in understanding the social issues, which are sensitive and personal, like health.

Medical anthropology is a branch of anthropology which studies all aspects of health-related phenomena (health, illness, and health care); considers cultural systems as well as the effects of local and worldwide social and political environments (Ember and Ember, 2004). Medical anthropology applies the anthropological knowledge, techniques and approaches to study health problems. In their studies, medical anthropologists focus on the description of the indigenous people's perspective of health and illness and their health seeking behaviour or what is also understood as ethnomedicine. Sometimes called folk medicine, primitive medicine, tribal medicine, indigenous medicine, "ethhno-medicine refers to the health-related beliefs, knowledge, and practices of an ethno-cultural group" (Ember and Ember, 2004). A vast number of anthropological studies have been conducted on the health, illness and disease around the world, especially focusing on the indigenous/tribal populations. These studies have established that the indigenous medicine is the main, and sometimes only source of health care for the indigenous population.

Understanding of Health, Disease, Indigenous Population, Epidemiology and Ethno-medicine

World Health Organization (WHO) defines health as "a state of complete physical, mental and social well-being and not merely the absence of disease and infirmity" (WHO, 1998: 1). This is the most quoted definition. However, the definition is not free from criticism. Qadeer (2011: 62) says "the definition tends to focus on ideal rather than actual, since it assumes the notion of absolute, i.e. complete well-being of an individual, rather than examine the relationship of the individuals with his/her social environment. It also ignores the fact that the health or well-being has a range and cannot be an absolute quantity (or quality). She shows the importance of social dimension and defines health as "a dynamic concept embracing biological and social dimensions of the well-being of a person" (Qadeer, 2011: 63). The concept of "absence of disease" is rather misleading because a disease free (or germless) society would be biologically unreal because everything around us is infected and diseased.

Disease, Illness and Sickness

According to Radley (1994) disease is something that physicians diagnose and treat. It refers to the pathological changes in the body. Illness is the experience of disease, including the feeling relating to the changes in bodily states and consequences of having to bear that ailment. It relates to a way of being for the individual concerned (Radley, 1994: 3). Illness is innately human experience of symptoms and suffering. It refers to a condition of poor health experienced by a person (Kleinman, 1988: 3). Sickness can be defined as "a social condition that applies to the people who are deemed by others to be ill or diseased. It refers to a particular status or role in society and is justified by reference either to the presence of disease or to the experience of illness" (Radley, 1994: 3).

Healing and Curing

The concept of healing is different from the curing. Healing deals with the body, mind, spirit and emotions whereas curing deals with the diseased parts of the body. The healing process indicates to the natural process by which a person feels or finds in a state of wellness. Hahn (1995: 7) defines healing as "not only the remedy or cure of sickness—that is the restoration of prior state, but also rehabilitation—the compensation for loss of health—the palliation—the mitigation in the suffering in the sick" (Hahn, 1995: 7). The focus of modern biomedicine is on curing while the indigenous or traditional medicine focuses more on healing than curing.

Epidemiology

The mortality and morbidity pattern varies from population to population. People from certain communities, geographical areas, caste or ethnicity, class, age, gender experience higher incidence of disease and higher death rate. Certain groups of people are at risk of some kind of diseases, because all types of disease are not equally distributed among all groups of the people. Some group experience the higher burden of disease and higher rate of morbidity and mortality. The distribution of a disease or an illness condition in a population and the factors that influence this distribution is the subject area of epidemiology. Epidemiology is the study of the incidence and distribution of diseases, and their prevention and control. Epidemiology is more conventionally defined as the study of the distribution and determinants of disease in human populations (Trostle, 2005: 5).

Ethno-medicine

Ethno-medicine refers to folk ideas and practices concerning the care and treatment of illness available within particular (usually non-western) cultures—that is, outside the framework of professionalized, regulated scientific medicine. They commonly involve empirically based natural remedies, frequently from plants, and healing rituals with supernatural elements. Often deemed unscientific, such methods of healing are increasingly shown to have some value (Marshall, 1998 : 202-203). Anthropologists often have used the term "ethnomedicine" to refer to the multiplicity of medical systems associated with indigenous societies as well as peasant communities and ethnic minorities in complex or state societies (Baer, Singer, and Susser, 2003 : 308).

Health Indicators for Indigenous Population

Indigenous population refers to the population of the native people or original inhabitants of particular territories who have been living with distinct cultural identities. Various terms such as 'tribal' people, 'native' people, 'primitive' people, ethnic groups, autochthonous, and aborigines are used to mean the indigenous people, which are laced with biases and demeaning. However, officially they are known as Scheduled Tribes (ST) or *Adivasi* people in India. The main characteristics of indigenous people are that, they generally have their own language, traditional rites and customs, distinct cultural identity, distinct social structure and written or oral history.

Virginius Xaxa (1999) in his article *Tribes as Indigenous People in India*, notes, features such as geographical isolation, simple technology and condition of living, practice of animism, tribal language, physical features etc. as criteria of tribes. He further states, "aspects of marginalization are built into the definition of indigenous people. Only those people that have been subjected to domination or subjugation have come to constitute the component of the indigenous people" (Xaxa, 1999: 3590). The essential characteristics, first laid down by the Lokur Committee, for a community to be identified as Scheduled Tribes are: indications of primitive traits; distinctive culture; shyness of contact with the community at large; geographical isolation; and backwardness (Ministry of Tribal Affairs, 2010).

Though they are the original inhabitants of the country they are still experiencing exclusion, discrimination and marginalization. They are deprived of their basic rights and access to fundamental resources. They have the least access to health care services and poor health status. Among the Scheduled Tribes or *adivasis* of India, mortality, morbidity and malnutrition rates remain particularly high, when compared to the Indian population at large. According to 2001 census, the tribal population of the country is 8.43 crore (i.e. 8.2% of the total population) and of them 91.7 per cent live in rural areas and 8.3 per cent in urban areas. Remoteness of villages, uncooperative attitudes among medical personnel, limited manpower, and a lack of awareness within tribal communities all pose difficulties in achieving adequate health care delivery (Ministry of Tribal Affairs, 2010).

Morbidity Patterns

The morbidity and mortality data show that there is a marked inequality in health between indigenous and non-indigenous populations worldwide (Haddad, Mohindra, Siekmans, Mak, and Narayana, 2012) and India is no exception. Indigenous people have higher morbidity and mortality rates and prevalence of diseases than the national average. Though the health status has improved over the years because of the government intervention on tribal development programmes, the gaps between indigenous (tribal) and non-indigenous (non-tribal) population remained wide (Mohindra and Labonte, 2010). Table 4.1 compares indigenous people with the national average in terms of some of the health indicators.

Table 4.1: Health Indicators of Indigenous Population and Total Population of India

Indicators	*Total Population*		*ST (Indigenous Population)*	
	1998-99	*2005-06*	*1998-99*	*2005-06*
Infant Mortality Rate (per 1000)	73.0	57.0	84.2	62.1
Under 5 Mortality Rate (per 1000)	101.4	74.3	126.6	95.7
% of Children undernourished (weight for age)	47.0	42.5	55.9	54.5
% of Children with full immunization	42.0	43.5	26.5	31.3
% of women with anemia	51.8	55.3	64.9	68.5
% of deliveries by skilled provider	42.3	46.6	23.3	25.4

Source: National Family and Health Survey (NFHS-2: 1998-1999), (NFHS-3: 2005-2006).
[*Note:* Cited in Mohindra and Labonte (2010), Reddy (2008), Ministry of Tribal Affairs (2010):

Table 4.1 shows that there is an improvement in health indicators between the second and the third NFHS period, however, for indigenous people there is not a single indicator, which is better than the national average. And in each of the socio-economic indicators, we can see a noticeable improvement in the total population than the tribal population (Ministry of Tribal Affairs, 2010).

Among the tribal population in India, there exists widespread poverty, illiteracy, malnutrition, and absence of safe drinking water, poor housing and unhygienic living conditions. There exists high rate of tobacco and alcohol consumption, low and poor food intake (resulting micronutrient deficiency), high rate of preventable diseases such as tuberculosis, diarrhea, asthma, goiter, anemia, physical injuries (cuts, burns) etc. (Ministry of Tribal Affairs, 2010).

There is a paucity of mortality and morbidity data, which can show us the variation across the states and across the indigenous people. Non-availability of disaggregated data, across tribes in various states, further restricts to take any concrete interventions (Reddy, 2008). However, it is quite clear that all the indigenous people (as there are 461 STs officially recognized) do not have similar circumstances and similar status. They do not have equal access to the health care services and equal morbidity pattern. Some groups are more prone to disease or to have more disease prevalence than others.

Globalization and Marginalization and Its Impact on the Health of Indigenous Population

Marginalization refers to a process whereby a group of people is devoid of assimilation, integration and inclusion. People are treated as insignificant and excluded from the nation making process. Marginalization is the opposite of mainstreaming. People do not have a say even on the decision-making process which affect them. In the *International Encyclopaedia of the Social Sciences*, Hanagan writes, "marginalization comprises those processes by which individuals and groups are ignored or relegated to the sidelines of political debate, social negotiation, and economic bargaining and kept there" (Hanagan, 2008).

Globalization is a free flow of goods and services around the world. It is also a free flow of finance and philosophy, idea and ideology, tools and technology. Goods and services produced in one country become easily available in other country. It breaks and crosses the national boundary. *The Encyclopaedia of Medical Anthropology* defines globalization as "the massive flow of goods, people, information and capital across huge areas of the earth's surface" (Ember and Ember, 2004). The main point is free play of finance, goods and services around the world and ideology of consumerism, democracy, liberty, individual choice and freedom.

Globalization has brought five new things:

- New markets (such as market outside the border and market for new goods and services)
- New tools (such as internet, mobile, i-pod, kindle etc.)
- New actors (such as world trade organization, transnational and multinational companies)
- New laws (such as trade related intellectual property right, multinational trade agreements, neoliberal policy)
- New practices (such as outsourcing and e-commerce)

Globalization is affecting each of us. We all are part of it. No one can remain in isolation or unaffected by it. It has both positive and negative effects. However, the globalization has done more harm than good to the developing countries and to the indigenous people. Indigenous people's life and living have been affected by the new technologies that have been imposed. Some of the adverse effects are seen in the agriculture, health care and production and consumption process. Indigenous people are finding it difficult with the newer technologies and increased cost of production. The rate and use of chemical fertilizer, insecticide and pesticide has been exponentially increasing. And more disappointing is that almost all types of seeds of indigenous variety are being disappeared with the introduction of newer (genetically modified) varieties. Though from these high yielding seeds and technology production has increased but the production cost has exceeded the value of produce. P. Sainath's reporting of Bt cotton suicide story of Maharashtra is one of the many examples of negative impact of globalization. It has increased dependency, indebtedness, and exploitation of farmers (Gruère and Sengupta, 2011).

Globalization has confiscated people's resources, altered food practices and lifestyle, shattered their knowledge base, forced them to be dependent on new products and newer technologies, and has enslaved people. For example, traditional/indigenous healers (*local vaidya*) used to prepare medicine for patients and the cost used to be minimal or affordable. With the impact of globalization, the reliance upon modern pharmaceutical drugs and technology has increased and which is far more expensive. The process of imparting traditional knowledge from old generation to new generation has been shattered. Multinational companies have trapped the herbal resources, knowledge domain and technical knowhow of the indigenous people.

Development and Displacement and Effect on Indigenous Population and their Health

By definition, the aim of development is to "improve the quality of all aspects of human life" (Phillips, 1990) however, the present development activities have resulted in the depletion of natural resources and displacement of human settlement. In the name of development, indigenous people have been displaced from their indigenous land. This has caused adverse effects on their life and living, health and well-being. Excessive use of natural resources, high tech production and consumption, too much dependency on technology, environmental pollution, climate change, and atomic energy have become the threat not only to human health but to the human existence. A hydro-electric project or a nuclear power plant, displaces people from their native lands. These projects on the one hand fulfil the energy needs and on the other hand displace indigenous population which can be termed as development with displacement (Hyma and Ramesh, 1994). Industrial pollution, air, water, land and noise pollution, fertilizers and chemical pesticides used in agriculture, domestic wastes, all are contributing to degradation of our environment. This also exposes us to newer health risks. Newer technologies like genetic modification have the potential of having several unintended health consequences. Industrial accidents like the explosion at the Chernobyl nuclear power plant in Ukraine or the pesticide plant disaster of Bhopal show how unmanageable technology can become dangerous (Giddens, 2009: 101) and these risks are not confined to certain geographical zones but can also be seen far from their places of occurrence.

In many states, the rich natural resource base, where the tribes have the proprietorship have been taken away by the government for development purpose, displacing them, without proper compensation and rehabilitation. Recently, some of the tribal populations have come forward for their rights. For instance, the resistance by the tribes of Niyamgiri hills could keep the developers at bay, who fought tooth and nail. With such resistance and rights movements, there is rising awareness and understanding of indigenous people's right as human right.

Issues of Accessibility and Availability of Health Care Services

Indigenous people in India are utilizing the available health care resources. They predominantly rely on the indigenous/folk healing systems and have the least access to formal health care services, both public and private. The issue of the availability and accessibility has been associated with the public provisioning, geographical location, distance to health facility, shortfall and absence of medical staffs, behaviour of health staffs, shortage or unavailability of drugs, overt and covert cost of care. There has been a huge shortfall of medical staffs in the tribal areas, they have been facing problems in accessing medical advice and treatment services from the health institutions and they have the lowest per cent (2.6%) of insurance coverage (Ministry of Tribal Affairs, 2010).

The health indicator points to the poor health status among the indigenous populations. There is a tendency to blame indigenous people and their cultural practices. These views hold that indigenous people are poor, illiterate, lack awareness, follow unhygienic practices, believe in superstitious beliefs, they are fatalists and they do not seek modern medical care. But the fact behind not utilizing and non-compliance by tribal is not because of individual problem, ignorance or the resistance of modern medicine, but because of social hierarchy and power differentials between the so-called modern doctors and indigenous population (Reddy, 2008; Zurbrigg, 1984: 68-69).

Ethno-medicine and Etiology of Disease Causation

The *Encyclopedia of Medical Anthropology* defines etiology as "the causes of a disease or illness" (Ember and Ember, 2004). Womack defines as "cause or origin of a disease or the study of the causes and origins of disease" (Womack, 2010: 330) and Pool and Geissler define etiology as the "explanations of the causes of sickness" (Pool and Geissler, 2006: 52). The cause of an illness or a disease or of sickness is simply referred as etiology.

Anthropologists have studied about how indigenous people explain, interpret and give a meaning to an illness and developed theories about how people give a reason or causation for an illness or disease. They have often made a distinction between two main types of illness etiologies: natural and supernatural or naturalistic and personalistic (Foster, 1976; Garro, 2000; Murdock, 1980). The former attribute to imbalanced natural equilibrium and cause-effect relationship, while the later to the superhuman or unseen forces such as evil spirits, ancestral spirits and the deities.

George P. Murdock's (1980) theories of illness is considered as a landmark in the study of illness etiology. Murdock distinguishes theories of natural causation from supernatural causation. By the theories of natural causation he means "any theory, scientific or popular, which accounts for the impairment of health as a physiological consequence of some experience of the victim in a manner that would appear reasonable to modern medical science" (Murdock, 1980 : 9). He also defines five distinct types of theories, which fall into this category, namely, infection, stress, organic deterioration, accident and overt human aggression. The other eight additional types of theories, which rest on supernatural assumptions, which modern medical science does not recognize as valid, fall into the theories of supernatural causation. He describes these theories of supernatural causation in three broad categories: mystical causation (fate, ominous sensations, contagion, mystical retribution), animistic causation (soul loss, spirit aggression) and magical causation (sorcery, witchcraft) (Murdock, 1980 : 17-22).

George M. Foster (1976) presents two principal etiologies of non-Western medical systems: naturalistic and personalistic. In the naturalistic system, disease is explained in terms of "natural forces or condition, as cold, heat, winds, dampness and above all, by an upset in the balance of the basic body elements". In the personalistic system, disease is explained in terms of "the active purposeful intervention of an agent, who may be human (a witch or sorcerer), non-human (a ghost, an ancestor, an evil spirit), or supernatural (a deity or other very powerful being)". In the naturalistic system religion and magic are largely unrelated to illness while in the personalistic system illness, religion and magic are inseparable. Naturalistic system requires curers or doctors whose primary role is therapeutic while personalistic system requires healers with supernatural and/or magical skills or shamanic healers whose primary role is diagnostic though, Foster does not see the two types of systems mutually exclusive (Foster, 1976: 775-779).

These theories also indicate that the meaning and perception differs because what is illness to one community may not be regarded as illness to another. And even in the same community what is not considered an illness in one point of time can be considered illness in another.

Classification of Medical Systems

Scholars have classified the medical systems variously. The medical system across the world has been basically classified into two broad categories (Stoner, 1986: 44).

1. **Biomedicine,** which is invariably understood as allopathic, scientific, western and modern medicine; and
2. **Indigenous medicine,** which is variously referred as folk medicine, ethno-medicine, traditional medicine, complementary and alternative medicine.

Frederick L. Dunn classifies medical systems into three categories based on their geographical and cultural settings (Dunn, 1976: 139).

1. Local medical systems
2. Regional medical systems
3. Cosmopolitan medical system

By **local medical systems** he means 'primitive' or 'folk' medicine of small-scale communities. The local medical system tends to be popular and non-scholarly. Regional medical systems are the systems distributed over a relatively large area such as Ayurvedic, Unani and Chinese medicine. The **regional medical system** tends to be scholarly. **Cosmopolitan medicine** refers to the global medical system, which is often referred to as modern, scientific or western medicine. However, Dunn abandons the terms modern, scientific or western and favours the term of cosmopolitan medical system because these terms are misleading; local and regional medical systems are also scientific, modern and western medicine is no more western.

Arthur Kleinman (1978) explains about the three are interconnected and overlapping sectors:

1. Popular sector
2. Folk sector
3. Professional sector

The popular sector consists of health care conducted by sick persons themselves, their families, social networks, and communities. In both Western and non-Western societies somewhere between 70 and 90 per cent of sickness is managed solely within this sector. **The folk sector** consists of non-professional healing specialists who function informally and often on a quasi-legal or even illegal basis. These include shamans, mediums, magicians, herbalists, bonesetters, and midwives. **The professional sector** consists of professional scientific ('Western' or 'cosmopolitan') medicine and professionalized indigenous healing traditions (e.g. Chinese, Ayurvedic, Unani and Chiropractice) (Kleinman, 1978: 86-87).

Classifications of Traditional Healing Systems

In most of the (indigenous) societies there exists a cadre of indigenous healers. By indigenous healers we mean shamans, magico-religious healers, faith healers, herbalists, bone setters, snake-bite healers, poison healers, midwives, massagers or any other practitioners who are experienced enough and are recognized as healers by the community people. These healers are not trained in any formal educational systems; however, cater to most of the health care needs of the people. The indigenous medical system is largely an unregulated, informal, unorganized, non-codified, non-scholarly, popular traditional medical system. This system has no written text and the healing knowledge is handed down from one generation to the next, usually through oral tradition.

In classifying these traditional healing systems basically there can be three categories:

1. Healing activities that employs the methods of *mantra* or follow shamanic healing practices or magico-religious methods or faith healing, which is also described as **shamanism**.
2. Healing activities that uses herbs or plant, animal and mineral resources which is also known as **herbalism**.
3. Those who use body manipulation methods such as **massage**.

The indigenous healing system is comprised of naturalistic, animistic and shamanic practices. Some of the healers blend together natural medicine and spiritual medicine.

Naturalistic

Among indigenous people illnesses are generally classified as either naturalistic or personalistic. In naturalistic category, illness is explained by impersonal forces or conditions, including cold, heat, and other forces that upset the body's balance (Ember & Ember, 2004). Naturalistic agents identify what caused an illness, whereas personalistic agents recognize who caused the illness. If the illness is perceived as naturalistic they infer into impersonal agents as inadequate rest, poor nutrition, and germs cause illnesses (Ember & Ember, 2004).

Animistic

Animism involves beliefs in a soul or vital principle animating entities and producing their behaviours and observed properties. Animism is the term used by Edward Tylor to describe a belief in a dual existence for all things—a physical, visible body and a psychic, invisible soul (Ember and Ember, 2004).

Shamanic

Shamanism is an ancient form of healing tradition that employs ritualistic processes to mediating between community people and supernatural beings and to using *mantras* and means to deal the spirits. It refers to the activities and practices of the shaman. It is defined by the helping spirits who work through the shaman and the needs of the people, the shaman works for (Pratt, 2007 : viii). A shaman plays an intermediary role between people and spirits. Shaman may know and use herbs to heal illnesses.

Summary and Conclusion

When we hear the word "health" what comes into our mind? What clicks on our mind? What do we visualize? Yes, when we hear the word "health", most of us visualize a hospital, a doctor wearing white apron and hanging a stethoscope round his neck, a supporting nurse, an injection or saline water hanging on a side of hospital bed, a patient lying on the bed helplessly, packaged drugs, pills or varieties of bottles of medicine and so on. However, health in this picture narrows down our understanding of health. Health is a broad concept, consisting of physical, psychological, and social well-being. It incorporates social, economic, political and environmental consideration. A healthy person will function normally and lives a productive life whereas a person with disease or illness experience something uncomfortable or imbalance in the normal functioning of the physical body and in the state of mind and emotion. When we talk health, we generally mean physical health and not the social and psychological health. We often overlook the social determinants of health or show indifference on such factors.

The health of a particular person or a section of people depends on many factors such as where do they live, what types of food do they eat, what type of health care services are there in their locality, how much do they have access to rights and productive resources, what is their economic status, which caste do they belong, what occupation do they follow, which type of family or neighbourhood do they have, what type of policy their government follows, what type of programmes are there to empower and strengthen the weaker sections of society and how their state deals with privatization, commercialization, liberalization and globalization. Therefore, it is far more important to understand the social causes of illness and the social determinants of health.

Indigenous people's health should be observed in this context. There is a connection of the indigenous people's health and the socio-economic, political condition of the country at large. It depends on how serious is the Centre, State and local government to deal with poverty, hunger and disease of its people, particularly the poorer sections. The access to economic resources and their representation in the administrative body and political participations are also equally important to understand the health of the indigenous populations.

Acknowledgement: An earlier version of this chapter was written by the first author for a programme of Anthropology Department of IGNOU. The second author contributed in revisiting some parts and in referencing. We acknowledge the support of the Department of Anthropology, IGNOU.

References

Baer, H.A., 2003. "The Work of Andrew Weil and Deepak Chopra—Two Holistic Health/New Age Gurus: A Critique of the Holistic Health/New Age Movements", *Medical Anthropology Quarterly*, 17 (2): 233-250.

Baer, H.A., Singer, M., and Susser, I., 2003. *Medical Anthropology and the World System*. Westport: Praeger Publishers.

Dunn, F., 1976. Traditional Asian Medicine and Cosmopolitan Medicine as Adaptive System. In *Asian Medical System: A Comparative Study.* Charles Leslie, (ed.) (pp. 133-58). Berkeley: University of California Press.

Ember, C.A., and Ember, M., 2004. *Encyclopaedia of Medical Anthropology: Health and Illness in the World's Culture.* Carol R. Ember and Melvin Ember (eds.) (Vols. 1-2). New York: Springer Science and Business Media.

Foster, G.M., 1976. "Disease Etiologies in Non-Western Medical System", *American Anthropologist*, *78* (4): 773-782.

Garro, L.C., 2000. "Cultural Meaning, Explanations of Illness, and the Development of Comparative Frameworks", *Ethnology*, *78* (4): 305-334.

Giddens, A., 2009. *Sociology* (Sixth Edition). Cambridge: Polity Press.

Gruère, G., and Sengupta, D., 2011. "Bt Cotton and Farmer Suicides in India: An Evidence-based Assessment", *The Journal of Development Studies*, 47 (2), 316-337. http://doi.org/10.1080/00220388.2010.492863

Haddad, S., Mohindra, K., Siekmans, K., Mak, G., and Narayana, D., 2012. "Health Divide" between Indigenous and non-Indigenous Populations in Kerala India: Population based Study. *BMC Public Health*, 12 (390): 1-10.

Hahn, R.A., 1995. *Sickness and Healing: An Anthropological Perspective.* New Haven: Yale University

Hanagan, M., 2008. Marginalization. In *International Encyclopaedia of the Social Sciences.* William A. Darity Jr. (ed.) (Second Edition, Vol. 4, pp. 598-599). New York: MacMillian Company.

Hyma, B. and Ramesh, A., 1994. Traditional Medicine: Its Extent and Potential for Incorporation into Modern National Health Systems. In *Health and Development.* David R. Phillips and Yola Verhasselt (eds.) London: Routledge Publications.

Kleinman, A., 1978. Concepts and a Model for the Comparision of Medical Systems as Cultural Systems. *Social Science and Medicine, 12*, 85-93.

Kleinman, A., 1988. *The Illness Narratives: Suffering, Healing and the Human Condition.* New York: Basic Books.

Kottak, K.P., 2011. *Cultural Anthropology: Appreciating Cultural Diversity* (14th ed.). New York: McGraw-Hill Co.

Marshall, G., 1998. Ethnomedicine. *Oxford Dictionary of Sociology* (Second Edition). Oxford: Oxford University Press.

Ministry of Tribal Affairs, Government of India, 2010. *Statistical Profile of Scheduled Tribes in India 2010.* New Delhi: Ministry of Tribal Affairs.

Mohindra, K. and Labonte, R., 2010. A Systematic Review of Population Health Interventions and Scheduled Tribes in India. *BMC Public Health, 10*(438), 1–10.

Murdock, G.P., 1980. *Theories of Illness: A World Survey.* Pittsburgh: University of Pittsburgh.

Padgett, D.K., 2012. *Qualitative and Mixed Methods in Public Health.* Los Angeles: Sage Publications.

Phillips, D.R., 1990. *Health and Health Care in the Third World.* London: Longman.

Pool, R., and Geissler, W., 2006. *Understanding Public Health: Medical Anthropology.* New Delhi: Tata McGraw-Hill Inc.

Pratt, C., 2007. *An Encyclopaedia of Shamanism.* New York: The Rosen Publishing Group, Inc.

Qadeer, I., 2011. Health Services System in India: An Expression of Socio-Economic Inequalites. In *Public Health in India: Critical Reflection.* K. R. Nayar and Rama V. Baru (eds.) (pp. 61–91). Delhi: Daanish Books.

Radley, A., 1994. *Making Sense of Illness: The Social Psychology of Health and Disease.* New Delhi: Sage Publications.

Reddy, S., 2008. Health of Tribal Women and Children: An Interdisciplinary Approach. *Indian Anthropologist*, 38 (2), 61-74.

Stoner, B.P., 1986. Understanding Medical Systems: Traditional, Modern and Syncretic Health Care Alternatives in Medically Pluralistic Societies. *Medical Anthropology Quarterly*, 17 (2), 44-48.

Trostle, J.A., 2005. *Epidemiology and Culture.* Cambridge: Cambridge University Press.

WHO, 1998. *Health Promotion Glossary.* Geneva: World Health Organization.

Womack, M., 2010. *Anthropology of Health and Healing.* United Kingdom: Alta Maria Press.

Xaxa, V., 1999. Tribes as Indigenous People of India. *Economic & Political Weekly, XXXIV* (51), 3589-3595.

Zurbrigg, S., 1984. *Rakku's Story: Structure of Ill Health and Sources of Change.* Banglore: Published by George Joseph, on behalf of Centre for Social Action.

FIVE

HEALTH-RELATED QUALITY OF LIFE OF A GROUP OF WOMEN WITH POLYCYSTIC OVARY SYNDROME (PCOS)

A Study in West Bengal, India

DEBARUPA SEN GUPTA, NIVEDITA SOM, CHAITALI DUTTA ROY, SEBANTI GOSWAMI AND SUBHA RAY

Introduction

Polycystic ovary syndrome (hereafter PCOS) is a complex hormonal disturbance that appears to be one of the leading causes of infertility among women (Schmid *et al.*, 2004). Moreover, PCOS is found to be associated with other symptoms like, hirsutism, greasy skin, acne, obesity, amenorrhea/oligomenorrhea and dysfunctional uterine bleeding (Azziz *et al.*, 2006; Brassard *et al.*, 2008; Teede *et al.*, 2010). The symptoms of PCOS vary widely within and across the population (Franks, 1995; Conway, 1996). Presently, "Rotterdam criteria" (chronic anovulation, elevated androgen concentrations and the presence of polycystic ovaries) is used for the diagnosis of PCOS (Rotterdam ESHRE/ASRM-sponsored PCOS Consensus Workshop Group, 2004) and the treatment is aimed at symptomatic improvement. In the long run, PCOS also increases the risk for several non-curable diseases such as, type 2 diabetes mellitus, cardiovascular disease, depressive disorder and certain types of cancer (Balen, 2001; Kelly *et al.*, 2002; Ehrmann, 2005; Hollinrake *et al.*, 2007).

Thus, PCOS affects health and subsequently causes impairment in health-related quality of life of women (Jones *et al.*, 2002; Coffey *et al.*, 2006; Barnard *et al.*, 2007; Ching *et al.*, 2007; Li *et al.*, 2011).

Health-related quality of life is a multidimensional approach that involves physical, psychological and social aspects of life in association with a particular disease or its treatment (Naughton and McBee, 1997; Colwell *et al.*, 1998). Cronin *et al.* (1998) explicates health-related quality of life of PCOS women with respect to emotions, growth of body hair, body weight, infertility and menstrual problems. There are studies that report that the problems of acne, depression, obesity and menstrual disturbances are the major consequences of poor quality of life in both adolescent girls and adult women having PCOS (Sonino *et al.*, 1993; Barnard *et al.*, 2007; Jones *et al.*, 2011). Apart from these, quality of life in PCOS individuals becomes impaired with an increased response to stress, declined social activity and dissatisfaction with sexual and marital life (Elsenbruch *et al.*, 2003; Drosdzol *et al.*, 2007).

In India, clinical based studies reveal that a substantial proportion of women are reported with the problems of PCOS such as, hirsutism, acné, obesity, oligomenorrhea, infertility, spontaneous abortion, hyperinsulinemia, thyroid dysfunction and cardiovascular disease (Mandrelle *et al.*, 2012; Sinha *et al.*, 2013; Chakraborty *et al.*, 2013; Ramanand *et al.*, 2013; Guleria *et al.*, 2014; Thathapudi *et al.*, 2014). None of these studies draw attention to the quality of life of PCOS individuals. Thus, in our study we have attempted to assess the health-related quality of life of a group of women having PCOS.

Materials and Methods

Study Area

The present study was conducted in the city of Kolkata, the state capital of West Bengal, India. Two public health institutions, namely "Institute of Post-Graduate Medical Education and Research and Seth Sukhlal Karnani Memorial Hospital" (commonly referred to as PG Hospital) and "Medical College and Hospital, Kolkata", (commonly referred to as Calcutta Medical College) were selected to collect data on patients diagnosed with PCOS. The former hospital is located in the southern part of the city and the later is in the northern-central part of the city.

Both the hospitals are renowned in terms of infrastructure and facilities and cater to the needs of a large section of the people.

Study Participants

A total number of 80 individuals, diagnosed with PCOS using "Rotterdam criteria" by the medical practitioners of the two hospitals were recruited for this study. The participants were aged between 14 and 38 years. Informed written consent was taken from each of them. The protocol of the study was reviewed by the "Ethical Clearance Committee" of both the public health institutions. The study was conducted during the time period of April to July in the year 2014.

Data Types

Data were collected in person from the "out patient department" (OPD) of both the hospitals. The face-to-face interview was conducted by a same sex interviewer and one of the co-authors of this study (DSG).

Socio-demographic Characteristics and PCOS Health History

Information on socio-demographic profile includes age of the participants at the time of interview (in years), years of education, occupational types, marital status and monthly household income (in Indian rupees). Age at the time of interview followed normal distribution. However, years of education and monthly household income of the participants followed skewed distribution; hence these two variables were converted into normal distribution after performing the log transformation. We presented the mean and standard deviation values for the age at the time of interview, years of education and monthly household expenditure of the participants.

Further, the participants were asked to make an assessment about their perceived (present) health status (either 'good' or 'fair' or 'poor'), and also to report the years of botheration with PCOS and duration of treatment (in years) they received from the date of interview.

Health-Related Quality of Life

Health-Related Quality of Life Questionnaire for women with PCOS (PCOSQ) was employed in interviewer-administered format as suggested by Cronin *et al.* (1998) who originally developed this questionnaire. PCOSQ involves 26 items that are grouped into five domains such as, 'emotion' (8 items), 'body hair' (5 items), 'body weight' (5 items), 'infertility problems' (4 items) and 'menstrual problems' (4 items). Each of these items is rated on a 7 point scale, in which the optimal functioning is represented by the score 7, and the score 1 indicates the poorest level of functioning. Thus, the minimum and maximum scores for each item ranges between 1 and 7 respectively. Each domain was formed by adding the scores of its corresponding items. The minimum and maximum values for each domain depend on the number of items for the domain. For example, the minimum and maximum values for 'emotion' domain would range between 8 (8×1) and 56 (8×7). The lower score indicates the greater concern and the more adverse impact on woman's health-related quality of life.

Anthropometric Characteristics and Actual Weight Status

Height and weight were measured following standard protocol (Lohman *et al.*, 1988). Height was measured to the nearest of 0.1 cm using a portable GPM anthropometer and the weight was measured to the nearest of 0.1 kg for each participant in light clothing without shoes using weighing machine. Body mass index (BMI) was calculated using the formula: [BMI= weight (kg)/height (m^2)]. For the adolescent participants (aged 14-19 years), the calculated BMI was translated into age and sex specific BMI z score values using the cut-off points based on reference data of World Health Organization (WHO) (2007). On the other hand, the BMI of those participants whose age was beyond 19 years was classified following the proposition of World Health Organization (2004). Underweight/thin (BMI for age z score < -2 SD or BMI< 18.5), normal weight (BMI for age z score $= -2$ SD to 1 SD or BMI $= 18.5$ to 25.0), overweight (BMI for age z score = 1 SD to 2 SD or BMI = 25.0 to 30.0) and obese (BMI for age z score > 2 SD or BMI > 30.0) individuals were identified. Finally, the participants were grouped into overweight and non-overweight. The few obese participants were combined with overweight participants to make 'overweight group', while the underweight and normal weight participants were combined into another group 'non-overweight'.

Statistical Analyses

Descriptive statistics were conducted to show the socio-demographic characteristics of the participants. Student's-t test was applied to compare each of the domains indicating the health-related quality of life of PCOS participants with respect to their actual weight status. Furthermore, analysis of variance (ANOVA) was conducted to compare each of these domains with respect to perceived health status, years of botheration with PCOS and also with the duration of treatment received for the PCOS problems. A minimum p value of = 0.05 was considered statistically significant for all inferential statistics. Cronbach's alpha was calculated to judge the reliability of this questionnaire in this study population. The test result 'emotion' (0.59), 'body hair' (0.82), 'body weight' (0.80), 'menstrual problems' (0.36) and 'infertility problems' (0.84), indicates that the internal consistency of the domains such as, 'body hair', 'body weight' and 'infertility problems' proved to be acceptable. The entire data were analyzed with the help of Statistical Package for Social Science (SPSS) software version 20.0 (IBM Corporation, 2011).

Results

Table 5.1 shows the socio-demographic characteristics of the participants. The mean values for the age of the participants at the time of the interview and years of education were 23.50 and 12.79 years respectively. Close to half of the participants were students and around 60 per cent of the participants were unmarried. Mean monthly household income was 12,000 (in Indian rupees).

Table 5.2 shows that the mean score for 'body weight' domain and also for all the items pertaining to 'body weight' domain were significantly lower in overweight PCOS participants compared to their non-overweight counterparts. The score for the individual item like, late menstrual period (of 'emotion' domain), embarrassment about excessive body hair (of 'body hair' domain) and abdominal bloating (of 'menstrual problems' domain) were significantly lower for the overweight participants compared to those who were non-overweight.

Table 5.3 shows that the scores of five domains ('emotion', 'body hair', 'body weight', 'menstrual problems' and 'infertility problems') indicating health-related quality of life of the participants failed to differ significantly with respect to the years of botheration with PCOS.

Table 5.4 shows the similar trend in the results as found in Table 5.3. The scores of five domains ('emotion', 'body hair', 'body weight', 'menstrual problems' and 'infertility problems') of health-related quality of life failed to differ significantly among the participants with respect to the duration of treatment received for PCOS problems.

Table 5.5 demonstrates that the participants who perceived their health as good, had significantly higher scores for the domains like, 'emotion', 'body weight' and 'infertility problems'; and also for the individual items like, depression for having PCOS (of 'emotion' domain), concerned about being overweight, frustrated in trying to lose weight, felt less sexy for being overweight (of 'body weight' domain), concerned with infertility problems, worried of not being able to have children (of 'infertility problems' domain).

Discussion

We aimed to assess the health-related quality of life of a group of women with PCOS. Here, five domains (emotion, body hair, body weight, menstrual problems and infertility problems) of health-related quality of life were estimated with respect to the actual weight status, perceived health status, years of botheration and treatment received for the PCOS. The results revealed that the health-related quality of life of the participants differed significantly with respect to their actual weight status and perceived health status; however, it failed to differ significantly with respect to the years of botheration and the duration of treatment received for PCOS.

Literature revealed that the issues pertaining to body weight, menstrual problems, infertility, emotions and body hair were directly reflected in

Table 5.1: Socio-Demographic Characteristics of the Participants (N = 80)

Socio-demographic characteristics	*n*	%
Age of the participants (years) mean±sd	23.50 ± 8.55	
Educational levels of the participants (years) mean±sd	12.79 ± 2.17	
Occupational status of the participants		
Home-maker	25	31.2
Student	38	47.5
Working	17	21.2
Marital status of the participants		
Unmarried	50	62.5
Married	30	37.5
Monthly household income (Indian rupees) mean±sd	12,000 ± 4,569.48	

Table 5.2: Health-related quality of life of PCOS participants with respect to their actual weight status (n = 80)

Health-related quality of life	*Actual weight status*		*t value*	*p value*
	Non-overweight n = 38	*Overweight n = 42*		
	Mean ± se	*Mean ± se*		
Emotions	3.51±0.17	3.32±0.16	0.805	0.423
Depression for having PCOS	3.63±0.38	3.61±0.35	0.024	0.981
Easily tired	2.15±0.29	2.78±0.33	1.389	0.169
Mood swing for having PCOS	2.28±0.32	2.90±0.36	1.253	0.214
Low self-esteem for having PCOS	4.28±0.43	4.28±0.38	0.006	0.995
Felt frightened of getting cancer	6.36±0.26	5.85±0.29	1.297	0.199
Worried about having PCOS	3.10±0.34	2.47±0.25	1.488	0.141
Self-conscious for having PCOS	3.07±0.34	2.64±0.24	1.050	0.297
Late menstrual period	3.23±0.39	2.02±0.28	2.523	0.014
Body hair	5.29±0.24	4.79±0.26	1.384	0.170
Visible hair on chin	5.84±0.31	5.76±0.31	0.182	0.856
Visible hair on upper lip	5.21±0.30	4.35±0.33	1.882	0.064
Visible hair on face	5.52±0.29	4.88±0.33	1.442	0.153
Visible hair on body	3.55±0.37	3.64±0.35	0.173	0.863
Embarrassment about excessive body hair	6.34±0.26	5.33±0.39	2.080	0.041
Body weight	4.18±0.29	2.93±0.22	3.419	0.001
Concerned about being overweight	3.57±0.39	2.45±0.26	2.404	0.019
Felt trouble with body weight	4.60±0.37	3.07±0.31	3.181	0.002
Frustrated in trying to lose weight	4.97±0.39	3.73±0.35	2.331	0.022
Felt less sexy for being overweight	4.00±0.39	2.85±0.34	2.197	0.031
Felt difficulties to maintain ideal weight	3.76±0.39	2.54±0.32	2.388	0.019
Menstrual problems	3.38±0.20	3.27±0.18	0.392	0.696
Headaches	5.23±0.35	5.40±0.36	0.327	0.745
Irregular menstrual periods	1.31±0.18	1.83±0.28	1.473	0.145
Abdominal bloating	2.55±0.29	1.26±0.12	4.164	0.001
Menstrual cramps	4.42±0.44	4.59±0.41	0.284	0.777
Infertility problems	4.23±0.36	3.84±0.29	0.825	0.412
Concerned with infertility problems	4.39±0.42	3.76±0.37	1.125	0.264
Worried of not being able to have children	4.36±0.45	3.83±0.38	0.904	0.369
Lack of control over the situation with PCOS	3.68±0.38	3.90±0.38	0.405	0.687
Felt sad for infertility problems	4.47±0.40	3.88±0.37	1.074	0.286

the life experiences of PCOS patients (McCook *et al.*, 2005, Barnard *et al.*, 2007, Thomson *et al.*, 2010, Acmaz *et al.*, 2013, Khomani *et al.*, 2015). In our study, overweight participants more frequently reported the problems related to their own body weight than their non- overweight

Table 5.3: Health-related quality of life of PCOS participants with respect to their years of botheration (n = 80)

Health-related quality of life	*Years of botheration with PCOS*			*F value*	*p value*
	<2 years n = 37	2-5 years n = 26	>5 years n = 17		
	mean±se	*mean±se*	*mean±se*		
Emotions	3.31±0.16	3.47±0.20	3.55±0.31	0.315	0.731
Depression for having PCOS	3.62±0.39	3.23±0.41	4.23±0.56	0.968	0.384
Easily tired	2.32±0.33	2.57±0.41	2.70±0.49	0.238	0.789
Mood swing for having PCOS	2.37±0.33	2.80±0.42	2.82±0.63	0.383	0.683
Low self-esteem for having PCOS	4.32±0.38	4.38±0.54	4.05±0.68	0.087	0.916
Felt frightened of getting cancer	5.94±0.32	6.42±0.27	5.94±0.42	0.637	0.532
Worried about having PCOS	2.40±0.30	3.00±0.37	3.23±0.45	1.391	0.255
Self-conscious for having PCOS	2.56±0.30	3.00±0.36	3.23±0.44	0.877	0.420
Late menstrual period	2.97±0.39	2.34±0.38	2.17±0.52	1.002	0.372
Body hair	5.05±0.27	4.90±0.32	5.17±0.35	0.156	0.856
Visible hair on chin	5.78±0.33	5.53±0.42	6.23±0.34	0.648	0.526
Visible hair on upper lip	4.56±0.33	5.15±0.38	4.58±0.56	0.692	0.504
Visible hair on face	5.18±0.32	5.07±0.44	5.35±0.43	0.094	0.910
Visible hair on body	3.86±0.38	3.11±0.45	3.76±0.54	0.856	0.429
Embarrassment about excessive body hair	5.89±0.36	5.61±0.47	5.94±0.49	0.153	0.859
Body weight	3.62±0.31	3.44±0.30	3.44±0.39	0.098	0.906
Concerned about being overweight	3.10±0.37	2.92±0.39	2.82±0.53	0.116	0.891
Felt trouble with body weight	4.05±0.37	3.73±-.43	3.35±0.58	0.565	0.571
Frustrated in trying to lose weight	4.64±0.39	4.00±0.48	4.11±0.59	0.615	0.543
Felt less sexy for being overweight	3.27±0.38	3.23±0.43	3.94±0.67	0.554	0.577
Felt difficulties to maintain ideal weight	3.02±0.39	3.34±0.42	3.00±0.63	0.169	0.845
Menstrual problems	3.29±0.21	3.48±0.20	3.16±0.32	0.372	0.691
Headaches	5.16±0.37	5.50±0.41	5.41±0.62	0.179	0.836
Irregular menstrual periods	1.59±0.27	1.73±0.34	1.35±0.24	0.280	0.750
Abdominal bloating	2.02±0.26	1.61±0.21	1.94±0.44	0.573	0.566
Menstrual cramps	4.37±0.45	5.07±0.50	3.94±0.68	0.980	0.380
Infertility problems	4.03±0.33	3.87±0.42	4.25±0.52	0.164	0.849
Concerned with infertility problems	4.13±0.39	3.80±0.50	4.29±0.66	0.216	0.806
Worried of not being able to have children	4.10±0.42	3.73±0.53	4.58±0.65	0.538	0.586
Lack of control over the situation with PCOS	3.51±0.39	4.30±0.47	3.64±0.59	0.862	0.426
Felt sad for infertility problems	4.37±0.39	3.65±0.47	4.47±0.67	0.823	0.443

counterpart. For example, they often expressed their frustration in failing to lose body weight and found themselves to be less attractive. Apart from these, other symptoms like, abdominal bloating, late menstrual period and feelings of uneasiness with excessive body hair were reported to be higher among the overweight participants. It was found that the incidence of both overweight and obesity pose a strong implication on

Table 5.4: Health-related quality of life of PCOS participants with respect to duration of treatment received (n=80)

Health-related quality of life	*Duration of treatment received by PCOS patients*			*F value*	*p value*
	<2 years n = 52	2-5 years n = 22	>5 years n = 6		
	Mean ± se	*Mean ± se*	*Mean ± se*		
Emotions	3.28±0.13	3.80±0.25	3.10±0.51	2.106	0.129
Depression for having PCOS	3.48±0.32	3.95±0.49	3.66±0.84	0.320	0.727
Easily tired	2.38±0.27	2.59±0.48	3.00±0.57	0.281	0.756
Mood swing for having PCOS	2.36±0.28	3.18±0.50	2.66±0.48	1.067	0.349
Low self-esteem for having PCOS	4.28±0.33	4.40±0.62	3.83±0.54	0.116	0.891
Felt frightened of getting cancer	6.03±0.26	6.54±0.20	5.00±0.93	1.934	0.152
Worried about having PCOS	2.53±0.26	3.22±0.35	3.16±0.98	1.155	0.320
Self-conscious for having PCOS	2.63±0.24	3.45±0.44	2.50±0.50	1.650	0.199
Late menstrual period	2.57±0.30	3.09±0.50	1.00±0.07	2.162	0.122
Body hair	5.00±0.23	5.22±0.29	4.60±0.49	0.377	0.687
Visible hair on chin	5.75±0.28	6.00±0.36	5.50±0.92	0.198	0.821
Visible hair on upper lip	4.65±0.28	5.22±0.40	4.00±0.28	1.047	0.356
Visible hair on face	5.21±0.28	5.27±0.41	4.66±0.80	0.220	0.803
Visible hair on body	3.59±0.32	3.50±0.50	4.00±0.85	0.108	0.898
Embarrassment about excessive body hair	5.78±0.31	6.13±0.39	4.83±0.22	0.824	0.443
Body weight	3.65±0.25	3.33±0.33	3.10±0.64	0.452	0.638
Concerned about being overweight	3.19±0.30	2.54±0.41	2.83±0.90	0.708	0.496
Felt trouble with body weight	3.94±0.30	3.13±0.49	5.00±0.89	1.916	0.154
Frustrated in trying to lose weight	4.53±0.33	4.13±0.52	3.16±0.77	0.945	0.393
Felt less sexy for being overweight	3.42±0.33	3.72±0.51	2.00±0.81	1.257	0.290
Felt difficulties to maintain ideal weight	3.19±0.33	3.13±0.48	2.50±0.95	0.231	0.794
Menstrual problems	3.32±0.16	3.59±0.24	2.37±0.53	2.419	0.096
Headaches	5.21±0.31	6.00±0.40	3.83±0.34	2.389	0.099
Irregular menstrual periods	1.63±0.23	1.63±0.31	1.00±0.04	0.442	0.645
Abdominal bloating	1.84±0.20	2.00±0.36	1.66±0.66	0.137	0.872
Menstrual cramps	4.59±0.37	4.72±0.54	3.00±0.26	1.022	0.365
Infertility problems	3.97±0.28	4.31±0.48	3.41±0.85	0.482	0.619
Concerned with infertility problems	4.01±0.34	4.27±0.56	3.88±0.68	0.155	0.857
Worried of not being able to have children	3.96±0.36	4.45±0.57	3.83±0.66	0.294	0.746
Lack of control over the situation with PCOS	3.78±0.34	4.22±0.51	2.33±0.71	1.462	0.238
Felt sad for infertility problems	**4.13±0.33**	**4.31±0.52**	**3.83±0.27**	**0.098**	**0.907**

the development and progression of the syndrome (Diamanti-Kandarakis, 2007). A higher proportion of obese women with PCOS reported the symptoms of hirsutism and menstrual irregularities (Gambineri *et al.*, 2002). Moreover, the fat accumulation in the abdomen could stimulate the production of androgen in the body that possibly developed the menstrual abnormalities and the growth of body hair (Dale *et al.*, 1992). Our study also implied that the domains of 'emotions', 'body weight' and 'infertility problems', of PCOS health-related quality of life remained

Table 5.5: Health-related quality of life of PCOS patients with respect to perceived health status (n=80)

Health-related quality of life	*Perceived health status*			*F value*	*p value*
	Poor n = 15	*Fair n = 56*	*Good n = 9*		
	Mean ± se	*Mean ± se*	*Mean ± se*		
Emotions	2.97±0.29	3.39±0.13	4.31±0.31	4.833	0.011
Depression for having PCOS	3.00±0.54	3.50±0.30	5.44±0.72	3.641	0.031
Easily tired	2.53±0.49	2.28±0.25	3.66±0.88	1.834	0.167
Mood swing for having PCOS	2.60±0.59	2.42±0.28	3.77±0.86	1.474	0.236
Low self-esteem for having PCOS	3.13±0.61	4.46±0.34	5.11±0.88	2.167	0.121
Felt frightened of getting cancer	5.26±0.60	6.21±0.22	6.77±0.22	2.537	0.086
Worried about having PCOS	2.33±0.48	2.73±0.25	3.77±0.59	1.698	0.190
Self-conscious for having PCOS	2.26±0.35	2.96±0.26	3.11±0.56	0.934	0.397
Late menstrual period	2.66±0.61	2.53±0.28	2.88±0.88	0.104	0.901
Body hair	5.20±0.39	4.98±0.20	5.04±0.76	0.101	0.904
Visible hair on chin	6.26±0.39	5.73±0.26	5.44±0.85	0.602	0.550
Visible hair on upper lip	5.06±0.52	4.60±0.26	5.22±0.84	0.542	0.584
Visible hair on face	4.93±0.49	5.25±0.26	5.22±0.84	0.145	0.866
Visible hair on body	3.66±0.58	3.46±0.30	4.33±0.86	0.551	0.579
Embarrassment about excessive body hair	6.06±0.48	5.87±0.28	5.00±0.87	0.724	0.488
Body weight	2.36±0.24	3.69±0.24	4.44±0.41	5.419	0.006
Concerned about being overweight	1.66±0.23	3.25±0.30	3.55±0.68	3.795	0.027
Felt trouble with body weight	3.13±0.47	3.76±0.32	5.11±0.56	2.210	0.117
Frustrated in trying to lose weight	2.93±0.57	4.50±0.32	5.55±0.68	4.039	0.021
Feltless sexy for being overweight	2.00±0.40	3.53±0.31	4.88±0.88	4.888	0.010
Felt difficulties to maintain ideal weight	2.06±0.49	3.41±0.32	3.11±0.71	2.000	0.142
Menstrual problems	3.11±0.26	3.31±0.16	3.72±0.46	0.689	0.505
Headaches	5.33±0.54	5.37±0.30	5.00±0.92	0.102	0.903
Irregular menstrual periods	1.40±0.19	1.50±0.20	2.44±0.86	1.534	0.222
Abdominal bloating	1.20±0.20	2.05±0.21	1.88±0.51	1.906	0.156
Menstrual cramps	4.53±0.70	4.33±0.36	5.55±0.86	0.772	0.466
Infertility problems	3.43±0.48	3.93±0.28	5.61±0.46	3.479	0.036
Concerned with infertility problems	3.40±0.59	3.91±0.34	6.11±0.56	3.862	0.025
Worried of not being able to have children	3.53±0.70	3.91±0.35	6.11±0.51	3.280	0.043
Lack of control over the situation with PCOS	3.13±0.56	3.91±0.32	4.22±0.87	0.760	0.471
Felt sad for infertility problems	3.66±0.62	4.00±0.33	6.00±0.50	3.074	0.052

impaired among the participants who perceived their health as poor. These participants were found to be concerned with the problems of overweight and remained worried of not being able to have children and reported depression for having PCOS more than those who perceived their health as either good or fair. The psychosocial health of the participants was more affected than physical health (Coffey *et al.*, 2006) since the clinical symptoms and its effect significantly caused the impairment in quality of life among PCOS women. Likewise, the psychosocial factors were believed to develop a profound emotional distress among these women (Eggers *et al.*, 2001). Hahn *et al.* (2005) reported that irregular menstrual cycles were perceived as the primary reason for infertility and hirsutism among PCOS women. In a qualitative study, it was found that PCOS women who had hirsutism were mostly dissatisfied with body image and perceived themselves as ugly and unattractive that consequently lowered their self-esteem and increased the level of depression (Ekback *et al.*, 2009). Thus, disease related changes such as, hirsutism, acne and obesity, hormonal disturbances, fear of infertility and psychosocial distress may impinge on the female identity grasping all the pleasure and confidence in the sexual life of PCOS women (Elsenbruch *et al.*, 2003).

Studies showed that the baseline treatment of PCOS using the medicine (like, metformin) is highly recognized by the medical practitioners (Zisser, 2007) as this medicine was found to improve the lipid profile and the insulin sensitivity by shedding the body weight that subsequently prevents the progression of metabolic and reproductive abnormalities (Glueck *et al.*, 2006). Furthermore, this medicine could restore the ovulation and often reduce the risk of miscarriages among the PCOS patients (Fleming, 2006). Thus, it is expected that the treatment received for a longer period of time could reduce the botheration of PCOS symptoms and improve the health-related quality of life. On the contrary, our study demonstrated that the participants who received the treatment for a longer period of time were similarly bothered like the ones who have recently started receiving the treatment. Medical practitioners suggested that along with medicine lifestyle modifications (like, moderate physical activities and diet control) are required as the first-line treatment for PCOS management (Essah *et al.*, 2007; Thomson *et al.*, 2010). However, the PCOS participants of this study neither have control over their diet nor do they exercise regularly (Sen Gupta *et al.*, 2015). It is probable that the lower educational attainment of the participants failed to develop fair amount of awareness about how healthy food habit and exercise help to mitigating PCOS health-related quality of life.

Strength and Limitation of the Study

Studying the health-related quality of life among the PCOS women is a maiden attempt in Indian context. Previous research on PCOS conducted within a medical framework could not provide the psychosocial aspect of PCOS quality of life. Inclusion of qualitative approach to explore the women's self experiences on PCOS symptoms may add the adequate information in the body of existing literature.

Conclusion

We concluded that the perceived health status and actual weight status of PCOS women are likely to determine the health-related quality of life. Therapeutic intervention alone would not help much to improving the PCOS health related quality of life; generating awareness in bringing lifestyle change might be required in addition.

References

Acmaz, G., E. Albayrak, B. Acmaz, M. Baser, M. Soyak, and G. Zararsiz, 2013. "Level of Anxiety, Depression, Self-esteem, Social Anxiety, and Quality of Life among the Women with Polycystic Ovary Syndrome", *Scientific World Journal*, 1-7.

Azziz, R., E. Carmina, D. Dewailly, E. Diamanti-Kandarakis, H.F. Escobar-Morreale, W. Futterweit, O.E. Janssen, R.S. Legro, R.J. Norman, A.E. Taylor, and S.F. Witchel, 2006. "Androgen Excess Society. Positions statement: Criteria for Defining Polycystic Ovary Syndrome as a Predominantly Hyperandrogenic Syndrome: An Androgen Excess Society Guideline. *J. Clin. Endocrinol. Metab,* 9: 4237-4245.

Balen, A., 2001. "Polycystic Ovary Syndrome and Cancer", *Hum. Reprod. Update,* 7: 522-525.

Barnard, L., D. Ferriday, N. Guenther, B. Strauss, A. H. Balen, and L. Dye, 2007. "Quality of Life and Psychological Well-Being in Polycystic Ovary Syndrome", *Hum Reprod.,* 22: 2279-2286.

Brassard, M., Y. AinMelk, and J.P. Baillargeon. 2008. "Basic infertility including polycystic ovary syndrome", *Med. Clin. North Am.,* 92: 1163-1192.

Chakraborty, P., S.K. Goswami, S. Rajani, S. Sharma, S.N. Kabir, B. Chakravarty, and K. Jana, 2013. "Recurrent Pregnancy Loss in Polycystic Ovary Syndrome: Role of Hyperhomocysteinemia and Insulin Resistance", *PLoS One,* 8: 64446.

Ching, H.L., V. Burke, and B.G. Stuckey, 2007. "Quality of life and psychological morbidity in women with polycystic ovary syndrome: body mass index, age and the provision of patient information are significant modifiers", *Clin. Endocrinol (Oxf),* 66: 373-379.

Coffey, S., G. Bano, and H.D. Mason, 2006. "Health-related Quality of Life in Women with Polycystic Ovary Syndrome: A Comparison with the General Population using the Polycystic Ovary Syndrome Questionnaire (PCOSQ) and the Short Form", *Gynecol. Endocrinol.,* 22: 80-86.

Colwell, H., S. Mathias, D. Pasta, J. Henning, and J. Steege, 1998. "A Health-related Quality of Life Instrument for Symptomatic Patients with Endometriosis: A Validation Study. *Am. J. Obstet. Gynecol.*, 179: 47-55.

Conway, G.S., 1996. "Polycystic Ovary Syndrome: Clinical Aspects", *Baillieres Clin Endocrinol Metab.,* 10: 263-279.

Cronin, L., G. Guyatt, L. Griffith, E. Wong, R. Azziz, W. Futterweit, D. Cook, and A. Dunaif, 1998. "Development of a Health-related Quality-of-life Questionnaire (PCOSQ) for Women with Polycystic Ovary Syndrome (PCOS)", *J. Clin. Endocrinol. Metab.,* 83: 1976-1987.

Dale, P.O., T. Tanbo, S. Vaaler, and T. Abyholm, 1992. "Body Weight, Hyperinsulinemia, and Gonadotropin Levels in the Polycystic Ovarian Syndrome: Evidence of Two Distinct Populations", *Fertil., Steril.,* 58: 487-491.

Diamanti-Kandarakis, E., 2007. "Role of Obesity and Adiposity in Polycystic Ovary Syndrome", *Int. J. Obes. (Lond). Suppl.* 2: S8-13.

Drosdzol, A., V. Skrzypulec, B. Mazur, R. and Pawlińska-Chmara. 2007. "Quality of Life and Marital Sexual Satisfaction in Women with Polycystic Ovary Syndrome", *Folia Histochem. Cytobiol.,* 11: S93-S97.

Eggers, S. and S. Kirchengast, 2001. "The Polycystic Ovary Syndrome—A Medical Condition but also an Important Psychosocial Problem", *Coll. Antropol.,* 25: 673-685.

Ehrmann, D.A., 2005. "Polycystic Ovary Syndrome", *N. Engl. J. Med.,* 352: 1223-1236.

Ekback, M., K. Wijma, and E. Benzein, 2009. "It is Always on my Mind: Men's Experiences of their Bodies when Living with Hirsutism", *Health Care Women Int.,* 30: 358-372.

Elsenbruch, S., S. Hahn, D. Kowalsky, A.H. Offner, M. Schedlowski, K. Mann, and O.E. Janssen. 2003. "Quality of Life, Psychosocial Well-being, and Sexual Satisfaction in Women with Polycystic Ovary Syndrome", *J. Clin. Endocrinol. Metab.,* 88: 5801-5807.

Essah, P.A., E.P. Wickham, and J.E. Nestler, 2007. "The Metabolic Syndrome in Polycystic Ovary Syndrome", *Clin. Obstet. Gynecol.,* 50: 205-225.

Fleming, R., 2006. "The Use of Insulin Sensitizing Agents in Ovulation Induction in Women with Polycystic Ovary Syndrome", *Hormones (Athens)* 5: 171-178.

Franks, S., 1995. "Polycystic Ovary Syndrome", *N. Engl. J. Med.,* 333: 853-861.

Gambineri, A., C. Pelusi, V. Vicennati, U. Pagotto, and R. Pasquali, 2002. "Obesity and the Polycystic Ovary Syndrome", *Int. J. Obes. Relat. Metab. Disord.,* 26: 883-896.

Glueck, C.J., D. Aregawi, M. Agloria, M. Winiarska, L. Sieve, and P. Wang, 2006. "Sustainability of 8 per cent Weight Loss, Reduction of Insulin Resistance, and

Amelioration of Atherogenic-metabolic Risk Factors over 4 years by Metformin-diet in Women with Polycystic Ovary Syndrome", *Metabolism.,* 55: 1582-1589.

Guleria, A.K., S.K. Syal, A. Kapoor, S. Kumar, P. Tiwari, and P. Dabsadghao, 2014. "Cardiovascular Disease Risk in Young Indian Women with Polycystic Ovary Syndrome", *Gynecol. Endocrinol.,* 30: 26-29.

Hahn, S., O.E. Janssen, S. Tan, K. Pleger, K. Mann, M. Schedlowski, R. Kimmig, S. Benson, E. Balamitsa, and S. Elsenbruc, 2005. "Clinical and Psychological Correlates of Quality-of-life in Polycystic Ovary Syndrome", *Eur. J. Endocrinol.,* 153: 853-860.

Hollinrake, E., A. Abreu, M. Maifeld, B.J. Van Voorhis, and A. Dokras. 2007. "Increased Risk of Depressive Disorders in Women with Polycystic Ovary Syndrome", *Fertil. Steril.,* 87: 1369-1376.

IBM Corporation. 2011. IBM SPSS Statistics for Windows, Version 20.0. Armonk, NY.

Jones, G.L., J.M. Hall, H.L. Lashen, A.H. Balen, and W.L. Ledger, 2011. "Health-related Quality of Life among Adolescents with Polycystic Ovary Syndrome", *J. Obstet. Gynecol. Neonatal Nurs.,* 40: 577-588.

Jones, G.L., S.H. Kennedy, and C. Jenkinson, 2002. "Health-related Quality of Life Measurement in Women with Common benign Gynecologic Conditions: a Systematic Review", *Am. J. Obstet. Gynecol.,* 187: 501-511.

Kelly, C.J., A. Speirs, G.W. Gould, J.R. Petrie, H. Lyall, and J.M. Connell, 2002. "Altered Vascular Function in Young Women with Polycystic Ovary Syndrome", *J. Clin. Endocrinol. Metab.,* 87: 742-746.

Khomami, M.B., F.R. Tehrani, S. Hashemi, M. Farahmand, and F. Azizi, 2015. "Of PCOS Symptoms, Hirsutism has the most Significant Impact on the Quality of Life of Iranian Women", *PLoS One.,* 10: e0123608.

Li, Y., Y. Li, E.H. Yu Ng, E. Stener-Victorin, L. Hou, T. Wu, F. Han, and X. Wu., 2011. "Polycystic Ovary Syndrome is associated with Negatively Variable Impacts on Domains of Health-related Quality of Life: Evidence from a Meta-analysis", *Fertil Steril.,* 96: 452-458.

Lohman, T.G., A.F. Roche, and R. Martorell, 1988. "*Anthropometric Standardization Reference Manual*", Human Kinetics Books, Champaign, IL.

Mandrelle, K., M.S. Kamath, D.J. Bondu, A. Chandy, T. Aleyamma, and K. George. 2012. "Prevalence of Metabolic Syndrome in Women with Polycystic Ovary Syndrome Attending an Infertility Clinic in a Tertiary Care Hospital in South India", *J. Hum. Reprod. Sci.,* 5: 26-31.

McCook, J.G., N.E. Reame, and S.S. Thatcher, 2005. "Health-related Quality of Life Issues in Women with Polycystic Ovary Syndrome", *J. Obstet. Gynecol. Neonatal. Nurs.,* 34: 12-20.

Naughton, M.J. and W.L. McBee, 1997. "Health-related Quality of Life after Hysterectomy", *Clin. Obstet. Gynecol.,* 40: 947-957.

Ramanand, S.J., B.B. Ghongane, J.B. Ramanand, M.H. Patwardhan, R.R. Ghanghas and S.S. Jain, 2013. "Clinical Characteristics of Polycystic Ovary Syndrome in Indian Women", *Indian J. Endocrinol. Metab.,* 17: 138-145.

Rotterdam ESHRE/ASRM-sponsored PCOS Consensus Workshop Group, 2004.

"Revised 2003 Consensus on Diagnostic Criteria and Long-term Health Risks related to Polycystic Ovary Syndrome", *Fertil. Steril.,* 81: 19-25.

Schmid, J., S. Kirchengast, E. Vytiska-Binstorfer, and J. Huber, 2004. "Infertility Caused by PCOS-Health-related Quality of Life among Austrian and Moslem Immigrant Women in Austria", *Hum. Reprod.,* 19:2251-2257.

Sen Gupta, D., N. Som, C. Dutta Roy, S. Goswami, and S. Ray. 2015. "Polycystic Ovary Syndrome: A Study from West Bengal, India", *J. Indian Anthropol Soc.,* 50.

Sinha, U., K. Sinharay, S. Saha, T.A. Longkumer, S.N. Baul, and S.K. Pal, 2013. "Thyroid Disorders in Polycystic Ovarian Syndrome Subjects: A Territory Hospital based Cross Sectional Study from Eastern India", *Indian J. Endocrinol. Metab.,* 17: 304-309.

Sonino, N., G.A. Fava, E. Mani, P. Belluardo, and M. Boscaro. 1993. "Quality of Life of Hirsute Women", *Postgrad. Med. J.,* 69: 186-189.

Teede, H., A. Deeks, and L. Moran. 2010. "Polycystic Ovary Syndrome: A Complex Condition with Psychological, Reproductive and Metabolic Manifestations that Impact on Health across the Lifespan", *BMC Med.,* 8: 41.

Thathapudi, S., V. Kodati, J. Erukkambattu, A. Katragadda, U. Addepally, and Q. Hasan, 2014. "Anthropometric and Biochemical Characteristics of Polycystic Ovarian Syndrome in South Indian Women using AES-2006 Criteria", *Int. J. Endocrinol. Metab.,* 12: 12470.

Thomson, R.L., J.D. Buckley, S.S. Lim, M. Noakes, P.M. Clifton, R.J. Norman, and G.D. Brinkworth., 2010. "Lifestyle management improves quality of life and depression in overweight and obese women with polycystic ovary syndrome", *Fertil. Steril.,* 94:1812-1816.

World Health Organization Expert Consultation, 2004. "Appropriate Body-mass Index for Asian Populations and its Implications for Policy and Intervention Strategies", *Lancet.,* 363:157-163.

World Health Organization, 2007. Growth reference data for 5-19 years. Available on http://www.who.int/growthref/en/

Zisser, H.C., 2007. "Polycystic ovary syndrome and pregnancy: Is metformin the magic bullet?" *Diabetes Spectr.,* 20: 85-89.

SIX

FOOD AND GENDER
A Case Study of the Matrilineal Garos

QUEENBALA MARAK

Introduction

Gender permeates all aspects of life including food life. The relation between the sexes, their gender definitions and their sexuality are some of the significant domains of meaning embodied in food. In many cultures, eating is a sexual and gendered experience throughout life (Counihan, 1999). Some research suggests that gendering of food is largely culturally constructed rather than biologically based. Foods are gendered differently in different cultures and historical periods (Jansen, 1997; Counihan and Kaplan, 1998; and Counihan, 1999). For instance, Caplan (1997: 3) points out that 'entitlement' to food differs between men and women, in terms of the type of food as well as the quantity itself. Again, 'real men' are thought to need meat, particularly red meat while women were much more likely to be vegetarians. Some conclude that men adopt unhealthy behaviours and beliefs in order to demonstrate their masculinity (Moynihan, 1998; Courtenay, 2000; and Watson, 2000). However, most of these studies on food and gender have been done by women on women respondents. On the other hand, a study on male carpenters, drivers and engineers in Oslo revealed that there was no homogeneous pattern in male food choices; rather social class played a role in the selection or rejection of food (Roos and Wandel, 2005).

The gendering of food in any society is remarkable. The present study assumes importance since the people studied are a matrilineal people though wrongly referred many times as matriarchal. Nevertheless, it would be interesting to see gender dimensions in a matrilineal society through the microcosm of food and food ways. The Garos are a tribe living in the North-eastern part of India and Northern Bangladesh, more distinguished for their matrilineal system. In India, they are found predominantly in the state of Meghalaya in the districts of East, West and South Garo Hills; however, they are also found in small pockets in different states such as Assam, Tripura, Nagaland and West Bengal. In Bangladesh, they mostly reside in the Northern districts of Mymensing and Tangail. In India, they call themselves 'Achik' while in Bangladesh they refer to themselves as 'Mandi'. As in other matrilineal systems, lineage, succession, transmission of property and residence after marriage is through the female line, i.e., from mother to daughter. However, unlike some other systems, succession of leadership and transmission of property does not follow any rules of ultimogeniture or primogeniture; instead it is laid in the hands of the favourite and capable daughter. The head of the family generally is the father, and in his absence, the son-in-law who is married to the inheriting daughter. The authoritative position normally is held by the maternal uncle and the clan, whose authority over his sister's children and use and disposal of her property is second to none. However, only in mitigating cases, a maternal uncle (and the clan) will come in the way of decisions made by the husband of a sister.

Methodology

The data incorporated herein is original and empirical collected throughout a period of three years during the Ph.D. work. The study area is a village called Gohalkona situated in the state of Assam in India. The village has 258 Garo households, with a total population of 1367, males numbering 632 and females 735 (from personal census data collected by the researcher). They are all Christians, majority of them being American Baptists.

Garos were originally shifting cultivators, now cultivating a large amount of crops in their plots, starting with the staple, which is rice, and followed by other crops such as millet, tapioca, pumpkin, varieties of gourd and bean, sorrel leaves, chillies and others. However, at present the people depend on wet paddy cultivation for their livelihood. There are a few families in the village who have started cultivation of cash crops, such as betel nut, pepper, cashew nut, oranges and pineapples. Besides, cultivated food, Garos forage in the wilds for food such as arum, ferns, bamboo shoot and mushrooms. Animals domesticated include pig, cow and chicken. Livestock is reared invariably for food even though bulls are kept for agricultural work. Dogs and cats are also commonly reared, but these are only kept as pets and not meant for food. Besides the above, some amount of hunting for wild animal food and birds also take place. Fishing is very common.

Food, Masculinity and Feminity

A number of authors mention that in the US and other Western post-industrial societies, men's foods are considered masculine and typically include beef (especially steak), hamburgers, potatoes and beer, while women's foods are considered feminine and often include salads, pasta, yogurt, fruits and chocolate (Bender, 1976; Logue and Smith, 1986; Jensen and Holm, 1999). Among Garos, there is no such clear-cut distinction between men's food and women's food. Men and women eat the same food and show a liking for all types of food consumed. However, some understated differences can be witnessed on close observation. In order to find out the gender perspective, if any, inherent in Garo food, the researcher administered two simple questionnaires on 20 individuals of each gender.

Why We Eat?

The question, "*Maina cha·a*?" (Why do you eat?), was asked to 20 men and 20 women randomly. Table 6.1 shows the responses given as reasons why they ate.

Table 6.1: Reasons behind Eating

Reasons	*No. of Men (In %)*	*No. of Women (In %)*
I am hungry	100.0*	70.0
It is tasty	20.0	–
It is filling	40.0	–
It gives strength	40.0	–
It is good for body	–	30.0

Source: Field Data.

*All 20 men-respondents also gave a second reason why they ate.

Irrespective of sex, both men (100%) and women (70%) eat because of hunger. Hunger is the basic urge that leads to gratification through food. This response also indicates that eating is a routine habit connected to physiological changes, i.e., body craving for food, rather than for social or cultural reasons. This is rather interesting for the supposed physiological change (craving for food) is also culturally reasoned. A Garo is always "hungry" if he/she has not eaten rice. One of my informants narrated:

> "I have gone many times to visit my Assamese[1] friends, especially on weddings. They offer *lucee-bhaji*[2], some pieces of *lucee* (fried flat bread) and fried vegetables together with *dal* (lentils) and one sweet tomato preparation. I like the food. I always eat many *lucees*, such that my friends tease me always on such occasions. But do you know? Even after eating my fill, when I come home I am always hungry. I go directly to the kitchen and search for rice and curry".

However, the stress on reasons other than hunger seems to be gendered. Men follow their senses. Taste (20%) is an important factor. Implicit in this response is the fact that if they do not find the food tasty, they would not eat, though that is never the practice. A feeling of fullness (40%) and strength-giving (40%) were other reasons given by them. Garo men are seen valuing those food items which give them a feeling of "fullness" over others. These food items include rice, tapioca and jackfruit. "Fullness" and "strength-building" are again characteristics which emphasize the importance laid on physicality by men. On the other hand, women eat when they are hungry (70%) and also because it is good for the body (30%). In effect, it showed the emphasis that women laid on health, which the men did not. Strength-building food and beneficent food are not the one and same. For instance, *matchu-be·en* (beef) is a supposedly strength-building food, which however is not too beneficial for the body (in terms of how it is avoided during fever, malaria, cough and cold).

What We Eat?

The question, "What food do you eat?" put to men-respondents elicited the answer, "Everything." This gives the impression of an indifference to food and portrayed eating as a necessary routine. However, in practice,

Garo men are actively concerned about food and have also been seen taking pride in informing one and all that they eat everything. Meat occupies a very important position in Garo's food. When asked men listed eating elephants, tigers, monkeys, wild boars, deer, dogs, rats, squirrels, mongooses, sparrows, crows etc. In fact, it is a conquest for eating as many varieties of animal-species as one could.

Women, on the other hand, are found to be conventional meat-eaters, eating only that meat with which they are familiar since childhood. In fact, there are many women who refused to entertain the idea of eating dogs and monkeys, which are not traditional food. The reasons are cultural in nature: One informant said she got a very obnoxious odour (*kaltenteng senga*) from dog-meat even after it was well-cooked. Another pointed out that a monkey looks like a human baby when de-skinned. "How can one even think of eating that?"

Here I need to explain the concept of indigenous and non-indigenous food among Garos. In Garo cuisine, a distinction is made between indigenous food or local food, called *a·chik samjak* (Garo vegetables) and non-indigenous food or non-local food. *A.chik samjak* refers to traditional vegetables which are either collected from jungles, forests and marshes or grown in shifting/slash-and-burn plots of land. These include varieties of plant food like tubers, roots, stems, leaves, and flowers, which are believed to have been consumed since times immemorial. These are also at times grown within the margin of the dwelling places in the form of gardens both tended and untended. On the other hand, non-local food items are pulses (except the black lentil), legumes and vegetables like tomato, cabbage, cauliflower and potato which are also grown in the village, but which according to local perception, are food items that their forefathers did not know. There is no term to refer to non-local food, but in every Garo's mind there is a sharp distinction between *a·chik samjak* and others. Again, those foods are considered indigenous which are prepared in an indigenous style. For instance, food cooked in alkali (*kalchi*[3]) is local food. Bamboo shoot fermented in the local indigenous way is also a local food.

In terms of indigenous food items, men are seen to eat every variety to establish their masculinity. On the other hand, many women in Assam avoided food items for supposedly health and other reasons. A twenty-three year old mother of a baby boy is considered an "odd" woman in Gohalkona. She refuses to take *kalchi* (alkali), one of the most important ingredients in Garo food, so much so that others tease her that she is not a Garo: "*A·chik ongja biade, Bangal sa*" (Not a Garo, but a non-Garo). She cooks food separately for herself from her family. The reason behind her not eating *kalchi* is because she felt it gave her stomach ache when she was a child. She has since never taken any food cooked in *kalchi*, and now she gets a detestable smell emanating from food cooked in alkali. Another instance in point is a woman of 57 years who suffers from arthritis. She avoids eating beef, which she feels makes her sickness acute. However, her husband, aged 65 years, who also suffers from arthritis and constipation (and has been told to stay away from beef by a traditional healer), is still a consummate beef-eater. Again, their granddaughter who stays in the city refuses to eat because she feels disgust at the very sight even after it is cooked de-skinned.

In essence, even though men are hard to please in terms of the type of food consumed, it is women who are actually fastidious when it comes to eating food for supposedly health and cultural reasons. Interestingly, in the case of non-indigenous food items, women are seen to be more forthcoming and interested than men.

Gendering of Food Items

There are certain foods or parts of foods that are associated in some manner with gender. Hunted meat such as venison, elephant-meat and tiger-meat are found associated with men probably due to the association of such meat with hunting, an activity generally associated with men. Meat portions such as head and intestines of any animal, whether domesticated or otherwise is also associated with men. This might be explained as men who are "strong" would have an affinity to "unpleasant" parts[4] of meat. Chicken head is always served to the head of the family who is a male. In his absence, it is served to the eldest male member, the son or the son-in-law. Again cleaning of intestines (which, when cooked is a delicacy) of slaughtered cows or pigs is done mostly by men. Portions of food partaken such as a large share of cooked rice are also gendered. The amount of rice consumed in a meal is termed many times as either "male" or "female" with males supposedly consuming more. "*Bangkhale songbo, biade pante podaldal*!" (Cook more rice, he's a bachelor), is very often quoted when a man is invited for food. This does not mean that bachelors eat more than married men. Even married men are referred to as "*pante srek-srek*" meaning "like a bachelor" in terms of food consumption. If a woman consumes more rice, “She eats like a man”, is the comment often made.

There are a few food items which are considered more or less “feminine” in nature. Shrimps, cockles and crabs are associated with women since they are foraged by them. Tubers, leaves, shoots, flowers and fruits are gathered by women and therefore associated with them. Sour citrus fruits like *jambura*, *jambil* (pomelo), *cheng* (tamarind), *kangkil* (berry) and *ambare sigun* (gooseberry) are said to be “*mechikni cha·ani*” (female’s food). Interestingly, vegetables such as cabbages, cauliflowers, carrots and french beans are also found associated with women. These are non-indigenous food items and are many times encouraged by women in their daily meals, despite subtle objection by men and children. Finally, flour (wheat and gram), noodles and store-bought cookies, since introduced in the family by the mother or the wife, are therefore associated with them.

Thus, a subtle gender difference is also noticeable in Garo food items. Table 6.2 generalizes food items according to gender:

Table 6.2: Gendered Food items

Male Food items	*Female Food Items*
Hunted meat	Fish, shrimps, cockles
Large share of food	Vegetables and fruits
Indigenous Food	New food

Source: Field Data.

In short, men are seen to make food choices based on the state of the body and work capacity than about healthy food choices. According to Moynihan (1998), the association between masculinity, success, and strength makes it difficult for men to talk about their health. This also seems to be true for men in the present study, who were perhaps projecting a version of hegemonic masculinity, which promotes reason and strength; whereas women, besides reasons of strength-building, seem to make food choices based mainly on health. Many studies of gender and food choice have actually described women as more food and health conscious than men (Charles and Kerr, 1988; Counihan, 1999; Jensen and Holm, 1999).

Food: Feminine and Masculine Activities

The question of food and gender is complex. In the West, gender is in part a status ascribed by biology, but it is also achieved through 'performance' (Butler, 1990, 1994; Moore, 1994). This would not only include practices of food and eating, including smoking in public, but also the preparation of meals and the clearing-up afterwards.

Even though Garos do not have a clear distinction between men's food and women's food, there exists a distinct bifurcation between male and female behaviour regarding food acquisition and its allied activities. This distinction is culturally defined even before the birth of a new born. It is believed that if a foetus is felt on the left side of the womb it is a female and if felt on the right side it is a male. The reasoning for such a belief is rather revealing. Since the woman (and would-be mother) carries the *basing* (water pitcher) on the left hip, the unborn female foetus tries to help her hence her positioning on the left side. Similarly, since the woman carries *ate* (chopper) and *godal* (spade) over the right shoulder the unborn male foetus similarly tries to help by positioning himself on the right (Marak, 2010, 2012). Thus, the society defines all work connected with the chopper and spade, such as cutting/clearing jungle and tilling the soil as men's work and fetching water as women's work.

Interestingly, the left-right classification sees parity with Indian philosophy. "... whilst left and right signify female and male, in Tantrism they are a part of a totally different spectrum in which the principles of impure/pure and inauspicious/auspicious, rather than evil/good, matter/spirit etc. were central" (Knott, 2005: 198). Among Garos, the left-right classification is significant. Garos shake each other's hands in greeting. In such a greeting, the right hand is always forwarded and not the left hand. Again, eating, writing and all 'clean' tasks is done with the right hand. Children are mildly and later strongly rebuked and even rapped on their knuckles for transgressions to this norm (Marak, 2014).

Food Producing Activities

For centuries, Garo women have been primary cooks at home and nurturers and the ones who store plant-seeds for progeny. One of the most feminine of food related activities is food gathering. Men are rarely food collectors, except when collecting honey. They are considered hunters than collectors as shown in Table 6.3. Sixteen men and twenty four women were randomly selected for data on food foraging activities.

Table 6.3: Division of Labour: Food Foraging

Activity	*Men (In %)*	*Women (In %)*
Hunting		
Set up snares and traps	100.0	–
Hunt with spears, guns and catapults	100.0	–
Fishing		
Large fish with spears and nets	75.0	–
Small fish with traps	12.5	100.0
Eels, snakes and frogs	75.0	–
Cockles, crabs and shrimps	12.5	100.0
Fishing in running water	100.0	–
Fishing in man-made dam	12.5	100.0
Food Collection		
Honey	75.0	–
Leaves, shoots, fruits, flowers, roots and tubers	100.0	–
Firewood	50.0	91.6

Source: Field Data.

Hunting is clearly a male endeavour. All interviewed men had used snares and traps to catch prey such as mongoose, squirrels, deer and foxes. Six men-informants hunted big game with guns, two with spears and all with catapults to catch birds and squirrels, in their lifetime. None of the women interviewed had ever gone on a hunting expedition. "Even if a woman wants to go along as a part of the hunting party, there are no takers", one woman informant lamented.

Interestingly, fishing is seen as a feminine activity, although 'big' fish, caught with the help of spears and nets, is supposedly caught by men, and not women (Marak, 2014). As a result among Garos, women's fishing usually entails catching of small fish and collection of cockles, shrimps and crabs.

Food collection is a woman's activity. All women informants collected food from the jungle and swamps, while none of the men interviewed had taken part in food collection. Whenever bee-hives were located in the jungles by women who are foraging for food, men go and collect them. Collection of firewood was also done mostly by women (91.6%) compared to men (50%).

Just as in food foraging, activities connected to cultivation are also gendered. Table 6.4 gives the list of such specific activities. Data collection for this section was done at the household level between men and women (husbands and wives). Care was taken to collect data only from those households (8 each) who were following a specific type of cultivation, and whether the husbands or wives ever contributed towards it.

Table 6.4: Division of Labour in the Household: Cultivation

Activity	*Men (In %)**	*Women (In %)**
Slash-and-Burn		
Clear and burn jungles	100.0	12.5
Construct way to plot	100.0	–
Harrow soil	50.0	100.0
Sow seeds	12.5	100.0
Weed	–	100.0
Harvest	–	100.0
Wet Paddy		
Ploughing with bullock	100.0	–
Soil preparation	100.0	–
Construction and repair of irrigation canals	100.0	–
Sowing seedlings	12.5	100.0
Transplantation	–	100.0
Harvesting	100.0	100.0
Transportation	100.0	–
Thresh of paddy by bullocks	100.0	–
Collect paddy after threshing	–	100.0
Dry rice grains under sun	–	100.0
Unhusk rice	–	100.0
Carry unhusked rice to store	–	100.0
Vegetable Garden		
Clear up jungle, bush and shrub	37.5	87.5
Harrow soil	–	100.0
Plant seeds, seedlings and tubers	–	100.0
Weed	–	100.0
Harvest	–	100.0
Cash Crops (Besides Rice)		
Clear jungle, bush and shrub	100.0	–
Plant crops	100.0	–
Weed	100.0	–
Harvest	100.0	–
Carry home	100.0	–

Source: Field Data from Gohalkona.

* The statistics refer to role of men and women (1 husband and 1 wife) of 8 households respectively. 8 different households were selected randomly (for each cultivation) on the basis of type of cultivation practiced.

In slash-and-burn cultivation, it is seen that except in preparation of the soil (clearing and burning jungles and constructing the way to the plot), all other activities such as preparation of soil, sowing of seeds, weeding and harvesting are done by women. Fifty per cent of the men also helped in harrowing the soil. This information seems to indicate that slash-and-burn is women-specific, while men are less inclined towards it. In reality too men are seen putting in more time and labour in other forms of cultivation than slash-and-burn.

Even though the agricultural output is very less in slash-and-burn, women are nonetheless seen cultivating a small plot where indigenous vegetables are grown. One woman-informant said,

> "The food we procure from *a·ba* (slash-and-burn) is very less. The rice is not sufficient even for one month, while the vegetables finish in distribution to *songsul-noksul* (co-villagers and neighbours). However, if we are lucky to get rice over two *mon*[5] (60 kilograms), we invite *mahari* (matrilineal kin) and *songsul-noksul* for the *mi-gital* ceremony (literal translation, "new rice"; referring to a ceremony that precedes the first consumption of the year's produce). Everyone looks forward to it, more than the *mi-gital* of *patal* (wet cultivation). *Atchu-ambini mi, tobata, nambata, smilbata, okabata*" (It is our forefathers' rice, it is tastier, better, more fragrant and fills you more).

In wet paddy cultivation, contribution of both men and women is seen at the household level. Interestingly, however besides the tasks being gendered, the assignments occur at sporadic intervals. At the preparation stage prior to sowing, men are seen performing heavier tasks such as soil preparation, ploughing, and construction and repairing of canals. Once the soil is prepared, women take-up the tasks of sowing seedlings, transplantation of seedlings and weeding (once rice-plants grow). Again, when crops are ready for harvest, it is men who undertake harvesting, transportation of the crops and threshing of paddy by bullocks. Once again, after threshing of rice, it is women who collect, clean, dry, unhusk and store rice.

In the village, all households have a vegetable garden attached to the homesteads. These gardens vary in sizes, some with just a small patch near the kitchen while others with gardens spread up to 1 *bigha*[6] or more. Eight families, which had some form of vegetable gardens, were studied. Of these, except in three households where men helped in clearing up bushes and shrubs, others did not take any part in the maintenance or tending of the gardens. These were all looked after by women.

Interestingly, when cash crops come into play, it becomes the domain of men. In all the eight households who had a cash crop garden, it was looked after by men alone, and women had no role to play in it. These crops included betel nut and leaves, cashew nut, oranges, pepper, pineapple and coconut.

It is thus seen in the above that men are involved in heavy-duty tasks such as clearing of jungles, ploughing of land, construction and repair of terraces, threshing of paddy by bullocks, while women take part in sowing of seedlings, transplantation, weeding and harvesting, which are considered time-consuming and meticulous tasks. In terms of activities, it is also seen that women are mostly and solely (in many cases) involved with slash-and-burn cultivation and tending of vegetable gardens, while men are involved in wet paddy and cash crop cultivations. It is interesting that women play no role in cash crop productions where men do all the work. It shows that with the introduction of cash crops, the role of women in economic activities seems to have declined or disappeared altogether, which in turn, can have serious consequences on gender relations as well.

Food Consuming Activities

Food consumption among Garos appears to be gendered. At the household level, women do all work related to food and cooking. However, while serving food, men gets precedence over women whether it is the husband, father or son. Table 6.5 shows the division of labour in the household. Data has been collected from men and women from ten households.

Table 6.5: Division of Labour in the Household: Consumption of Food

Activity related to consumption	*Men (In %)*	*Women (In %)*
Domestic Sphere		
Preparing and processing rice	–	100.0
Preparing vegetables	–	100.0
Preparing meat/fish	25.0	100.0
Preparing cockles and shrimps	–	100.0
Cooking	–	100.0
Serving	–	100.0
Cleaning up afterwards	–	100.0
Public Sphere		
Preparing and processing rice	25.0	75.0
Preparing vegetables	50.0	50.0
Preparing meat/fish	100.0	–
Cooking	100.0	–
Serving	100.0	–
Cleaning up afterwards	75.0	–

Source: Field Data.

Garo women process and cook all kinds of food at home. These foods include vegetable foods as well as meat, fish and other aquatic fauna. In a family meal, the mother/wife does the serving. The father/husband is served first. If the children are young they eat before the adults do. If they are adolescents and eating with the father, then they are served next. Only after everyone has been served the mother/wife takes her plate and serves herself. Even while eating if anyone needs a second helping it is the mother who serves. If the *mama* (maternal uncle) is present, he is first served. Even if other kin members are present, the first spoonful of rice goes to the *mama*'s plate. Four of the men-respondents also helped out in preparing meat and fish. These men helped in cutting and cleaning hunted meat, "big" fish, snakes and eels.

On the other hand, on ceremonial occasions, men perform activities connected to food preparation, cooking and serving. Such ceremonial occasions are many in Gohalkona and include the Christmas feast, the New Year's feast, clan meetings, weddings and funerals. On such occasions, except for cleaning and processing rice which is mostly done by women (75%), all other activities are undertaken by men. All the men interviewed took part in preparing meat, fish, cooking and serving, while the women declined having taken part in such activities.

A bifurcation of the domestic and public spheres among Garos in terms of commensality is noticed. All domestic activity connected to food is done by women. This includes fetching water, cleaning and cutting vegetables and meat, cooking, serving and cleaning up afterwards. On the other hand, all activity connected with food in the public sphere is done by men who are at times helped by women. On such occasions, men do the preparation, cooking, serving as well as cleaning up afterwards.

Food Distribution Activities

Food distribution among Garos is very common. Whatever the produce and whichever the cultivation, some amount is shared with neighbours and relatives. Table 6.6 shows the distribution of food that take place in ten households. These are the same households that were interviewed earlier for consumption of food.

Table 6.6: Distribution of Food

Food Items being Distributed	*Men (In %)*	*Women (in %)*
Produce from paddy fields		
Deciding to sell to trader	100.0	50.0
Actual selling to trader	100.0	–
Produce from slash-and-burn plots		
Selling to co-villagers	–	100.0
Sharing it with kin	20.0	100.0
Produce from vegetable garden		
Selling to co-villagers	–	100.0
Sharing with kin	20.0	100.0
Cash crops		
Deciding to sell to trader	100.0	–
Actual selling to trader	100.0	–

Source: Field Data.

Distribution of food among Garos can be studied at two levels: distribution without cash returns and distribution with cash returns. The former takes the shape of sharing food with relatives where the decision-making and actual distributions are in the hands of women. On the other hand, distribution with cash returns takes the shape of selling to a co-villager or a trader. If distribution (or selling) to a co-villager takes place, women make the decision and actually sell them in many cases as Table 5.6 reveals. However in the case of selling to traders, it is men who interact and do the actual selling.

Interestingly, in terms of food distribution, just as in consumption pattern, a distinction is seen between two worlds: the public and the domestic one. Women do the sharing and selling at home (for vegetables from slash-and-burn and homestead garden) to relatives, and if surplus, to co-villagers. Men, on the other hand, do the selling of rice and cash crops to traders, even though some women might participate in the bargaining process. Men at times do the actual selling of rice, betel-nut, coconuts, meat etc. in the village market. Women rarely do the selling of vegetables even in the village square.

The decision of selling rice to traders is made by men, even though sometimes women (50%) also take part in the decision-making. The actual selling and passing of money from one hand to the other are between men only. The sale of cash crops like oranges, pineapples, betel-nut and leaf, pepper and coconut are totally the domain of men.

Conclusion

"Men, the hunter, and women the forager": this is a much debated concept. Nonetheless, in the studied areas, men were seen to be solely hunters; while women foraged (men helped them only to collect honey). Ethnographies from around the world have shown that women do hunt, and hunting is not solely undertaken by men. Notwithstanding such examples, Garo women are not known to take part in hunting, even of small animals like squirrels, hares and rats. Even among aquatic fauna, they are known to catch only "small" fish and collect crabs, cockles etc. and are not known to catch "big" fish with the net, nor catch frogs, tortoises, eels etc.

A Garo household is an economic unit. In terms of food-getting activities, it is seen that activities are greatly divided on gender lines. Men are seen performing "masculine" activities like hunting and catching "big" fish. Very rarely are men seen foraging for vegetable food, except if they have to collect honey combs. On the other hand, women collect vegetable items from the wilds, which are considered indigenous. These include bamboo shoot, mushrooms, and numerous roots, shoots, tubers, leaves and fruits. Interestingly, hunted meat (and unpleasant parts of meat) is associated with men, while women are found associated with small fish, shrimps, cockles and crabs. However, even though women sow (in the slash-and-burn plots), and collect indigenous food, it is men who are associated with it, while women are contrastingly found associated with new food. Just as in the hunting-gathering sphere, men and women have assigned tasks in the other food acquisition methods. There are stages in cultivation (both slash-and-burn and wet paddy) which are gender-specific. Thus, a household is clearly gendered, but also dependently reciprocal.

Interestingly, though landed property ownership is with Garo women, but it is men (husbands) who actually "own" them—deciding what to grow in wet paddy and cash crop gardens and deciding how to dispose the produce. Women do have a say in it, nonetheless it is men who make the abiding decision. On the other hand, women have full ownership of those food production activities that subsists for less time and has very little or no cash value. Through sole monopoly over hunting, men seem to reiterate their dominance over women who have control over a "less-prestigious" task, i.e., food foraging. This seems to be reiterated at home too, where men are the *nokgipa* (owner of the house) and make decisions for the house and children, which the wives adhere to even though they hold the dubious distinction of being the "actual owners" of land and property, and through whom the lineage passes on. This position seems highly ironical in a matrilineal society.

This is reiterated in the divide between the public and private domains which is very apparent. Men play a bigger role in public life (such as selling and buying, and cooking and serving) and therefore are the public faces. On the other hand, women perform all private or domestic works, inclusive of selling and buying at home, and cooking and serving at home. Therefore, women play out roles only at the domestic and private arenas. Similarly, when the prospect of something "new" appears, such as a new technology (as in ploughing), new economy (as in wet paddy and cash crops) and new people (traders), men take a bigger role.

Notes

1. Assamese refers to people or culture belonging to Assam (India). The mentioned informant had many friends belonging to caste Assamese groups staying in the nearest town of Boko, 7 kms away from the village. These friends were not "tribal", nor Garo. Therefore, their food habits were considerably different from the Garos, whose feasts comprised of rice and meat curries.
2. *Lucee-bhajee* is an Assamese snack preparation, comprising of deep-fried flat bread of wheat flour and potato fry. This is also served in weddings, with accompanying vegetable curries of many varieties.
3. *Kalchi* refers to liquid alkali procured after filtration of special ash of dried plantain stems and bamboo stumps. This is an ingredient that is added to food while cooking for its flavour. Cooking with alkali is an everyday food, in which local vegetables together with one or two pieces of dry fish is cooked. This type of cooking is much favoured over others such as boiling, steaming and cooking in oil. *Kalchi* food is also referred to as typically Garo in nature.
4. These are considered "unpleasant" since these are parts of the meat which are not typical meat pieces. Interestingly, these "unpleasant" meat parts become delicacies when cooked.
5. *Mon* is a corrupt form of *maund. Maund* is a unit of weight used in India. By the definition of the Standard Weights and Measures Act of 1956 (amended 1960, 1964) one *maund* weighs exactly 37.3242 kilograms. In the studied village, 1 *mon* referred to 30 kilograms approximately.
6. *Bigha* is a unit of measurement of area of land, commonly used in a few states of India like Bihar, West Bengal, Assam and Gujarat. The precise size of a *bigha* appears to vary considerably. However in the village, a *bigha* is 14,400 square feet.

References

Bender, A.E., 1976. "Food Preferences of Males and Females", *Proceedings of the Nutrition Society*, 35:181-89.

Butler, J., 1990. *Gender Trouble: Feminism and Subversion of Identity*. New York and London: Routledge Publications.

______. 1994. *Bodies that Matter*. New York and London: Routledge Publications.

Caplan, P., 1997. "Approaches to the Study of Food, Health and Identity", (pp. 1-31) in P. Caplan (ed.), *Food, Health and Identity*. London/New York: Routledge Publications.

Charles, N. and M. Kerr, 1988. *Women, Food and Families*. Manchester and New York: Manchester University Press.

Counihan, C., 1999. *The Anthropology of Food and Body: Gender, Meaning and Power*. New York: Routledge Publications.

Counihan, C.M. and S.L. Kaplan, 1998. *Food and Gender: Identity and Power*. Amsterdam: Harwood Academic Press.

Courtenay, W.H., 2000. "Constructions of Masculinity and their Influences on Men's well-being: A Theory of Gender and Health" *Social Science and Medicine*, 50: 1385-1401.

Jansen, W., 1997. "Gender Identity and the Rituals of Food in a Jordanian Community", *Food and Foodways*, 7(2):87-117.

Jensen, K.O., and L. Holm. 1999. "Preferences, Quantities, and Concerns: Socio-cultural Perspectives on the Gendered Consumption of Foods", *European Journal of Clinical Nutrition*, 53: 351-59.

Knott, K., 2005. *The Location of Religion: A Spatial Analysis*. London/Oakville CT: Equinox.

Logue, A.W. and M.E. Smith, 1986. "Predictors of Food Preferences in Adult Humans", *Appetite*, 7: 109-25.

Marak, Q., 2010. "Sex Typing of Children's Tasks: A Study among the Garos of Assam", *The Oriental Anthropologist*, 10 (2): 301-10.

______. 2012. "Are Daughters Preferred in a Matrilineal Society? A Case Study of the Garos from Assam", *The Anthropologist*, 14 (1): 49-56.

______. 2014. *Food Politics: Studying Food, Identity, and Difference among the Garos*. New Castle: CSP.

Moore, H., 1994. *A Passion for Difference*. Cambridge: Polity Press.

Moynihan, C., 1998. "Theories in Health Care and Research: Theories of Masculinity", *British Medical Journal*, 317: 1072-75.

Roos, G. and M. Wandel, 2005. "I Eat because I am Hungry, because its Good and to become Full: Everyday Eating Voiced by Male Carpenters, Drivers and Engineers in Contemporary Oslo", *Food and Foodways*, 13: 169-80.

Watson, J., 2000. *Male Bodies: Health, Culture, and Identity*. Buckingham/Philadelphia: Open University Press.

SEVEN

LANGUAGE OF THE SANTALS

It's Lyrical Expression

KUMKUM BHATTACHARYA AND R.K. BHATTACHARYA[1]

Introducation

The Santals who are numerically the largest tribe of eastern India and the third largest in the country have a beautiful and rich language. The Santals are spread beyond the country's boundaries. They are found in Northern part of Bangladesh and in Nepal. The Santals though spread far and wide display a strong adherence to their language and maintaining a relatively homogenous cultural pattern and traditional social systems. Their language has flexibility, expressiveness, poetry and large vocabulary. The language uses allegory, allusion, euphemism, metaphor and words that have multiple meanings and usage.[2] The language belongs to the Mundari group and has no known script from the historical perspective. There have been efforts at rectifying this situation through the discovery of Alciki ('*Al/Ol*' means drawing or writing and '*ciki*' meaning speak) that is supposed to be an ancient but, lost script of the Santals. However, there is practically no proof that this was ever in use by the Santals. Whatever written records available do not reflect the use of this script. The written records created painstakingly by the Christian missionaries are usually in the Roman script and some are in the scripts of the regional languages like Hindi, Bengali and Odia, the languages of the three Eastern States that the Santals in large numbers inhabit.

The quest for establishing Alciki has an interesting history.[3] Initially, it was a response to the need to have a script followed by an interim period of sporadic inventions and elaborations and finally mobilizing political will for inclusion of the language between the years 2003-2004 under the VIIIth Schedule of Languages[4] formally recognized in the Constitution of India. In its journey, the issues of language and script have meandered into channels that have not remarkably become more spouting or torrential in their spread. There seems to be a lesson here for language preservation—it is more than political will or victory that goes into the breathing of life into a language, it needs deeper and often intangible cultural elements for its sustenance and growth—it needs to be appreciated, encouraged and used. Language has to be in use, languages that have scripts have a higher survival rate but not necessarily so than languages that are widely spoken and used as a means of extension of one's social and cultural persona. It is this deep identification of the self with language that adds to its nourishing and flourishing! Identification of the self with one's language is almost an automatic process largely experienced unconsciously. This aspect is comprehensible when we think of our own identification with the language that we use. The situation becomes more complex when people experience the pressures of other dominant language(s) especially when that language is imposed because it enjoys currency in the economic sustenance of individuals.

Language and Socio-cultural Space

There is another factor that nurtures language, the social and cultural space within which one can with dignity and appreciation practise one's language, albeit with or without script! The phrase "social and cultural space" signifies the social and cultural environment within which the language (and other items/traits of culture) is used and enriched. India is a multiethnic country in which the communities can be classified along the dominant-minority continuum based on which some communities are marginalized. The marginalized communities have to contend with marginalization at various levels and social-cultural exclusion is one dimension that is experienced as restriction in social and cultural space in the broader public sphere. In the present situation of nation state in which polity plays a very significant role, the earlier seclusion of communities[5] has given way to communities being engulfed by the dominant one(s) in the context of the nation resulting in the former communities becoming peripheral. One of the reasons of the continuation of languages of the tribes and many of the other languages can be explained by cultural seclusion of communities that does not seem possible any more in the contemporary time except in rare ecological niches.

Oral *vis-à-vis* Text

Oral tradition develops an ear for the spoken word, its cadences and semantics. It provides the experience of deep engagement with the language that result in attraction and love for it in the user. It also ensures mass participation in the proliferation and sustenance of language; languages with written scripts may inhibit engagement of those who are unlettered or considered illiterate as also causing them to develop a 'blind' faith in those who 'know' the script of the concerned language. Orality preserves the pristine elements of intangible heritage and their transmission from one generation to the next is direct without necessarily having to be strained through the sieve of the cultivated written form of the language.

A Brief Ethnographic Note on the Santals

As mentioned earlier, the Santals are a dominant tribe of eastern India. They are found in Bihar, Jharkhand, Odisha, West Bengal, Assam and Tripura. They are the third largest tribe in India. Santals can be found in Bangladesh, Nepal and Sri Lanka in small numbers. Wherever the Santals are found, they speak their language, *Santali* with regional variations in dialect. The following details have been included, as they seem to have a bearing on the theme of this chapter, "the language, history and emotional world of the Santals". The Santals are found to occupy fringe areas of villages inhabited by other communities, predominantly so in the context of West Bengal. They like to live beside forests which they look upon as source of sustenance. The Santals are cultivators maintaining a subsistence level economy, some work as labourers in farms, factories and construction sites. The Santals refer to their village as *ato.* The village for a Santal is closely intertwined with individual and community identity. A typical Santal village is arranged along two sides of a central road, this *kulhi* (the Santali word for road) has an important role to play in their social lives; the meetings of the village council [*kulhi durup*, literally meaning a sitting (*durup*) on the road] and the community dancing at the time of festivals are also held on this road. It may be mentioned that some of the songs that are sung during these festivals are referred to as *kulhi dhuri* or literally dust from the village road that rises during the community dancing.

On one side of the village is situated a number of trees as in a grove and this place is called the *jaher* or sacred grove which plays an important role in the religious life of these people. Santal villages are characterized by settlement of kin and householders are related to each other in various ways.

The Santals usually live in nuclear families. Rules of inheritance and succession follow lines of descent patrilineally. Women do not enjoy right of inheritance. Women otherwise are not discriminated socially. They are free to choose their husbands, free to divorce and remarry. Couples living together and raising children are not stigmatized. There are no social taboos for women conversing with strangers (Baski, Boro 2007: 28). Women are normally earning members in a family. Children of both sexes are treated alike.

The Santals present "a state of timelessness" as if they are not in a hurry or under compulsion to race against time or punctiliously trying to maintain a strained time schedule. This can be observed in their daily activities, in discharging their chores, the calmness with which they discuss everything including urgent village and familial problems and issues and in the ways in which they entertain relatives and other visitors (Bhattacharya, K. and R.K. Bhattacharya, 2007: 40).

The Santals have the propensity to generate joy of living; the Santali word for this is *raska. Raska* is integral to how they conduct their lives and which they try to attain in whatever they do. Their language is a great source of *raska*. The capacity to generate a sense of joy is commonly found among most tribes. This has attracted the attention of scholars who have depicted in detail their pleasure complex (Culsahw, W.J., 1949; Grigson, W.V., 1949; Sinha, Surajit C., 1959; Orans, Martin, 1960; Archer, W.G., 1974; Somers, G.E., 1977; Bhattacharya, K., 1999). The Santals are relatively non-acquisitive and non-inhibitive. They maintain their needs within an area of limited dependency when they are confined within the bounds of the social systems found among them, i.e. within their own milieu. As a consequence there is a sense of peace, of inner well-being and a quiet belongingness to their surroundings.

The Santals are a dignified people and every member tries to preserve the dignity of each other. Children too have a sense of dignity and the adults around them endeavour to preserve this. The accepted conventions of behaviour are imbibed directly from older siblings and peer groups and from the social order prevailing in the environment; discipline is not imposed by force (Bhattacharya, K. and R.K. Bhattacharya, 2003: 161). More importantly, the child is made to feel that it has a position of contributing to the community and is expected to participate in all the community activities like ceremonies and festivities. Through the above and following vignettes we are presenting the presentation-of-self of the Santals primarily within the context of their community and habitation, both extremely important in shaping identity and perception of the world.

The Spoken Word and the Sung Tunes

When we talk about language in the context of this chapter, we refer to the spoken word, the manner in which people speak, the use of language in self-expression, in songs, stories and rituals and the role of language in characterizing the community. We get some idea about the large repertoire of lexis of the Santals from the five volumes, *A Santal Dictionary* by P.O. Bodding, a Norwegian Missionary. His volume *Santal Medicine: Studies in Santal Medicine and Connected Folk-lore*; and *Santal Folktales* in three parts stand testimony to the vast expanse of the language of the Santals.[6] Indications of the complexity of their language can be gauged from their usage of parts of speech like the "number of persons" (singular, dual and plural in case of first, second and third persons) and the distinctions that they make between human, animal and inanimate objects when using verbs (Majhi, Chaitanya Prasad, 2001: 89-99) and between animate and inanimate in the case of pronouns.

Language forms the very basis of identity and perception of the world and it is also the means that provide others insight and understanding of their ways of thinking or mind-set. Language represents "an entire way of life: a way of feeling, seeing and thinking" (Nagarkar, K. 2006: 551). Language preserves the full quantum of experience and culture of a people (*ibid.*) Language is also the channel of cultural expression.[7]

The language of the Santals expressed in songs, myths, stories and ways of speech tells us of the richness of their linguistic embellishments. The stories, songs and poems of the Santals play on words to create situations and incidents that amuse these people. As an example of the ways of speech, birth of a child is never announced directly, it is announced as the arrival of a new relative or *perahor* to which is asked if the new arrival carries (things) on the head or shoulder (for girl or boy respectively) and the answer is made according to the sex of the newborn.

In order to understand the social and cultural context of language of the Santals, it is necessary to probe into the aspects of belief systems that are found among them. The Santal world apart from human beings, fauna, flora and nature, is also composed of the world of spirits that are of numerous types. The spirits are referred to as *Bonga*. They occupy the whole atmosphere and are found in homes, forests, groves and hills. The *Bonga* have a special relationship to Santal life, society and culture. All the villagers including visitors come within the purview of the *Bonga* of the village. *Bonga* are polluted at the time of birth and death for removal of which there are rituals. There are various rituals that are performed for the propitiation of the *Bonga*. The relationship between the *Bonga* and the Santals is of fear, awe and avoidance and it is very difficult to predict the causes that could upset the *Bonga.*[8] This mind-set is reflected in their speech as in their actions. The circumlocution in their speech is most apparent in the references to *Bonga*. Their reticence in disclosing their points of origin or destination when they are journeying or making oblique references to events could be regarded as a few illustrations of the reflection of the effects of the *Bonga* on speech. There are many more illustrations that could be cited.

The following songs illustrate the inherent lyricism of Santal language expressed in a variety of songs.

Song 1: This is a song by a woman addressing the former lover who is now married; the dancing women sing this song during Sohrae. The situation of the song is that the line of dancing women has reached the door of the once-lover of a woman who is part of the dancing group. "In the dark, dark nights without a trace of fear (1) I have been your companion and have been the keeper of your heart; how is it that you have been able to now forget me and my charms? Do come out of the house once, come to the street (2), let us at least see each other once. We do not need to speak; we do not need to even smile at each other, oh, my old friend I just want to quench my longing for you with our meeting eyes."

Notes: (1) Refers to fear of the *Bonga* who are believed to inhabit the forests, trees and are believed to be more potent during the nighttime. The lovers overcome this very real fear. (2) Refers to the all-important road (*kulhi*) that runs through the village and is the scene for most of the gatherings of the community.

Song 2: This is a song in *dong* tune by a boy addressing a girl usually sung during *sohrae*. "On top of the hills, under the pair of *Sal* trees and keeping them as witness, we made a divine promise of ourselves to each other. Oh, my friend, that promise is no more. I am married; it is time for you to also be married."

Note: The pragmatic approach of the boy towards the loss of promise, love is worth noting. It is as if the exigencies of practical life cannot be overshadowed by romanticism of youth. It may also be noted that there are various classes of tunes used in Santali songs.

Song 3: This song in the *dong* tune is sung by a boy addressing a girl who he once loved. "Why are you holding the branches of the deeply shaded tamarind tree on the banks of the river and crying your heart out? We are no longer friends, do not take my name and cry."

Note: At the death of a loved one, the Santals mourn the dead in a sing-song manner in which the name of the dead person is mentioned over and over again and the memories of their time with the person is recapitulated. Also note that the essential message of the song is let bygones be.

Song 4: This is a song in the *sohrae* tune about rekindling the love between couples married or otherwise together. The wife/woman addresses the husband/lover, "Why do not you play the *madal* like before, your flute does not play the old tunes; please play the *madal* and the flute." The husband/lover answers, "Who will be my inspiration for playing the flute or raising beats on my *madal*?" The wife/woman answers, "Look at me and remember those days of our love, play your *madal* and your flute!"

Song 5: This is a song in the *dong* tune sung by women transplanting paddy that is a backbreaking task. "The first rains of the month of *Asadh*/I am in the middle of the field transplanting the paddy plant/My dear friend is playing his flute under a *Kadam* tree/Here the rain is falling in a musical rhythm/The sounds of my friend's flute is wafting towards me/My tired body and heart is rejuvenated."

Note: The symbols of flute, *Kadam* tree, the rainy season all suggest influences of the Radha-Krishna myths. The *Kadam* is not a common tree in the Santal Parganas.

Song 6: This song is also sung during festivals accompanied by dance. "There are ten drummers/There are twenty girls/The dancing ground is big and wide/Do not rouse me, drummer/Or I will make you drink/A river-full of water."

Song 7: "At night I slept on a verandah/And in a dream I found you/ How lovely you were/Swaying in the dew."

Note: The songs 6 and 7 in *large* tune allude to making love through the use of allusions "drinking a river-full of water" and "swaying in the dew". (Archer, W.G., 1974: 66).

These are only a few songs and few of the tunes that we have mentioned; there are countless songs and tunes that Santals know and sing on occasions by themselves or together. There are songs sung by women, by men, songs sung in public places, songs sung in the seclusion of forests during the annual hunt. The latter type of songs is confined to boys and men and it is a social breach of etiquette if these songs are sung in the village or directly addressing girls. Some of these songs as old as can be recalled are continued to be sung even today. There are some songs that have remained unchanged over time—songs related to rituals and social customs. We shall give some examples:

Song 8: This song is sung during religious festivals. "Who had identified this land of jungles that we call our own/Who had created our homes in the hamlet/It is Maran Buru (the Supreme God) who brought us to this land/It was He who taught us to live like a community/It was Jaher Era (or the deity of the grove) who taught us to live together in a hamlet."

Song 9: This is a song in *sohrae* tune of a social occasion, when groups of older women visit the homes of kin or neighbours during *sohrae*. The women have come to pay a social visit and to drink the traditional rice beer. The song is in the form of an exchange between visitors and hosts. This song is really ancient and variation of this can also be found in the collection of Bodding (1942: 144). "Stand a while, sit down/Though we do not have enough seats for all of you/These are bad times, there has been no produce in the fields/We were not able to preserve the paddy seedlings/Our children have become lazy."

Note: This song is an illustration of the play on wit that characterizes Santal speech. This song also indicates the genre of social songs in which there is no obsequious display of hospitality on the part of the hosts or fear of a social gaffe being committed by the guests yet there is no lack of welcome.

Song 10: This is a widely sung song when guests arrive. "Small and little are our fowls and pigs/Rich and wealthy are our guests and relatives/ I shall prepare the rice and curry/But father I shall certainly not serve it out."

Note: In this song too we observe that wit and play on words are important features of Santal songs. Santals are very hospitable people and in fact do everything in their means to play host. The guest is shown respect and welcomed with an assumed modesty so that the guest feels privileged.

Orality against the Trajectory of Modernity in the Santal Society

Psychologists recognize that emotions are constituted by three interrelated aspects, the physiological changes that are found to accompany the expression of strong or violent emotions; the cognitive undercurrent that informs emotions and the expressions and gestures that help others of the same culture in identifying the emotion. All these aspects help in interaction between people; using prediction of others' responses we automatically prepare our own that carries forward interaction. Facial expressions and gestures are culture specific thereby easing interaction between people belonging to the same culture. The physiological changes that accompany strong emotions can be explained as the functioning of the peripheral nervous system and the secretion of hormones. Of all the constituents, the most important in human beings is the cognitive factor. This is based on evaluations of past experiences, the individual life experiences that shape and form emotions, the ways people are socialized to think about emotions and their own understandings of social expectations regarding the expression of emotions. The intention of this very brief analysis is to show that emotions are largely cognitive in nature—they involve our cogitations and reflections. When we try to interpret the changing nature of Santal society against the trajectory of modernity, we cannot leave out the emotional ascriptions of the society in general and the community and its people in particular. If there are major shifts and changes in the cognitive base of the people and this is quite possible through changing aspirations and exposure to multiculturalism, we shall find that the essential aspect or the cognitive constituent of emotions will also undergo change. The very emotions that are reflected in the songs of the Santals will change as a result of which there will emerge changes in the quality of the lyrics that in turn reflect life and culture. Already, we find the introduction of techno beats, the effects of remix, the influence of Bollywood and Western and Indian pop music in the new music albums being released by Santals. There is a trend to compose songs on more topical issues with explicit and implicit undertones of 'message'—political and reformist in nature!

Tradition is dynamic in nature and over time makes gradual adjustments to changing times. It is true that people carry tradition within their consciousness putting the stamp of their individual and collective interpretation on it. This is why it changes and changes so imperceptibly. This is what that can be said to be true when there is a kind of stability in life and times. However, what we see today seems to reflect a state of upset in the equilibrium that exists between the aspects of culture and lives of people. Culture in most societies has assumed a distinct entity of its own, as a discrete category that could very well survive without it being integrated into lives of people. One of the reasons for this is that we have succeeded in putting culture between covers of books and journals and other media. The Santals however have managed to fare well in the face of the many challenges posed to their identity from many fronts in certain pockets. It is clear from the above discussion that the verbal expression of the Santals is shaped by and intertwined with their lives, experiences and ways of thinking—as the ways of their lives change so will their expression and somewhere along the way the lyricism of their language will be reduced to a play on words and not an expression of their ethos. Language cannot overcome this possibility, it may not become extinct but 'that something' will cease to connect with the lives of people. The beautiful songs that we still hear today will continue to haunt the people not as a living tradition but rather as "something of the past" like the "old unheard melodies" of yore.

Conclusion

Love and pining and their various manifestations and shades as verbalized are good indicators when we want to understand the relationship between emotions and language or *vice versa*. Among the Santals, it is seen that songs are the natural choice of emotional expression whereas their stories are not solely constructed around the themes of love, longing or separation. What is possible in poetry through allusion, euphemism and allegory in being able to comply with the social values of maintaining a certain kind of public civility and decency would not have been so possible in running prose—this may be one reason for the freedom of expression in Santali songs. Above all, it is through their songs that the range of emotional attachment and amorous behaviour is revealed. It is interesting to note that songs being generally a part of public domain there seems to be spontaneity and lack of inhibition in the portrayal of love and in many ways sex. However, it would be important to keep in mind, that the Santals use allusion and euphemism to such an extent that reference to sex does not appear objectionable or obscene. Songs and Santals are inextricably woven—there is probably not a time of day that they across all ages do not hum songs. They are adept at composing songs on the spur of the moment sometimes reflecting what they observe or about events in their environs. Just before the advent of their biggest festival, *sohrae*, music seems to be in the air and on everybody's lips as joy or *raska* is in their hearts.

Women working in the fields during rice transplanting, going to the forests for collection of leaves and twigs for the purpose of fuel, little children minding domestic animals when grazing or out for hunting birds or playing in the village—there is a humming sound that when listened to carefully can be deciphered as song, "The ever singing, ever flute-playing Santals" (Lewin, T.H., 1870; cited in W.G. Archer, 1974:9). The dominant themes of the songs concern love, longing, joy and the pangs of separation. The other themes are nature, fertility and traditional myths and legends. In many ways, the songs are the natural carriers of tradition, cultural ethos and the collective psyche of the people. Some of the songs are accompanied by dance—a line of girls dancing in complete harmony and unison with the men playing the musical instruments of which the flute is very important. It is interesting to note the use of flute that is regarded as eponymous with love and tryst almost universally in India. "On the hill of flutes/a flute is sounding..." (*ibid.*).

Notes

1. Kumkum Bhattacharya, Professor, Visva-Bharati University and R.K. Bhattacharya, former Director, Anthropological Survey of India, Government of India can be contacted at *kmkm.bh@gmail.com*
2. See *A Glossary of Literary Terms* by M.H. Abrams, 2000, India, Harcourt Asia Private Ltd. The terms used in describing the characteristics of Santali (the language of the Santals) are not exactly as enunciated in the glossary but have been borrowed as they come closest to the characteristic features of the language. The same characteristic features are present in the languages of the Mundas and the Mahalis who share the same linguistic roots, i.e. Mundari.
3. See Shyam Sundar Mohapatra, 2001: 74-88, *Formation of Ol Chiki Script and Process of its Transmission in Santal Worldview,* edited by Neeta Mathur, New Delhi, Indira Gandhi National Centre for the Arts.

4. Government list of official Indian languages – as of now the government has recognized 22 languages as being official in nature. There are certain rights enjoyed by such languages.
5. Seclusion of and social distance among communities within plural/multiethnic societies can be better understood from the nature of interaction between communities that has been described by J. S. Furnivall as being more a response to the "economic factor" (*Netherlands India: A Study of Plural Economy*, Library of Congress Catalogue Card no. 39-20815; 1967:449). This is further clarified by Fredrik Barth's (1959: 16) definition "...a society integrated economically under the control of a state system dominated by one of the groups leaving large areas of cultural diversity in the domestic and religious sectors of activity" in *Ethnic Groups and Boundaries: The Social Organization of Cultural Difference*, London: George Allen & Unwin Ltd.
6. P.O. Bodding, a Norwegian missionary spent 44 years, 1889-1933, in the Santal Parganas primarily engaged in missionary work. He developed a keen interest in the myths and tales of the Santals that he avidly collected and left for posterity.
7. See the Report of High Level Committee appointed by the Paridarsaka of The Visva-Bharati University, 2006: 91, Kolkata: Raj Bhavan Press.
8. "Although fields, houses, men and women seem to constitute a Santal village, Santals regard them as at a most a portion of their total world. From a dwelling "somewhere in the sky", the creator, Thakur Jiu, allots each Santal a term of life, rarely interferes and maintains a calm indifference. Sim Cando, the sun with whom he is sometimes identified has the same listless majesty. ...It is underneath the sun, beneath the clouds, that Santal rule is challenged. Here bongas or spirits roam and only by coming to terms with them can Santals be happy.... ... ...

   "All these bongas are, in a special sense, a Santal creation, monopoly or prerogative. ... ...

   "...To pass their days happily, to experience to the full of joys, of tribal existence, Santals must not only attune themselves to village customs but unite in honouring their ghostly protectors.

   "Such a double world, a world at once visible and invisible, has a number of repercussions on Santal behaviour." (Archer, W.G., 1974: 25-29—*The Hill of Flutes: Life, Love and Poetry in Tribal India;* London: George Allen & Unwin Ltd.).

   Also refer to Kumkum Bhattacharya (1995) "The Religion of the Santals" in *Sociology in the Rubric of Social Science*, pp. 253-261; edited by R.K. Bhattacharya and Asok K. Ghosh; Kolkata: Anthropological Survey of India.

References

Abrams, M.H., 2000. *A Glossary of Literary Terms*. India: Harcourt Asia Pvt. Ltd.

Archer, W.G., 1974. *The Hill of Flutes: Life, Love and Poetry in Tribal India*. London: George Allen & Unwin Ltd.

Barth, Fredrik, 1959. *Ethnic Groups and Boundaries: The Social Organization of Cultural Difference*. London: George Allen & Unwin.

Bhattacharya, Kumkum, 1995. "The Religion of the Santals", (pp. 253-61) in R.K.

Bhattacharya and Asok K. Ghosh (eds.), *Sociology in the Rubric of Social Science*. Kolkata: Anthropological Survey of India.

——. 1999. "Socialization in a Santal Village", *Journal of Comparative Cultures*, 4: 13-41.

Bhattacharya, Kumkum and Boro Baski. 2002, "The Various Experiences of Being Marginalized", *Journal of the Anthropological Survey of India*, 51 (1): 9-16.

Bhattacharya, K. and R.K. Bhattacharya, 2007. "Celebrating Life: The Santal Experiement in Freedom", in Boro Baski and Kumkum Bhattacharya (eds.), *Celebrating, Freedom: the Santal Way of Life*. Kolkata: Ghosaldanga Bishnubati Adibasi Trust.

——. 2003, "Tribes—State of Mind", *Journal of the Indian Anthropological Society*, 38, (2 & 3): 159-165.

Bodding, P.O., 1932-36. *A Santal Dictionary*, Kolkata: Asitic Society.

——. 1927. "Santal Medicine: Studies in Santal Medicine and Connected Folk-lore", *Memoirs of the Asiatic Society of Bengal*, 10 (2).

——. 1942. *Traditions and Institutions of the Santals* (Bulletin 6). Oslo: Oslo Etnografiske Museum.

Culsahw, W.J., 1949. *Tribal Heritage*. London: Litterworth Press.

Furnivall, J.S., 1967. *Netherlands India: A Study of Plural* Economy. Library of Congress Catalogue: Card no. 39-20815.

Grigson, W.V., 1949. *The Muria Gonds of Bastar.* London: Oxford University Press.

Majhi, Chaitanya Prasad, 2001. "Santhal Language and Culture", (pp. 89-99) in Nita Mathur (ed.), *Santhal Worldview*. New Delhi: Indira Gandhi National Centre for the Arts.

Mohapatra, Shyam Sundar, 2001. "Formation of Ol Chiki Script and Process of its Transmission", (pp. 74-88) in Nita Mathur (ed.), *Santal Worldview.* New Delhi: Indira Gandhi National Centre for the Arts.

Nagarkar, K., 2006. *God's Little Soldier.* New Delhi: Harper Collins Publishers India.

Orans, Martin, 1960. *The Santals: A Tribe in Search of a Great Tradition*. Detroit: Wayne State University Press.

——. 2006. Report of High Level Committee appointed by the Paridarsaka of The Visva-Bharati University, p. 91, Kolkata: Raj Bhavan Press.

Sinha, Surajit, C., 1959. "Tribal cultures of peninsular India as a dimension of the little tradition: a preliminary statement", in *Traditional India: Structure and Change* (Vol. X). Philadelphia: American Folklore Society Bibliographical Series.

Somers, G.E., 1977. *The Dynamics of Santal Tradition in a Peasant Society.* New Delhi: Abhinav Publications.

D. YOUTH

EIGHT

YOUTH, ACHIEVEMENT AND 'MUTUAL RESPONSIBILITY'

It's Time to Theorise on the Positive

ANAND SINGH AND SHEETAL BHOOLA

Introduction

Historically, among the social sciences and humanities, anthropologists have taken an early lead in the study of adolescence and youth, inspired largely by Margaret Mead's (1928) study on young women that was published as the *Coming of Age in Samoa*. Her subsequent publication in 1970 of *Culture and Commitment: A Study of the Generation Gap* stimulated widespread interest in youth studies of other cultures in various parts of the world. Mead's interests were emulated by Ruth Benedict (1931) when her seminal paper on pre-industrial societies transition from adolescence to adulthood as a continuum, was considered a landmark essay. As a chapter that looked positively at preindustrial societies it marked a significant moment in early twentieth anthropology because she compared their transitions more favourably than in Western societies. It reinforced the emerging anthropological notion that there is value in socialisation processes that are other than Western in orientation. Yet in retrospect, the anthropological contribution to studies about youth remains incidental. It was not until the latter years of the twentieth century that anthropological interest was reignited through the International Union of Anthropological and Ethnological Sciences *Scientific Commission on Children, Youth and Childhood.* Led by an Indian anthropologist, Deepak

Kumar Behera, this Commission arose of the renewed international interest on the subject. This was a first for Anthropology, and the network that this Commission brought together encouraged research about children in which they are themselves the active participants. The intent here was to transcend the then prevalent emphasis in enculturation and socialisation processes that saw youth as part of societies' broader make-up. Contemporary realisation stresses the need for youth and the issues they represent as being broad enough with sufficient depth to arbitrarily treat them as stand-alone subjects of inquiry.

Through introduction of five recent papers on youth studies, Elizabeth Lewis's (2012) summary of widely read interests in youth studies provide a succinct perspective on historical and contemporary interests in the subject. Lewis's assessment of the classical and subsequent studies on youth in anthropology and sociology are accurate and interestingly condensed into an appropriate introduction. Our reading of it provided a refreshing perspective to the issues at hand for this chapter. Apart from mention of Mead (1928) and Benedict (1938), Lewis's (2012) stringing together of Malinowski's (1929), Evans-Pritchard's (1969) and Turner's (1995) collective emphasis on youth as a liminal transitional stage, i.e. "no longer a child but not yet adult", demonstrated how more than a generation of anthropologists remained steadfast in a common approach on youth studies—restricting themselves to socialisation processes. Among sociologists early interests in children and youth studies, since the 1930s, focused mainly on social deviation rather than conformity to socialisation (Cohen, 1955; Becker, 1997). Despite this, sociologists Chandra *et al.* (2009) in their book as editors on *Childhood, Child Labour and Youth,* began their preface in these words: "*When Chris Jenks title 'The Sociology of Childhood—Essential Readings' appeared in 1982, the sociological understanding of it was in its infancy.*" Their book placed no emphasis on the 1970s and 1980s focus on youth studies consolidated through the United Kingdom's Centre for Contemporary Cultural Studies, which famously became known as "*The Birmingham School*" (Mungham and Pearson, 1976; Willis, 1981; Hall and Jefferson, 1990). Much of the Birmingham School data was gleaned from the rapid transformations that were occurring in British society at that time. The Marxist frameworks that they relied upon in their analyses of youth cultures and subcultures placed the notion of class at the centre of their attention. This approach, with viewing youth as social actors engrossed in contestations against dominant values and norms, ignored the place of crucial elements such as gender, religion, race, and ethnicity as equally worthy analytical tools (cf., Blackman, 2005; McRobbie and Garber, 1990; Maira, 1999).

The idea of youth as significant to the premise that they are social actors in their own right continued through the Deepak Behera led Scientific Commission on Children, Youth and Childhood. In a book that Behera edited with Margaret Trawick in 2007 on *Children and Youth in the Global Metropole,* the collection of 13 papers served as a virtual antithesis to the Birmingham School's avoidance with issues of gender, race and ethnicity. While these three issues were prevalent in the book, there was a glaring absence of focus upon youth and their association with armed conflict, religion and familial responsibilities. A major focus has been on children, adolescents and youth and the negativities they experience through issues such as underpaid labour and social inequalities (Cross *et al.,* 2007; de Castro, 2007; Mayer, 2007), survival strategies as street children and slum dwellers (Swart-Kruger 2007; van Santen; Invernizzi, 2007); reproducers of ethnic and social boundaries through influences from their own bounded circumstances (Sujoldzic, 2007; Tanner and Pawson, 2007; Singh, 2007), and not being heard or treated with the respect that they deserve as human beings (Boothroyd and Evans, 2007; Gregory *et al.,* 2007). Chandra *et al.*'s collection of edited papers also dominates with the trials and tribulations that children have to face with the challenges of the world. The importance of raising these issues cannot be emphasized enough even if researchers and policy-makers across the globe act in unison to confront the enormity of the scourge against children, adolescents and youth. But it is important to also recognize the "opposite" of what these three categories of people have in their multiple experiences in life and its challenges.

It is against the background of such emphasis that this chapter diverts to focus upon the positive issues in the lives of youth and their steadfastness in turning challenges into goals and outcomes. We begin from the position that the definition and age boundaries of 'youth' need to be identified and separated from their counterparts of children and adolescents. While the definition and age boundaries of youth are still not universally accepted, it stretches the United Nations definition of youth as those persons between the ages of 15 and 24 to those who are between 18 and 35. Our adoption of these limits arise from the fact that the United Nations itself, in Article 1 of the Convention on the Rights of the Child, defines children up to the age of 18.[1] We begin by from 18 because in the normal course of education most children in the world complete 12 years of formal education from the age of 6 to the age of 17-18. We arbitrarily cut off at the age of 35 years because as South Africans this is the case in the National Youth Policy. A major country like India too had a limit of up to 35 years, until their review in 2012 brought it down to 30 years. China presently views all those between the ages of 15 and 29 as belonging to the youth category, while the USA defines youth as all those below the age of 25 years. The issue here is that the determination of age categories remain country specific because of a range of reasons, spanning from economic and political realities[2] to sheer political expediency.

Our interviews were with individuals from whose ages ranged from 22 to 35 years, and the presentation of our data is through the extended case study method. We not only emphasize the anthropological focus on micro-level studies, but also believe in the added value of the case study method to convey the meaning of 'mutual responsibility' among youth in familial responsibilities. 'Mutual responsibility' is viewed here in the context of household dynamics across class backgrounds, where biological parental care, love and support are reciprocated by children's conformance to role and responsibility expectations. It is defined here as youth who are between the ages of 18 and 35 years and who are conscientious about at least four things: appreciative of parental guidance, upholding the good name of parents, living up to parental expectations, and feeling a deep sense of responsibility to improve the material circumstances of household conditions, irrespective of class background. The data below is drawn from individuals of varying class backgrounds, of parents who were either still living or privileged with just one of them, and their personal trajectories from early education to completion of tertiary education and paid employment. Both depth and breadth of case histories are crucial to the elements that are considered necessary to make-up the substance and meaning of the theory of mutual responsibility.

Methodology

Information gathering for this project began through bringing together anecdotal evidence that was initially not intended for any research purpose. At a much later stage, the intention was to make sense of what could possibly be done to add to the existing information that was still a part of memory, as well as to the existing body of literature on youth and work. It became anecdotal only when an idea of writing about youth who are successful in their studies and work could serve as a diversionary presentation to the often negative side of what youth generally have to endure in a world of peer pressure and social exclusion. The first three notations, taken over a two-month period provided explicitly divergent information that seemingly could not provide any common ground in the search for uniformity among academically high performing youth. But a point too obvious to mention at times eventually concretised as a convincing position to begin with: stable families and supportive parents, inclusive of single parents. Hence, the quest for information began with the idea that most youth who are successful in high educational achievements and follow through with high paying jobs work from the vantage point of stable households and supportive networks. Each of the first three youth came from such easily classifiable backgrounds. But each of them demonstrated different stages of a twofold continuum in personal responsibility and household pride. One of the youth for instance, spoke about how it was necessary to continue with a business that his father established, but which needed a university degree to ensure such continuity. Another of the three spoke about making a personal choice in career and for the sake of experience away from home. His idea was only to challenge himself, but to add to seeing new places and meeting new people outside of his immediate group in Durban. The third among this first three saw himself on a mission away from home. His was a commitment to permanently extricate his parents and only sibling from the cycle of poverty that was so characteristic of his parental background.

In instances where researchers want to build upon such anecdotal evidence there is only one option open to them to amplify their data gathering, and that is purposive sampling. Finding such information and lessening the burden of a long drawn out project would have required the assistance of another researcher.[3] Our attempts in gathering this information had to be along the lines of finding graduates who already sought employment in the fields of their choice. The search site was the city of Durban, and our social networks were mainly from within the Indian population resident here. Several individuals were easy to identify and to follow-up with, but others had to be located through people we knew that who could introduce us to such leads. While some of them were still in Durban, others were already away in South Africa's two other major metropolises: Johannesburg and Cape Town. Our initial target was to follow-up on four respondents more from each category, to arrive at a total of fifteen respondents in all. But the number did increase to 22 individuals in total over time. Each of the initial interviews had taken around an hour and twenty minutes to do, while several had lasted up to two hours. Most of them had to be contacted *via* cell phone, e-mail and *Whats App* for further information. In at least seven instances parents were spoken to as well, some of them wantonly joining the conversations.

From the 22 that were spoken to seven were employed in Durban, 13 had found employment in Johannesburg and two were working in Cape Town. All of them were personally interviewed over a six month period, although follow-up questions happened through e-mail or phone calls. Since, the project was not constrained by a submission date and it had emerged largely out of personal interest, the wait for sporadic interviews with individuals returning home for weekends or family gatherings were not as stressful. The responses were entirely positive and when availability was possible there was also willingness to talk. Meetings took place in homes and coffee shops where the atmosphere was generally congenial to illicit responses. However, the situation in homes were often interspersed with family members offering snacks and drinks, sometimes with the intention of wanting to overhear the nature of the conversation as well as to add their views on what it was to achieve good to excellent results and to acquire the "right job". Parents who joined in the interviews tended to talk in exaggerated tones and with a sense of pride about how their children tiresomely made their achievements. Since, the interviews were open ended and conducted in a casual manner, parents felt a sense of entitlement to contribute towards the discussion. Their inputs were often helpful in viewing responses with greater depth and breadth than was given by the targeted respondents.

The Family Continuum

Youth often tend to emulate parents in the things that they observe over time. Such imitative behaviour cuts across class lines and impacts upon how they may develop into adult individuals. The point has been succinctly articulated by Roger Keesing in his writing about people from diverse social backgrounds. It would be difficult to disagree with his persuasive statement that individual aspirations and career building are often dictated by class background (Keesing, 1981). There were 9 among the 22 respondents who were inspired by parental career choices to the extent that they finally decided to graduate in the same degrees. A major encouragement in these decisions lay with the fact that their parents were successful in what they did. In 7 of the 9 instances parents had moved from being highly paid employees of major companies, either multinational or regional, to being successfully self-employed. Their experiences in paid employment allowed them to build upon trusted networks that developed over time. In the setting up of post-employment businesses such networks provided the advantage of immediate business as well as referrals because they came with a recommendation. For instance, AP[4] a twenty-five year old Bachelor of Commerce graduate recalled how his father started off his business after resigning as regional manager for a multinational courier company. As a Chartered Accountant, his father was among the highest paid in his extended family. By comparison with other known professionals within their extended family and among known professional friends AP's father's salary was significantly higher. Much of their introductory moments to any social together usually started off with jokes about his earning capacity, the house in which they lived and the lifestyle they are known to enjoy. Reminders of these characteristics often surfaced because of his father's almost 'meteoric' rise in class status. AP's grandfather was a teacher who retired early, and who had a gift of producing custom made furniture. The grandfather began a home based initiative by doing a few orders: "*with tremendous success*". But his work slowed down because of his liking for alcohol. His making of furniture eventually stopped because his orders were not being completed in time and clients gradually ignored him. AP's grandfather's saving grace was the extended family he lived with, because his brothers were also hard working and brought in regular incomes. The principle of collective responsibility protected AP's father and his siblings from being relegated to a pauper status. AP's father felt the humiliation of being continuously dependent upon his uncles for support, because he knew that their wives and children were gossiping about him in their absence. His university education too had to be subsidised by his uncles, because his father was an irresponsible man. AP's father often spoke about the good times in the extended family but the embarrassment that went with it through his father's alcoholism. The cumulative impact of this was to divert AP's and his sister's attention away from dependence upon anyone in the future and to rely upon the merits and rewards of a good education. AP and his sister completed degrees in Business Science, having observed their father's pride in his profession and the success he was making out of it. AP's father began a consultancy in auditing, including forensic auditing, for which he was (at the time of the interview) still getting substantial state contracts. While AP could have joined his father's company, he chose to work for another multinational auditing firm: "*...for experience and independence...*" from his father. AP's first employment was in Johannesburg, and the firm had sent him to the Isle of Man in the United Kingdom for a year's work. Upon his return he continued with his original position and applied for a year's work in New York, for which he was preparing at the time of the interview. His aim was to work for as long as possible away from his father's successful practice for experience and an independent life. But he was not sure if he could entirely avoid getting into it in the longer term.

AP's upbringing was replete with illustrations of how to be a proud member of an extended family but yet remain aloof from dependence upon them in the future. While much of his achievements were essentially about his own determination to succeed, coupled with an admirable discipline, he continued to attribute his success to the parental love and guidance he received. He felt that he needed to succeed not only for himself, but for his parents reassurance that he was not going to lower his lifestyle by choosing a career that would either not match or improve upon his father's. AP stressed several times what a calculating mind his father had, which had impressed upon him the need to take their improved financial status higher than where they were. While they were a conservative Hindu family, AP's father hardly dwelled upon ritualism or spirituality as much as his extended family did. Their conservatism lay with them remaining a close knit nuclear family, more than a public display about their religion or class status, with AP's father's mother a permanent member of their household. AP and his sister, as well as his parents feel a sense of mutual responsibility towards the widowed father's mother and are unable to see her as part of another household, such as one of his father's brothers or sisters.

Such positive parental influence and emulative behaviour has become fairly widespread among Indian middle class families in Durban. A similar situation to AP's household circumstances prevailed with a youngster of similar age. He was 26-year old YM, younger than his sister and the only two children for their parents. Both YM and his sister followed their father into becoming civil engineers, and their mother eventually completed her degree in law while working with their father in the engineering consultancy. YM's father graduated in the early 1980s and helped to support his parents who lived in a farming area about 120 kilometres from Durban. After his mother died his father continued to stay in the family farm until it became too risky for him to remain there alone. YM's grandfather then relocated to stay at his nuclear family home. Civil engineering was an attraction for YM and his sister because his father's success as a consultant had turned him into an entrepreneur of renowned success. Their mother felt compelled to complete her law degree because legal fees to secure and watch over contracts were becoming astronomical. YM's father's background was a humble one, and his grandparents were part of an extended family that worked as farmers of fresh vegetables and sugar cane. His father was supported by his father for his education. But the multiple relationships YM's grandfather had with women during his grandmother's lifetime and after her death did not set a good example to his father or them as children. It was often the excuse his mother used not to have him at their home as a 'permanent guest'. When YM's sister completed her degree and the related formalities for her qualification, she immediately joined her father's consultancy. But YM decided not to do the same and opted to seek employment elsewhere. Despite this he considers himself an integral part of the business because he often worked with his father while studying, and he is an integral part of his parental home as well. Through a secondary source it was learnt that his mother is a "control freak", forcing YM to find employment strictly with a firm in Durban. As a softener against his urge to join his school friends in Johannesburg they bought him a business subtly diverting his mind away from the thought of leaving home to work and infusing within him a sense of self-importance. YM's work outside of the protected environment was however, as he responded, to gather experience and "*...to learn more about the real world....*" Much of YM's experiences in his employment was, in his words: "*...pretty ordinary...*" He was able to adjust to the work environment as well as share some of his experience and knowledge that he acquired through working with his father. Problems arose when his opinions with more experienced staff tend to clash with his, because as he feels: "*People don't like the fact that I am the son of a very successful engineer, and they feel that I am trying to override them...but in fact they are intimidated by my knowledge and the fact that I do not have to taught like the others who come straight out of universities and still need guidance.*"

In situations such as the above, doting parents find it difficult to part with their children even when they are in a position to fend for themselves. YM was bought a business under the guise of mutual responsibility to family interests, but it was more accurately an imposed form of added control over his adulthood. The ownership of such a business was a calculated risk especially by his mother, giving him a sense of egoistic pride and ownership over prime property. But he shielded himself from such an analysis during the interview, emphasising upon his academic achievements and the well paid employment he had sought. However, much his parents appeared to have restricted his movement away from home, he still felt a sense of duty and responsibility towards them. YM ended the interview stating: "*A child's happiness is always besides his/ her parents*". But his friends saw it as emphatic control by his mother over his personal decisions. In this sense, if the comments YM's friends were correct, the notion of mutual responsibility is in real terms a supra-imposed form of social control. Parental fear and anxiety of living in luxurious mansions without their children generates loneliness and often fear. In South Africa's prevalent climate of political uncertainty and violent housebreakings such mental states are obvious manifestations of precarious social conditions. It is however also an indirect way of rebuilding an extended family situation that is still so characteristic of the Indian mind-set.

Both of the case studies above were of situations where parents had already established their professions and incomes. They had extricated themselves from the working class backgrounds that constrained their parents, and chided their children with as much of the comforts and security that they had missed out on in their childhoods. Other interviewees had talked about a virtual opposite of these circumstances, where they themselves are in the process of providing the comforts and security that their parents had still not been able to provide when they had completed their degrees and went into employment. Their remaining within the parental household was a matter of personal choice.

From Working Class to Middle Class

Working class parents without substantive secondary education or knowledge of the dynamics in tertiary education seldom have either the experience or the know-how about guiding their children towards under-graduate studies and specified career building. Children who are learned and committed to rising above the constraints of menial or artisanal work strive towards at least two significant things. The first is capitalising upon their ability to complete their secondary schooling with strong enough grades for entry into tertiary education, and the second is to work within the limits of affordability within their households. The underlying expectation is to reciprocate with parents through good behaviour, attentive adherence towards their studies and demonstration of commitment to family values. All of these expectations were articulately spoken about by 29 year old AB, a female civil engineer who was the daughter of a father who was an artisan and a mother who remained as a domesticated housewife. It was of immense pride that AB's mother remained committed to their rearing since birth even though their father, a bricklayer, earned a "lower-middle" income, and was often out of work. Only by the third conversation it was learnt that her father was often out of work because he was a habitual substance abuser. It took a while for her to be more open about her father. Despite his weakness, he was "...a loving, caring man who looks after us with everything he has." She recalled that all her life her parents rented out spaces to live, always in two-bedroomed outhouses in Indian dominated suburbs. Their financial circumstances did not allow them anything more than the basic necessities to live on. For this reason she and her sister felt excluded from the better off girls in their neighbourhood. She avoided weddings and birthday parties because they could not match the outfits of their friends and relatives. AB and her sister consciously isolated herself from the social gatherings and accepted their lots by remaining introverted. They tried with great pain not to feel jealous about their neighbours' better comforts and resourcefulness. Some often tried to make their class statuses known to them, often enforcing a quiet avoidance from them. But within AB was a quiet resolve not to be intimidated by such circumstances. She was determined to complete her studies and acquire employment that would radically improve her parents' quality of life. Unlike other middle and upper class Indian girls whose targets age to marry is often in their mid-20s, AB excluded herself from such a possibility. Her aim was to ensure that she helped her sister to complete her education as well as to take her parents into a home of their own. After completion of her degree, AB found employment with her bursars, because it was condition that she will serve the company for 24 months before going out to work in any other place of her choice.

Within a year of her employment she was given a company van to use with benefits of 100 litres of fuel per week and a maintenance plan at the cost of her company. This perk saved her the cost of transport to work and gave her the privilege to transport her parents around during weekends to do their shopping and attend family gatherings. Her salary increased substantially after two years of her compulsory service, inclusive of a housing subsidy and a company van. This was her opportunity to realise her dream of providing a home of their own for her parents. As a young graduate in a highly sought after career that is well paid, AB sailed through the generally difficult situation of getting a home loan.

Inspiration from them is derived more from the commitment they showed as parents in a stable household that exuded with love and affection. Despite their father's irregular employment there was always food in their home. Unlike other equally poverty-stricken homes around them, their father did not fight with their mother when they were financially strapped and unable to provide more than a basic meal. AB was aware that her mother once attempted to hold her pots as security when borrowing from a wealthier but kinder woman. The lender told her to keep her pots, gave her two months to repay the debt, and then cancelled the repayment because she knew that her father was struggling to provide for them. But her mother avoided talking to her about the incident. Only several years later, when AB felt secure in her earning and asked her mother about the issue because she felt that she was now relaxed enough to talk about it, that her mother opened up. The marvel through their childhood and early adulthood was the fact that their parents did not turn against each other when they reached points in their lives that were close to complete bankruptcy.

A similar situation prevailed in the household of NM, a 35 year old pharmacist who prolonged her marriage because of her domestic situation. NM's father had left school in 1961 soon after he completed 'standard 6' (equivalent of the 8th grade). Her parents, both of who were from an upper caste (Brahmin) background, were a reasonably happy couple together, although the stress of having to live continuously from "hand to mouth" led her mother to developing multiple physical afflictions. By the age of 47 years her mother was already a diabetic and pressure patient, and at the age of 52 years she was diagnosed with cancer. She attributes this to her father being an alcoholic and a low-wage earner, while their relatives around them were excelling in business and professional jobs. During this period introductions to "suitable boys" by NM's extended family for marriage, did not help because she was not prepared to leave her parental home. On at least two occasions NM agreed to test the commitment and strength of relationship with young men who agreed to marry her. The first relationship lasted only two months because she felt that the suitor "…was not genuine…" in his initial promise to live with her in her parents' home after marriage. She was forced to terminate the relationship to avoid an unhappy marriage later. In her second suitor, she found a genuine interest in him, allowing their relationship to continue for more than two years. Over time NM learnt about a much deeper commitment that her suitor had towards his parents and the difficulty he would have to leave his home. After bringing up the issue with him, he suggested that she can take as much time as she needed with her parents after marriage because his ageing parents needed home too. Herein lay the first strains of what seemed to have been a working relationship. In the process her mother became increasingly ill and had to be taken to doctors more regularly. This strained their relationship even more so, eventually forcing their break-up. NM was caught between being a responsible daughter to her parents and a good sister to her younger siblings. Her choice was one of self-sacrifice and delayed any further relationship with suitors until she felt comfortable in one. Two years later NM's mother died, forcing an abandonment of marriage until the situation in her parental household stabilised. As an attractive young girl with a good education and job, it was difficult for her, but she avoided any further introductions *via* her family until her mother's one-year ceremony was done. Soon after this event she was introduced to another suitor, and her wedding took place 13 months later. Her condition to marry was based on an agreement that her earnings were not to be interfered by her husband to be, for as long as her two siblings education was complete and her father needed her financial help. As a man of means her husband-to-be did not have any problem with that, and NM by the time of her marriage no longer had the compulsion to remain in her parental household. After more than a year in marriage her husband and she did not have any financial disputes over how they spent or invested their money because they had entered into an anti-nuptial contract and both of them "…showed responsibility towards each other…" and their common household, in which only two of them lived.

Mutual responsibility in the two cases above, have in the proverbial sense been "turned on its head". It was the children, both young girls, who endured and persevered more for their parents than the other way around. A major saving grace in both instances is that the principal respondents were academically inclined and high achievers with a firm sense of duty towards their parents and siblings responsibilities. Their indigent circumstances prior to their graduation and subsequent employment placed them in rather precarious positions. In AB's situation a failure to pay their rent would have led to them being thrown out into the street, because nobody in the neighbourhood would have wanted to take on an errant tenant. While her father often paid his monthly rent late, it was always his first priority. Having realised this through her quiet and defenceless observation over the years, AB's determination to change her parents' circumstances after qualifying as a civil engineer was resolute. And for her to achieve this marriage had to be abandoned until her parents were in a home they could call their own. To NM marriage was conditional too, because failure to pay their regular property rates, electricity and water bills could have caused them to either lose their home or live without it in sheer embarrassment. NM's determination not only arose out of her care for her parents, especially her sick mother, but the ways in which extended family members used to look down upon her father because of his alcohol addiction. AB and NM failed to stop their fathers' addictive habits, but they remained steadfast in ensuring that they turned their household circumstances positively turned around, taking the notion of mutual responsibility away from an implicit male gender biased paradigm.

Hard Won Professional Choices

Youth with a conscience who are generally well cared for and are not compelled to live with or care for their parents when they are able to live independently, continue to show mutual responsibility in whatever ways they can. Demonstrating appreciation for parental love often takes on a path that can simultaneously be a source of annoyance and pride for parents at once. But it is the choice of career, choice of partner in marriage and the sobriety with which they live their lives that matter the most. In the situation of DP, an unmarried 26-year old male who rose to a senior position in a major South African bank within a short space of time because of his strong abilities, his affection for his parents was shown in the opposite from they wanted him to do. As ex-Durbanites, DP's parents worked as warders in a major Medium-B security prison. As soon as DP graduated and found employment in Johannesburg, they too decided to leave Durban to work in the vicinity of Johannesburg because he was their only child. Their purpose was to be close to DP, but they disguised the truth to him about relocating as promotions to better positions. Both sought transfers to Pretoria, which in effect were promotional positions, especially since they were receiving better salaries. But the high cost of living in that part of the country does not make them any better off. However, before DP's parents could relocate from Durban, he had already secured an apartment for himself in Johannesburg. By the time his parents got to Pretoria and found a three bedroomed apartment for themselves, DP had already grown used to being alone and enjoying a new sense of freedom with many of his graduate friends who also sought employment in Johannesburg. He was however taken by surprise when his parents told him to relocate from Johannesburg to Pretoria because they had sought an apartment with space for him too. They allegedly expected him to commute to work in Johannesburg daily through the use of the Gautrain, South Africa's new model train service for that region only. DP refused because as a prison warder his mother worked shifts, but despite this she persistently laboured to care for and feed him. His refusal to stay with his parents was because he believed they needed to work their way towards retirement and enjoy that period of their lives because they earned it. While there appeared to be a distinct conflict of interest between parents and child, DP's mutual treat him like a child. "*They baby me too much...and forget that that I am now a grown boy and I can fend for myself. They need to take a rest from me now.*"

Yet the other case of KS, a 34-year old male, demonstrated a differing instance of motherly love. KS's mother, a widow, preferred her son to live with her after he married, which he did. Responsibility towards his parents was for them not to continually take care for him.

But soon marriage after KS and his wife began quarrelling to a point of virtual breakdown of their marriage. His wife could not understand or tolerate his mother, and wanted to leave to stay on their own. KS continuously resisted moving out and after realising the costs of living on their own, the demand to leave subsided, although the quarrelling did not. He made his wife realise that living with his mother was sacrosanct because being widowed early in her life enforced upon him, as he then saw it as "a divine responsibility" to now take care of her for all that she did for him and his two younger siblings "under extreme hardships". But his mother had a different view from what KS and his wife should do as a newly wedded couple. She was encouraging in her words to them that they could relocate to Johannesburg since so many of their friends and relatives were already working there. She too was anxious about KS acquiring a more financially rewarding job than he had in Durban and was loathe to be seen by her daughter-in-law as a mother who stifled her son's progress. Their house was freehold and expenses were manageable within the complex in which they lived. Food was not an issue since they had a simple lifestyle and depended more on home cooked meals than the expensive option of eating out. KS's mother had informed all of her wider family and her daughter-in-law's parents that they must feel free to leave to either live on their own or relocate to Johannesburg if that is what they wanted. KS gave his mother an emphatic response: that he was not leaving to either stay on his own with his wife or relocate to Johannesburg. He believed that his wife, the younger of two daughters, was experiencing adjustment problems after their marriage "*...because she was missing her parents' home and their ways of doing things....everything in my house, although we are Hindus, seemed different to her. Everything that my mother did was different to her, or it was not good enough. I saw it as an adjustment problem for her. If I was weak and the fighting type we would not have lasted...but I was right. Everything she once complained about, whether it was cooking, our family prayers, our guests that came home was a problem. Now she is fine, and she does everything our way. Our relationship is perfect, my mother is happy that we are still in Durban although she does not admit it, and I am now in a good place. All we needed was patience, and now we are there.*"

In DP's and KS's cases mutual responsibility was seemingly diametrically opposed to each other. But their points of convergence remain with how they felt towards their respective mothers. While one was a working mother and the other a domesticated housewife, both mothers were appreciated for their hard work and dedication to their children. In turn both DP and KS recognised their affection for them but demonstrated it through different ways. DP believed that by staying away from his mother he would be giving her chance to rest and tend to his father, without him being an added responsibility to her. "*She never sits when we are at home...always cleaning something or making, baking and cooking something. My mother really believes the girl I marry will do the same things for me as she does for me! She does not know that she is so wrong.*" KS believed that by staying with his mother he was fulfilling his obligation as a son. "*Yes my mother loves playing independent like she does not mind me not being around. But when I am missing for a few hours she will be phoning to see where I am, with who I am, what I am doing.*" He viewed living and providing for his mother as an uncompromising necessity because it was now his time to demonstrate his mutual responsibility, considering what she had done as an unemployed single parent for him and his two younger brothers.

Conclusion

Each of the six case studies above represents levels of sincerity that is not uncommon to the average middle and working class households. The world is replete with such examples in every society. Hence in many ways they do not constitute instances of the unusual. But against the background of a preoccupation among anthropologists and sociologists of the negativities that are ever so present among the youth of the world, such positive instances do help to provide fresh perspectives of what we are often inclined to ignore. Anthropologists other interests of discussing broad patterns of socialisation processes do not bring out the dynamics of individual circumstances and the dynamics of personal inhibitions brought out through poverty and limiting circumstances because of single parenthood. Searching for aspects of normative behaviour that will facilitate generalisations about socialisation processes actually ignores the very essence of what anthropologists have ably convinced the world about, i.e. bringing out the positives and regularities in human behaviour from the most tribal to the most modern. Upon closer scrutiny the intention is to show a greater degree of universalism in human habits that are often wrongfully thought about as too exotic to be able to identify with. While generalisations through micro-level studies have been convincing over the years, the case study method brings to the curious mind ever more detail that demonstrate almost 'microscopic' variations of how socialisation processes operate at the level of the individual. The theory of mutual responsibility, as it is applied here, can be a useful tool of analysis in such exercises. Such analyses that emphasize upon the positives of human relations need to be used concurrently with other tools of analyses which bring to our attention the social afflictions that are prevalent in the world. Illustrations of mutual responsibility should conceivably have a two-fold effect: of balancing ethnographies on the positive side of human relations with its negative side, as well as infusing positive energy into the minds of readers in future ethnographic studies. Balancing the negative with more positive studies will serve as instructive lessons to cognate disciplines such as social work and rehabilitation exercises.

Notes

1. See Editorial, by Anand Singh (2007), editor of *Youth and Migration,* Special Volume of *Journal of Social Sciences* – No. 10, Kamla-Raj Enterprises, Delhi, India.
2. Countries such as India and South Africa have raised the age levels of youth in order to address equity issues against discriminated segments of society. But South Africa's political leadership also has a record of manipulating age categories for political advantage over the challenging youth against senior politicians.
3. Hence Sheetal Bhoola, a post-doc affiliate.
4. Respondents will henceforth be referred to in such acronyms.

References

Becker, H.S., 1997. *Outsiders: Studies in the Sociology of Deviance.* Free Press.

Behera, Deepak Kumar and Trawick, Margaret (eds.) 2007. *Children and Youth in the Global Metropole.* New Delhi: Manak Publications.

Blackman, S., "Youth Subcultural Theory: A Critical Engagement with the Concepts, Its Origins and Politics, from the Chicago School to Postmodernism", *Journal of Youth Studies* 8 (2005): 1-20.

Boothroyd, Roger A. and Evans, Mary, E. (2007). "Environmental Safety and Exposure to Violence of Inner City Children Experiencing: A Psychiatric Crisis", (pp. 162-178) in Deepak Kumar Behera and Margaret Trawick (eds.) *Children and Youth in the Global Metropole.* New Delhi: Manak Publications.

Benedict, Ruth, 1931. *Tales of the Cochiti Indians.* Bureau of American Ethnology.

Chandra, Vinod; Jain, Mahaveer; and Sharma, Sunil Dutt (eds.) 2009. *Childhood, Child Labour and Youth.* New Delhi: Manak Publications.

Cohen, A.K., 1955. *Delinquent Boys: The Culture of the Gang.* Free Press.

Cross, E. Jamie, Sharma, Murari and Shrestha, Shraddha, 2007. "Weaving Carpets, Weaving Lives: Childhood and Ethnicity in Downtown Kathmandu", (pp. 33-52) In Deepak Kumar Behera and Margaret Trawick (eds.), *Children and Youth in the Global Metropole.* New Delhi: Manak Pubications.

de Castro, Lucia Rabello, 2007. "Cities and Social Participation: Social Inequalities from Children's and Youth's Point of View", In Deepak Kumar Behera and Margaret Trawick (eds.) 2007. *Children and Youth in the Global Metropole.* New Delhi: Manak Publications, pp. 92-105.

Evans-Pritchard, E.E., 1969. *The Nuer: A Description of the Modes of Livelihood and Political Institutions of a Nilotic People* (First American Edition) Oxford University Press.

Greogory, Janet, Robert Gregory, and Carrol-Lind, Janice, 2007. "The Wisdom of Children-in-Context". Deepak Kumar Behera and Margaret Trawick (eds.) 2007. *Children and Youth in the Global Metropole.* New Delhi: Manak Publications, pp. 179-193.

Hall, S., & Jefferson, T., 1990. *Resistance Through Rituals: Youth Subcultures in Post-War Britain.* Routledge Publications.

Keesing, M. Roger, 1981. *Cultural Anthropology: A Contemporary Perspective.* New York: Holt, Rinehart and Winston.

Lewis, Elizabeth, 2012. *Youth. http://www.culanth.org/curated_collections/7-youth*

Maira, Sunaina, "Identity Dub: The Paradoxes of an Indian American Youth Subculture (New York: Mix)." *Cultural Anthropology,* 14.1(1999): 29-60.

Malinowski, B., 1929. *The Sexual Life of Savages* (1st ed.), Beacon Press.

Mayer, Danila, 2007. "Growing-up in a Multi-Ethnic City (A Youth Worker's Perspective)". In Deepak Kumar Behera and Margaret Trawick (eds.) *Children and Youth in the Global Metropole.* New Delhi: Manak Publications, pp. 106-117.

McRobbie, A., & Garber, J., 1960. "Girls and subcultures." In S. Hall & T. Jefferson (eds.), *Resistance Through Rituals: Youth Subcultures in Post-War Britain* (pp. 209-220). Routledge Publications.

Mead, M., 1928 *Coming of Age in Samoa: A Psychological Study of Primitive Youth for Western Civilisation* (1st ed.). New York: Harper Collins Publishers.

Mungham, G., & Pearson, G., 1976. *Working class youth culture.* Routledge & Kegan Paul.

Singh, Anand, 2007. "The Reproduction of Ethnicity through Children and Childhood: Education in Post-Apartheid South Africa". Deepak Kumar Behera and Margaret Trawick (eds.) *Children and Youth in the Global Metropole.* New Delhi: Manak Publications, pp. 145-161.

Sujoldzic, Anita, 2007. "Adjustment of Adolescent Refugees in Croatia". In Deepak Kumar Behera and Margaret Trawick (eds.) *Children and Youth in the Global Metropole.* New Delhi: Manak Publications, pp. 118-129.

Swart-Kruger, Jill., 2007. "*IsikhathiSokulala:* How Boys and Girls in a South African Squatter Camp Experience Bedtime." Deepak Kumar Behera and Margaret Trawick (eds.) *Children and Youth in the Global Metropole,* New Delhi: Manak Publications, pp. 16-32.

Tanner, R.E.S. and Pawson, C.J., 2007. "The Moral Understandings of Urban Children in Sub-Saharan Africa: Some Preliminary Observations", Deepak Kumar Behera and Margaret Trawick, (eds.) *Children and Youth in the Global Metropole,* New Delhi: Manak Publications. pp. 130-144.

Turner, V., 1995. *The Ritual Process: Structure and Anti-Structure,* Aldine Transaction.

Van Santen, Josée, C.M., 2007. "Not Just Any Street Child: Universals and Particulars of Childhood in North Cameroonian Society", (pp. 54-70) in Deepak Kumar Behera and Margaret Trawick (eds.) *Children and Youth in the Global Metropole.* New Delhi: Manak Publications.

Willis, P., 1981. *Learning to Labour: How Working Class Kids Get Working Class Jobs.* New York: Columbia University Press.

E. MISCELLANEOUS

NINE

SOCIAL INCLUSION AMONG THE LODHAS A VTG:

An NGO Initiative

PRADIP K. BHOWMICK

I

Introduction

'Social exclusion' first originated in Europe, where there has tended to be a greater emphasis on spatial exclusion. There is also a policy focus on those living in 'deprived areas', where poor housing, inadequate social services, weak political voice and lack of decent work all combine to create an experience of marginalisation. However, there are various understandings of social exclusion and integration. In the seminal article below, Hilary Silver highlights these, and illustrates how they stem from analysts' own backgrounds and political traditions.

Social exclusion is a socially constructed concept, and can depend on an idea of what is considered 'normal'. In many developing countries, where most people do not enjoy an acceptable standard of living, defining what is 'normal' is not a simple task, especially given the lack of the welfare state and a formalised labour market. Indeed, as social exclusion can be structured around hierarchy, the exclusion of people on the basis of their race, caste or gender, may be viewed by the society excluding them as 'normal'. As such, the concept of social exclusion is contested, in that it is often difficult to 'objectively' identify who is socially excluded, as it is a matter of the criteria adopted and the judgements used. Social exclusion is multidimensional, and can encompass a lack of access to employment, legal redress and markets; a lack of political voice; and poor social relationships. Therefore, it is not enough to examine these issues individually; the links between must be explored. Social exclusion should be clearly differentiated from poverty. The causes of social exclusion have been attributed to the economic and social changes in free-market economies, and to weaknesses in government policies and services. Because people who are socially excluded are vulnerable, some may choose to assert themselves or to push back in inappropriate ways. A study in the United Kingdom found that a disproportionate number of crimes are committed by people who are socially excluded.

But social exclusion can happen to anyone. As our society speeds forward to new technological and economic heights, it elevates some people and leaves others behind. Individuals who belong to underprivileged groups or minority social groups are at higher risk of facing social exclusion. In developed countries social exclusion has been defined in relation to the welfare state and formal employment. Attempts to adapt the concept for the developing world have led to the repetition and relabelling of earlier poverty studies. Rather than trying to transplant the concept, therefore, elements such as its helpful focus on process could be incorporated into existing frameworks.

Some minority ethnic groups voluntarily exclude themselves from wider society. This phenomenon should be distinguished from social exclusion, which occurs for reasons that are beyond the control of those subject to it. Many studies emphasise the need for broad institutional reform, others call for greater inclusion into the benefits of development without necessarily challenging the mainstream policy agenda.

Social exclusion can encompass life and livelihood as a whole and can severely restrict participation in social services, welfare, security networks, consumer culture, political choice, bases of popular solidarity and also in the understanding of the circumstances surrounding the people at large. Social exclusion is the process by which individuals or households experience a deprivation either of recourses or of social links to the wider community or society. Same (2000) holds that exclusion from social relations can lead to other deprivations that further limit our living opportunity. It can thus be constitutively a part of capability deprivation as well as instrumentally a cause of diverse capability failures.

In the Indian context, exclusion revolve around institutions that discriminate, isolate, shame and deprive subordinate groups on the bases of identities like caste, religion and gender (Throat and Newman, 2007). According to Kabwer (2000), social exclusion revolves around social identities of people or groups and reflects the cultural devaluation of people based on their identities. Caste, ethnicity, religion and gender are examples of such group identities. Thus, social exclusion is more than an economic phenomenon. It refers to the alienation of or living out certain people within a society, which has consequence of social and cultural dimensions. It is argued that social exclusion based on identities is a process independent of income characters or the merit of an individual. The excluded are resorting to such strategies as low aspirations, despair, apathy, fatalism, migration etc. Social exclusion is synonymous with the concept of marginalisation and is related to poverty, unemployment, deprivation, withdrawal, underclass, alienation and disable.

Since independence, the Government of India as well as State Government introduced a number of policies and programmes for the empowerment of marginalised people. Besides, the effort of Government of India a few NGOs engaged themselves to provide better facilities and opportunities for providing those marginalised people in the process of social inclusion. In spite of consistent and continuous effort by the government as well as the NGOs, these marginalised groups have not progressed on the expected line. They continue to experience exclusion at various levels and in different context. The reservation policies have undoubtedly affected a considerable change in the lives of the oppressed section but the majority is still found to be outside the realm of the progress and economic empowerment.

In the context of social inclusion it can be understood as contextual and situational. In consonance of the idea of social upliftment through directive principles, the government formulates an inclusive policy. Constitutional safeguards and provision extended to weaker sections by the government are also considering inclusive policies in this context. The development policies and programmes are another kinds of measurements in order to achieve inclusive growth among the excluded social categories of India. The Indian Constitution provides equality to all citizens, irrespective of caste, creed, religion and gender. It also directs the state to take various measures to remove the different forms of discrimination and inequality and thereby helps to eradicate social exclusion. Keeping in view the above the present chapter makes an attempt the NGO initiative for social inclusion of the Lodha a Vulnerable Tribal Group in the state of West Bengal.

II

An NGO Initiative

The chapter will make a analysis of various welfare activities for the overall socio-economic transformation of Lodha through a organisation namely, Samaj Sevak Sangha and the Institute of Social Research and Applied Anthropology located under Narayangarh Development Block, Bidisa, Paschim Medinipur District in the State of West Bengal. The Lodhas were considered being a criminal tribe till the revocation of the Criminal Tribe Act in 1953. They are mainly food gatherers, depending on and exploiting the forest products from the neighbouring forests along the Bengal-Jharkhand-Odisha border in the rugged terrain of the Chotanagpur Plateau. These groups of people had regular social intercourse with the neighbouring tribes and other caste through markets where they sold their commodities. Possibly through this interaction which continued for a long time, most of them were assimilated gradually into the greater regional Hindu style of life as is evident from their dialect of corrupt Bengali with an admixture of Oriya. This can be also further substantiated from the surnames they use like Kotal, Digar, Dandapat etc. Anyway, this smooth process of gradual Hinduisation which may be described as Hindu method of tribal absorption (N.K. Bose, 1953) continued undoubtedly for a long time. But it took a different course when East India Company penetrated into the district of Midnapur after the Battle of Plassey (1757). The jungles which were exploited by the Lodhas were encroached by other land grabbing tribals like Santhals, Mundas, Bhumijs etc. The Lodhas thus faced different adverse situation. Besides, they had no knowledge of agriculture. As such they could not re-orient their style of life to meet this contingency. Thus, they became territorially and economically displaced (Bhowmick, 1963). They had no other alternative means of livelihood to fall back upon, because the forest were they used to live were strictly guarded by the police and forest guards and they were not allowed to go elsewhere. Thus, these peoples have had to indulge in criminal and antisocial activities for their survival. Due to this they are being socially excluded.

At as time rolled on this unfortunate victims of historical circumstances were declared as a Criminal Tribe or as "Branded Criminals" in 1871 (Daley, 1916). After independence however, various welfare schemes have been framed for their uplift and this are now being implemented both by the government and a few voluntary organisations, and assessment of the results of which has been made with a philosophy of social work done by Prof. P.K. Bhowmick through his "Bidisa Experiment".

To meet the problems of the Lodhas, a few welfare measures have been adopted by the State and the Central Government jointly as well as by a few NGOs. The impact of the uplifting activities of such NGOs as an inclusive policies have also been discussed and assessed in this chapter.

In 1954, the State Government and the Central Government jointly adopted certain schemes for the rehabilitation of the Lodhas. At the initial stage, the authorities selected 50 families for experiment at Auligaria in Jhargram Police Station through the Harijan Sevak Sangh, Bengal Branch. At that time, a sum of Rs. 1500 per family was allotted under various heads of expenditure like house building, land purchase, purchase of bullocks, goats, agricultural implements, goat rearing etc. Initially, the scheme seems to give the expected results, but ultimately it failed for lack of a "People-oriented and need-based plan" due to lack of sincere efforts on the part of the administrators. Later, the State Government entrusted the work to the Bharat Sevasram Sangh, a religious institution dedicated mainly to serve the afflicted humanity during floods, epidemics and other natural calamities who undertook the charge of implementing the Lodha Rehabilitation Scheme at Dholkat in the same Police Station after a year. The Sangh authority selected a site near their centre under Jhargram town and constructed 25 residential huts with iron shed roofs. The lands that were purchased were of inferior type, since good cultivable lands are not available in the locality. Everything was done in a cautious and calculated manner so that they may be directly involved and derived maximum benefits from these schemes but the food gathering Lodhas could not be moulded and attracted to agricultural pursuits because they are generally averse to hard labour and have no experience or aptitude for agriculture. One of the NGOs functioning in this district for rehabilitation of the Lodhas is Bidisa Samaj Sevak Sangh which is functioning as a 'growth-centre' in the Narayangarh development Block under the leadership of Prof. P.K. Bhowmick, who was initiated various socio-economic activities for the welfare of the Lodha communities.

III

Bidisa Initiative

The various social work activities were carried out since 1950. The Samaj Sevak Sangh was organised by a group of anthropologists and social workers in 1953. Since then it is doing experiments not only for proper uplift and rehabilitation of Lodhas, but also for other downtrodden communities and marginalised people in this locality. The Centre is situated at Daharpur in Narayangarh Police Station and the project is popularly known as "Bidisa Project". The State Government had entrusted them with the work of organising a colony for resettlement of the Lodhas. Altogether 39 families (on the basis of an average expenditure of Rs. 1500 per family) were resettled at that place. At the primary stage, the Sangh authorities took the following measures for proper supervision and implementation of the scheme—

(a) A rehabilitation sub-committee was formed for planning and supervision with three nominees of the government from block, district and state-level.

(b) A community hut was constructed to provide shelter to those who may require it for some reason or the other.

(c) Bullocks were purchased, not on individual family basis, but on the basis of total estimated needs for all these plots of land.

(d) Good type of agricultural land was purchased for this family.

(e) Arrangements were made to revitalize their recreational life through games, sports, dance and songs maintaining their tradition, and for imparting basic education to both children and adults.

Later on, a multi-purpose cooperative society was formed and responsibly for all these activities and programmes for development was entrusted with for developing local leadership from among them. The cooperative society, according to the direction of the Tribal Welfare Department has purchased and distributed lands for resettlement of the Lodhas, on family basis, to make them domestic minded. A Junior Basic School has also been opened for them. At present the same school being upgraded into the Doharpur Adhaypak Probodh Kumar Bhowmick High School. Three Ashram Hostels, one for the girls and two for the boys, have been established and are now accommodating a total of 70 students of both categories. A separate community centre has also been established to change their narrow psycho-emotional traits into broader social outlook, where some tribal boys and girls who could not been accommodated in this school are taught the modes of social behaviours and integration. They have been segregated from their dismal, drab and stunting domestic environment to infuse into them a zeal for education and ambition to lead a better life. Again, a Senior Basic School has been started along with a library for imparting employment oriented training in various trades. Improved agricultural methods are being taught in a school. Initially, a Bengal Khadi Board took-up a social and economic programme of development in this area by teaching, spinning and weaving to some tribal men and women and buying their products. Through this endeavour and sincere effort, the Lodhas learned to prepare their own napkins, clothes and some other garments they use. The criminal Lodhas thus apparently showed some sort of change in their mode of living involving themselves with this type of activities. This type of activities have been carried out by the Sangh bringing some change now and then in tune with changing system. Later on after 2003 due to inclusion of new energetic scholars having zeal of social work some new activities had been carried out by the Institute of Social Research and Applied Anthropology a sister organization of the Bidisa. The activities are mentioned below:

1. A project entitled "Empowerment of Tribal Women through Batik Print: Training-*cum*-Production" was implemented by the Institute by getting duly sponsorship from Department of Science and Technology, Government of India, New Delhi with a aim to provide livelihood opportunities for the tribal women forming 10 self-help groups (SHGs).
2. Imparting training for tribal youth mainly to Lodhas in particular and other tribal communities in general one Vermi-compost training was organised by the Institute duly sponsored by District Industries Centre, Paschim Medinipur, Government of West Bengal.
3. Keeping in view of the tribal women entrepreneurship, a Bee-keeping programme was organised by the Institute duly sponsored by District Industries Centre, Paschim Medinipur, Government of West Bengal.
4. Very recently the District Sericulture Department, Paschim Medinipur encouraged the authority to take up Taser and Mulberry cultivation in view of providing alternative economic opportunities.

This way Sangh from its inception are actively engaged to perform some kind of social action for overall socio-economic transformation of the Lodhas in particular and other tribal communities in general. Due to this inclusive process made by the NGOs, the Lodha at present are at comfortable position.

Conclusion

The impact of this project undertaken by the Sangh and the Institute has been tremendous on the minds of the local people not only the Lodhas but other tribals and non-tribals as well. Through integration process these groups of people are tried to be grafted or articulated into the middle class norm of the society. Thus once the enemies of the society, this people have now turned into friends of the society.

References

Shuttlesworth, Guy (2015). *Social Work and Social Welfare*. Cengage Learning. p. 31. ISBN 130548066X. Retrieved 22 February, 2016.

Lymbery. "The History and Development of Social Work" (PDF).

Popple, Philip R. and Leighninger, Leslie. 2011. "*Social Work, Social Welfare: American Society*." Boston: Allyn & Bacon. Print

"What is the History of the Social Work Profession?" socialworkdegreeguide.com.

Peter Higginbotham. "www.workhouses.org.uk". www.workhouses.org.uk. Retrieved 2010-12-20. "The Old Poor Law 1795–1834". Historyhome.co.uk. 2009-01-19. Retrieved 2009-05-17.

"A Short Explanation of the English Poor Law". Mdlp.co.uk. Retrieved 2009-05-17. Retrieved June 5, 2014.

TEN

UNIVERSE OF WOMEN IN THE MOBILE THEATRE OF ASSAM

BIRANCHI KUMAR MEDHI AND SANGEETA KAKOTY

Introduction

Gender is a socially constructed definition of women and men. Sex is the biological characteristics of men and women while gender is defined by the functions, tasks and roles attributed to men and women in society. Wijk and Francis (1999:1) write, the gender approach is distinct in that it focuses on women and men, and not on women in isolation. It highlights the differences between women's and men's interests even within the household and how these interact and are expressed; the conventions and hierarchies which determine women's and men's position in the family, community and society at large, whereby women are usually dominated by men; the differences among women and among men, based on age, wealth, ethnic background and other factors; the way gender roles and relations change, often quite rapidly, as a result of social, economic and technological trends. Gender equity means the equal enjoyment of the socially valued opportunities, goods, rewards and resources by both men and women. It means that the opportunities and chances in life should be equal for both men and women.

In this chapter, a humble attempt has been made to evaluate the universe of women in the very popular and unique mobile theatres of Assam. It is a fact that women in Assam have been relatively less visible or relegated to a background position as far as performing arts were concerned. The passage of time stands witness to the various trials and tribulations that women has had to go through in a patriarchal set-up to be able to carve a niche in the arena of performing arts (in this case, mobile theatre). What were these trials? What was the mind-set of society? How much of it has actually changed? Today, can we say that women hold a position of equality in the mobile theatres of Assam? These are some of the questions that are being probed into.

Subbiah (2013: 24-26) in her research paper writes, India is among the countries that has the highest number of women professionals in the world. They juggle between work and family, striving to strike a balance between the two. However, in Indian Theatre, women representation/participation as an actor/script writer/director/performer or a technical designer is very less and even though they are very much interested in theatre. Because of the social construction of our society, the discrimination of women in folk performing arts and in theatre is continued. Research scholar Gairola (2015:68-69) has pointed out that the dramatic creations in world drama have been overshadowed with the plays written by the male playwrights and comparatively fewer plays have come down from the hands of women playwrights. The factors preventing women from venturing into this field appear to be the social, cultural, economic, traditional and political barriers women have faced since the beginning of the history. The common factors that culminated in preventing women were poverty, lack of education, subjugation and suppression etc. It is not that women have never endeavoured to break away from these barriers, rather feminist movements and revolutions for equality of women around the globe have been making news time and again. Women playwrights like Poile Sengupta (English), Varsha Adalja (Gujarati), Manjula Padmanabhan (English), Dina Mehta (English), Tripurari Sharma (English and Hindi), Dr. Kusum Kumar (Hindi), Gitanjali Shree (Hindi), Irpinder Bhatia (Hindi), Neelam Mansingh Chaudhury (Punjabi), Binodini (Telegu), B. Jyashree (Kannada), Shanoli Mitra (Bengali), Usha Ganguli (Hindi), Shanta Gandhi (Gujarati), Sushma Deshpande (Marathi), Veenapani Chawla (Marathi), Qudsia Zadie (Urdu), *et al.*, became common names of Indian drama. Towards 1970s of post-independence period, the feminist theories and arguments were gaining ground throughout the world including India. The subdued and marginalized sections were also raising their voices against the age-old subjugation and marginalization in society. Obviously, women were also craving for the articulation of their voices and drama, besides other genres of literature, was a perfect tool for the representation of their lives. The women playwrights with their commendable contribution to Indian English as well as regional drama have not only enriched this field but also have paved the way for future generations of feminine geniuses to plunge into the exciting world of drama.

The history of Assamese drama is very long and old indeed older surely than the drama of any Indian modern language and older than even the regular English dramas by at least a century. The first drama is certainly *Chihna Jatra* (a play with the painted scenes) and the first theatre is the performance of it in 1468. As a matter of fact, neither introduction of scenes nor the regular drama in Europe in general can be ascribed to a period earlier than the seventeenth century, and in England in particular regular dramatic work really began in the later part in the sixteenth century with such predecessors of Shakespeare as Marlow, and the Globe Theatre which Shakespeare had immortalized was actually established in 1599 (Neog, 1982). It is said that just as the cradle of European drama rested on the altar, Assamese drama was also born under the shadow of the *namghar,* the Vaishnavite community village prayer house and was nurtured for religious purposes. The *Kathaguru Carita* and *Bardowa Carita*, the two biographies of the Vaishnava gurus of Assam, mention that, after returning from his first pilgrimage, Sankaradeva, the founder of Vaishnavism in North-East India, composed and staged his first play against the backdrop of painted scenes of *vaikuntha* (heaven) in 1468. It was called *China-jatra*, or play with the painted scenes (Neog, 1965). The acting process or presentation of *Ankiyanat* (the Vaishnavite ritualistic one act plays) which contributed to the foundation of Assamese drama and stage, is called *bhaona.* One of the striking feature of *bhaona* was that, the female roles were played by effeminate boys.

Assam is rich in folk performing arts but there was no space for women in most of these performing arts. To understand why, we will have to look into the social condition of the time. Mishra (1987:117) points out, the process of Hinduization or Aryanization of the Mongoloid people began in Assam, as elsewhere in India, under the influence of the Brahmin priests, the Hindu military adventurers and merchants. But this process was a slow and gradual one and even the influence of Sankaradeva and his followers in the *satras* (the Vaishnavite monastery) did not succeed in transforming the cultural base of Assam to give it a predominantly Brahmanical Hindu base. On the other hand, the Hindu culture and religion underwent significant changes under the impact of the Indo-Mongoloid influence in Assam. A study of the tribal culture of Assam reveals the position of importance occupied by women. As opined by Nath (1978: 3-4) in all primitive societies, women by virtue of their vital role in procreation and in agricultural activities, occupied a position of supremacy. The matrilineal system, or the system of recognizing women's rights in the matter of inheritance and of social administration, was the natural outcome of the practice of apportioning to the women the primary position in social production.

It is significant that even after Aryanization brought about the overthrow of the mother's rights and the establishment of a patriarchal form of society, the matrilineal system continued to be prevalent amongst certain sections of the tribals of North-East, like the Austro-Asiatic Khasis and the Mongoloid Garos. Neog (1965:368) writes, the final elimination of women from all important positions in the religious and social life of the Assamese Hindus for over five centuries was effected by the great Assamese Vaishnava saint, Sri Sankaradeva (1449-1568). Sankaradeva had successfully counteracted the influence of Brahmanical Hinduism and of tantrism in Assam and had established a broadly egalitarian base for Assamese religious and social life. He made no distinction of caste in accepting disciples from amongst the tribal, Ahoms and even from amongst the Muslims. However, in case of women, his attitude was marked by a strange intolerance. Considering women to be an evil influence on the male devotees, he advised his devotees to avoid attachment to women (Sarma, 1966: 65). In the ascetic order established by Madhavadeva, one of the greatest disciples of Sankaradeva, strict restrictions regarding women were imposed on the monks (*op. cit.*: 329). Sankaradeva himself was adverse to accepting women, kings and Brahmin priests as his disciples and though he was himself a twice-married man, he never gave women any position in the whole religious and cultural set-up created by him.

In the *satras* established by the followers of Sankaradeva, women were virtually excluded from all aspects of the religious and cultural life and even the lowliest of duties, like wiping the prayer-hall were denied to women (*Ibid.*: 338). Together with the Vaishnava influence, Bengali Brahmanism which was introduced in Assam during the reign of the Ahom King Rudra Singha, proved utterly detrimental to the position of women in Assamese Hindu society. The introduction of Bengali customs and prejudices, only served to strengthen the latent caste prejudices in Assam and to give legitimacy to such evil practices as child-marriage, prohibition of widow remarriage, ill-treatment of widows and seclusion of women (Nath, 1978: 145). The positive fact here is, that in spite of this dark picture, the condition of women in Assam, in comparison to other parts of India, was better. The intermixing of the non-tribal society and tribal culture resulted in the Assamese society attaining a unique identity and social evils targeting women like *sati*, female infanticide, dowry system and kulinism could not gain ground in Assam. Gogoi Nath (1992:22) writes, in such a scenario it was no wonder that women had no space in the *Ankiya bhaona,* i.e., the one act ritualistic Vaishnavite play performances since these plays were an instrument of religious propagation and women had been consciously kept away from the core of this religious movement. The only common women having some attainments in art and culture were the *natis* or temple dancers who were proficient in cultivation of fine arts like dance and music. The fine arts of the period portray female figures as playing on musical instruments and dancing. The references to the *natis* or *devdasis* as proficient in these branches of arts in ancient literature or in those of medieval times as Ananta Kandali's *Kumara Harana*, Sankaradeva's *Rukmini Harana* and other works like *Yogini Tantra*; and also the rock-cut remains of this remote part of India with the female figures bear testimony to this. It is interesting to note that the dancing girls are neither condemned for dancing nor prevented from cultivating the arts. This was because the males of a particular class, who could have condemned them, could enjoy their beauty for their satisfaction; in fact the dancing girls cultivated fine arts for the pleasure of man.

It was only in 1933 that *Abhinayacharya* Brajanath Sarma, one of the pioneers in the field of theater in Assam, dared to introduce co-acting on the stage of the Assamese theatre in Doomdooma in upper Assam breaking the shackles of a conservative society. Sixty years after Sarat Chandra Ghose, on the advice of Michael Madhusudan Dutta had introduced co-acting in Bengal by bringing three girls, *viz*., Jagattarini, Elokeshi and Shyama on the stage, Brajanath Sarma took this revolutionary step that etched his name in golden letters forever in the history of Assamese drama (Sarma, 2011:43-45). This was certainly not an overnight achievement and Brajanath Sarma had to work hard for more than three years to make his dream successful. He found support and encouragement when the legendary Phani Sarma (another stalwart in the field of Assamese theatre) joined the Kohinoor Opera Party. Together they went to the Parihareswar temple in Doobi near Pathsala, a township of lower Assam, which was famous for its *devdasi* (temple dancer) tradition. Here they met two dancers, Savitri and Sajani, who, after prolonged discussions agreed to act on stage. All arrangements were made for the ladies to go to Barnagar, then a village in lower Assam, for the rehearsals, but the shackles of the conservative society proved stronger and Savitri and Sajani changed their mind.

The days rolled by and Brajanath Sarma's search went on. Finally, after a lot of hard work, from Puranigudam area of Nagaon district, Assam, was found Sarbeswari Das and Golapi Das, from Chamuguri was found Phuleswari Das, from Jorhat was found Sailabala Debi, from North Gauhati was found Labanya Das and from Nazira (Sivasagar) was found Binoda Gogoi. Considering the plight of education, particularly for females, it was not surprising that these girls had not seen beyond primary school. However, it is said Sailabala had completed Middle Vernacular School (M.V.S.). As such, it was not possible to present them on stage immediately. A lot of stage, diction, pronunciation etc. training had to be given before they were ready. Brajanath Sarma tutored them in all these aspects. At last in November 1933 *Moran Jiyari*, literally, the daughter of the Moran community, was staged which inaugurated co-acting in the history of Assamese stage (*Ibid.*, 2011).

The backlash of this daring endeavour was not surprising. Brajanath Sarma expressed the bitter experience thus to Phani Sarma—"You know very well how I have managed to bring out these girls to the stage from within the interiors of a conservative patriarchal society. By introducing co-acting on stage I have suffered so much humiliation, criticism and bitterness even my own brother and nephew deserted the theatre party. The newspapers have criticized that I am trying to push the society towards destruction by inaugurating co-acting. I am propagating evil. Today, they are not being able to understanding what I am doing but one day the people of Assam will understand that I am not destroying the society, instead, I have taken the culture of Assam and the drama movement fifty years ahead" (Choudhury, 1983:15). Eminent stage actor Uday Bhagawati has mentioned in book *Jatrar para Bhramyamanoloi* how a strong protest was staged against Brajanath Sarma and his co-acting in Nalbari. Sarma (2011: 53) narrates societal criticism of co-acting coupled with other management problems saw the closing down of the Kohinoor Opera Party in 1936. With that came to a standstill co-acting on the stage of theatre. Twenty years later in 1957, that co-acting was seen on the opera stage for the second time when Tulika Das acted in Surjya Opera produced by

Late Surjya Das of Rangamati in South Kamrup of Assam. After that it was in 1960-61 that co-acting was revived on the stage by Purandar Talukdar of Nityananda, near Pathsala of Assam and since then, the trend of co-acting has been continuing without any break till now.

The revolutionary work of Brajanath Sarma had inspired the thoughts of Rupkonwar Jyotiprasad Agarwala who, at that time was busy with the making of *Jaymati,* the first Assamese movie. Agarwala sat in elaborate discussions with Phani Sarma, who had assisted Brajanath Sarma in inaugurating co-acting, before searching out actresses like Aideo Sandikoi and Mohini Rajkumari and in these discussions, the actresses found by Brajanath Sarma, Golapi, Sarbeswari, and Phuleswari also featured (Agarwala, 1996:105). Agarwala, in an article titled '*Asamar Film Silpa'* has written "In our nation, it is very difficult to get girls to perform in films: more so to select an able actress from among them. During the filming of *Jaymati*, about 28-30 girls were brought to the camp in Chitrabon (which housed the laboratory and shooting sets in Bholaguri Tea Estate in Tezpur, Assam). Most among them were uneducated village girls. From among them, only one could be considered for the film. But even then, this girl had to be continuously taught about acting for almost a year, but of course she had the face and talent for acting". The story of Aideo Sandikoi is well known in Assam. Sharma (2014: 124) talks to this pioneer, the first heroine in the first Assamese movie, and gets to know how she lived a life of loneliness because she dared to go against the social norms. It may be mentioned here that Aideo, in her role as *Jaymati*, had to address her husband Gadapani as '*bangahar deo*', literally 'my husband'. This was her offence in the eyes of a conservative society that believed that a girl should not address anyone as '*bangahar deo*' other than her husband. Her family was ostracized for three years by the village where they resided and even her own mother would not allow her entrance into the kitchen. The feeling of having done 'something wrong' resulted in Aideo never getting married. It was a very heavy price paid by a thirteen year old girl who never understood what she would have to face post-*Jaymati.* The other girls who acted in the movie were 'fortunate' that they got married and settled down to domesticity.

When, one of the stalwarts in theatre production in Assam, Sadananda Lahkar's Nataraj Opera (1959) was transformed and launched by his elder brother Achyut Lahkar as Nataraj Theatre in 1963, it was beyond anybody's wildest imagination that this was the beginning of a new era in the history of Assamese theatre. As narrated by Achyut Lahkar his creation was christened as 'mobile theatre' by Radha Gobinda Baruah. It is pertinent to mention here that Radha Gobinda Baruah was one of the most prominent figures of the Assamese society. An entrepreneur par excellence, he founded the first English daily newspaper in Assam, *The Assam Tribune* in 1939. He was the first Mayor of Guwahati and started the Assam Flying Club as well as the Guwahati Tea Auction Centre. A social worker and eminent sports enthusiast, the Nehru Stadium in Guwahati was built under his leadership. Today, the entire Stadium complex has been named R.G. Baruah Sports Complex. He played a key role during the freedom struggle ensuring that Assam and the North-East went to India during the partition of the country. He is called the architect of modern Assam. Lahkar wanted to take theatre to the common people by breaking away the shackles that had kept theatre city-centric and elitist. That was the reason why he thought of a travelling set-up that would take theatre to the nook and corners of Assam. This set-up was mobile in every sense of the term—right from the stage, auditorium, seats, sound system, light, kitchen, bedding, everything was to move. Nataraj Theatre pioneered a journey that has completed 52 years. Among the many questions that automatically come up like what developments took place in this half century? What has changed in the most popular Assamese form of theatre? What has been the socio-economic impact of mobile theatre on Assam? One particular question that this chapter seeks an answer to is—What is the space of women today in mobile theatre *vis-à-vis* fifty years back?

When Nataraj Theatre, the first mobile theatre of Assam, was established by Achyut Lahkar, women had already made their foray into the Assamese stage and cinema. So, finding actresses and female dancers was not a challenge that Lahkar had to face unlike Jyotiprasad Agrawala. In fact, when he advertised for artists in the newspapers in 1963-64, the first female playback singer of mobile theatre, Ms. Renu Phukan, who later on went on to become the first lady police officer of Assam, came out from a remote village of Sivasagar in upper Assam to join Nataraj Theatre in Pathsala, of lower Assam, in its second year. As was narrated by Ms. Phukan, this was not as easy as it sounds, back then. In that historic first venture of Nataraj Theatre, the female cast included names like Jyotsna Devi, Anupama Bhattacharya, Banita Borthakur, Manjil Bordoloi, Swarnalata Bora; dancers: Bina Borthakur and Pabitri Kakoty (Kalita, 2011:31).

The path that was shown by Nataraj Theatre was followed by almost a hundred mobile theatre groups in the fifty years of its existence, though not all of them survived the vagaries of time. It needs mention here that the participation of women in these three departments only, that is acting, dancing and singing are still largely the scene in the mobile theatres. It is not only surprising but sad that only one female director and one playwright can be named in this history of mobile theatre of Assam. The production scenario is as poor. One saving grace (if one may call it that) was when in 1977, an all-female mobile theatre named "Moon Theatre", was established by Smt. Abala Barman under the patronage of her husband Mr. Dharani Barman, renowned actor-director and proprietor of Suradevi Theatre. Kalita (2011: 117) mentions, on 8th June, 1977, Moon Theatre presented their maiden performance. The direction of the four chosen plays *Maju Baideu, Ila'r Binani, Kanika'r Sapon* and *Pushpalata* was done by Smt. Pushpa Devi, the first graduate actress in the mobile theatre of Assam and arguably the only female director till date in mobile theatre history. She was also the female playback singer. Interestingly, the single male character in *Pushpalata* was enacted by an actress. This was the antithesis of what had been going on in Assamese drama since ages, males portraying female characters but unfortunately Moon Theatre never lived to see a second season.

The only other such attempt of an all female mobile theatre named "Kalpana Women's Theatre" was made by producer Jadab Sen Deka in Nalbari town of lower Assam, where Smt. Mukta Barman was a director along with Bhairab Barman. Here too, the male characters of Dushyanta in the play *Sakuntala* and Gadapani in the play *Jerengar Sati* was enacted by Ms. Bhagyabani Pathak. The theatre did not survive for a second year (Kalita, 2011: 120). These, it must be admitted, had been daring ventures way back in the seventies, something producers today have never dared to try.

It is ironical that if one goes through the list of plays performed on the stage of mobile theatres in the last fifty years, or at least whatever is available, there are many plays based on strong female characters (protagonist). Mr. Achyut Lahkar, in his interview, proudly mentioned how the play *Beula* created records as the longest running show in the history of mobile theatre and it was staged by Nataraj Theatre for 40 years. But the question is what was the lens through which these female characters were looked at? Obviously, the male directors in a male dominant medium sketched the parameters of the female characters to suit the existing norms of the patriarchal society. *The Huffington Post* in association with *The Times of India* Group focused on work written and often also performed by women at the 2015 Fringe Festival in New York City. Here, some of the playwrights who featured included Ms. Tessa Keimes, Ms. Christine Howey and Ms. Ann Starbuck. Reacting to the question, how to combat the gender gap in the field of theatre, each of these ladies had their say. Kiemes opined, "I think the way to go about it is giving women the chance. It's not often women are given the opportunities. I mean obviously there are tons of actresses out there, but in terms of taking the reins, we are definitely way behind. So, in our community called Shooting Jane, we are going to give women the chance to do that—tell stories that women want to hear, but it will speak to everybody. It's not like we are anti-men, it's just about the quality of work that you produce".

Similarly, however (who changed sex to become a woman) said, "I think many men who run theaters do not take female playwrights seriously. They often can not relate to stories told from a female perspective. If theaters took a more proactive role in encouraging female playwrights, such as sponsoring workshops for play readings and play development, it might help change the atmosphere for women. In order to speak, it helps to know that you will be heard. Commenting on the reality of the gender gap in theatre in the US, Ann Starbuck added, "You know, in the writer's rooms, the ratio of men to women is a joke. There are so many more men than women. Men just have a lot more opportunities to go into the writer's rooms than women. It's probably one of the most sexist businesses out there." (*www.huffingtonpost.com/entry/theatre-gender-gap-US* accessed on 09/05/2016 at 10.00 a.m).

If this is the scene in the US in 2015, then it is true that we are in the same boat. Women playwrights, directors and producers across the world probably will have similar stories to share. Here we can look into some case studies which were taken up during the research for this chapter.

Ms. Pakiza Begum, renowned award winning actress of Assam, who has experience in amateur (proscenium) theatre, mobile theatre, radio and screen and has also ventured into direction in her own proscenium theatre group 'Ba' (breeze) opines that "changing the mindset of a society is not an easy task. We, women, got our opportunity quite late in time, so no wonder it will take time for us to get there. Change is taking place, no doubt, but very gradually."

Another prominent female director in the theatre scenario in Assam today, is Ms. Rabijita Gogoi, who has carved out a space with her distinct style of work. On the issue of the gender divide she accepted the fact that theatre is a male dominated sphere in Assam and as in most areas of work, a woman has to make that extra effort to prove her worth and talent. She narrated her own experiences about how she had to "act like a male" to make the people she was working with, listen to her and take her seriously. Ms. Gogoi opined that "gender division in the arena of theatre was as much a reality as in any other field of work. The mindset of the society at large must change".

Veteran Odissi dance exponent, Ms. Garima Hazarika, who was associated with mobile theatres as dance director, settings director and costume designer also stated that "the gender division is there. The reins are never given in the hands of women."

When questioned about the gender division, acclaimed Assamese film-maker, Ms. Manju Borah, replied that "gender division is there in every field, so why single out cinema and theatre? In spite of being an independent woman working on my terms, I am also bound by the social terms and conditions. For example, I try that much more to be a good wife and mother also. Our entire conditioning is such that it is very difficult for us to break out." On the question of very few women in decision-making positions in Assamese cinema and theatre, Ms. Borah explained, "See, in Assamese films my predecessors were Ms. Suprabha Devi, Ms. Kuntala Devi and Ms. (Dr.) Santana Bordoloi. This is a very time consuming field of work with no fixed working hours. Add to that the fact that it is a male dominant scenario. How many women get the support from their spouse to venture into and sustain in this line of work? Let us be realistic. Look at the field of politics also, the thirty-three per cent reservation which has been given to us, is it utilized? Ground reality is very harsh. The patriarchal mindset is there, no point denying it. Even in bollywood and hollywood, in the big league, how many women producer-directors can you count? However, if a woman wants to make herself visible, she will have to take up the challenge and never compromise on anything on the pretext of being a woman. From physical fitness to in-depth study about her field is a must. Otherwise she will not be taken seriously".

It is heartening to see that with time several women have ventured out to make a space for herself in the arena direction of cinema and theatre in Assam. Apart from the established names like Dr. Santana Bordoloi, Ms. Manju Borah, Ms. Bhagirathi, Ms. Pakiza Begum, Ms. Rabijita Gogoi and Ms. Prerona Barbarooah, a new generation of female directors have come-up like Ms. Bobby Sarma Barua, Ms. Enisha Sarma, Ms. Sanchita Talukdar, Ms. Papari Medhi, Ms. Ujjala Barman, Ms. Bidyabati Phukan, Ms. Pranami Bora, Ms. Rayanti Rabha, Ms. Manimala Das, Ms. Dipika Deka, Ms. Pari Saraniya *et al.*

Gender division is a fact and the real challenge is how to wipe it off. Almost all male producer/directors prefer to shy away from this topic. Replying to the question about women missing as decision-makers in mobile theatre, Mr. Ratan Lahkar, producer of Kohinoor theatre pushed the ball onto the women's court by saying—Women themselves will have to come out. This is precisely what 'The Kilroys', a Los Angeles based group of women producers and playwrights which was formed in 2013, says "we are done with talking about gender parity and are taking action." They have opted to funnel their distaste with their industry into an annual project titled "The List" that brings together the names of female and trans playwrights who have written plays in the past year. To do so, the Kilroys survey artistic directors, literary mangers, professors, producers, directors and dramaturges who nominate plays they have seen, specially works written by female or trans authors, that have yet to be produced. The 2015 list (which narrowed down a field of 755 suggested plays to 53) is meant primarily as a tool for those contemporary producers who claim they want to showcase under represented writers, but believe female playwrights are hard to find (*www.huffingtonpost.com/entry/theatre-gender-gap-US* accessed on 09/05/2016 at 11.15 a.m.)

In the course of their interviews both Ms. Pakiza Begum and Ms. Rabijita Gogoi lamented about the lack of such a common platform for women producers, directors, dramatists, scriptwriters, music directors, singers, dancers and actors where various issues related to these arenas may be voiced. This idea of "The Kilroys" is a fine example that can be adopted here in Assam also. When we talk of women playwrights in mobile theatre, the only name that can be mentioned is that of Smt. Minoti Acharjee, who wrote the play *Lakhimee Bowari* for Abahan Theatre in 1991, directed by Mr. Sebarata Barua (informed by Mr. Krishna Roy, producer of Abahan Theatre on 11-05-2016). The question that automatically comes-up is when we have so many prolific female litterateurs in Assam, why this dearth of playwrights? No doubt that writing literature and scripting a play are two completely varied fields, but if we have male litterateurs (Dr. Bhabendranath Saikia) taking-up play writing, what has stopped the ladies (litterateur or not) from venturing into this area? Krishna Roy opined that "writing a stage fit play is a very time consuming job and one must have the knowledge of stage. May be this could also be a reason that we do not find women playwrights in mobile theatre." This opinion of Sri Roy brings up another question—if scripting plays for mobile theatre is so tough and time consuming, how is it that today a single male playwright has almost monopolized the mobile theatre scenario, churning out dozens of plays each season? Is it humanly possible? Is that the reason why now most mobile plays remind us of some or the other Hindi, Bengali or south Indian movie? This can probably be another study in itself.

Talking about women in mobile theatres as a whole, few names (apart from the long list of actresses and dancers) can be counted who left their mark—Ms. Renu Phukan (first female singer), Ms. Pushpa Debi (only director), Ms. Abala Barman (first producer), Ms. Garima Hazarika (Dance director/settings designer/costume designer), Ms. Arati Das Bairagi (playwright and director of dance drama), Ms. Tarali Sarma (Music Director). But the question remains have these women been decision makers in the real sense of the term? Or did they simply adhere to the norms set by the male producer/director of whichever theatre group they worked with? In our society the "female" has always been defined through the male gaze. Thus, theatre and cinema also has been no exception. The self-sacrificing silent (voiceless), dependent, virtuous "heroine" *versus* the bold, self-confident, independent (with a voice and an opinion) "vamp". Who has sketched these images of the female? A mobile theatre of Assam has come a long way. It is time that new concepts, ideas and perceptions are experimented with. Feminist theatre can also be such an experiment. But the question is: will the producers dare to take up such experiments? As Ms. Rabijita mentioned "mobile theatre of Assam is a topic of great curiosity for theatre lovers outside the state". As such it is the duty of the producers to keep up its standards and what it has to offer to society at large. If earning profits become the sole motive of mobile theatre (as seems the trend nowadays), will mobile theatre of Assam be able to preserve its unique identity?

References

Agarwala, J. P., 1996, *Asamar Film Silpa*, in *Jyotiprasad Rachanavali*: *The Complete Works of Jyotiprasad*, S.N. Sarma, Navakanta Barua, Birendranath Dutta and S.P. Barua (ed.), Guwahati: Publication Board, Assam.

Choudhury, Natyasamrat Chandra, 1983, "Brajanath Sarmar Xilpi Manor Sapon" in *Souvenir, All Assam Brajanath Sarma Memorial One Act Play Competition,* Tezpur.

Gairola, Ishan, 2015, "Advent and Role of Female Dramatists in the Growth, Evolution and Development of Indian English Drama", *Indian Journal of Research*, Vol. 4, Issue 1:68-69.

Gogoi Nath, Jahnabi, 1992, "Social Attitude Towards Women in Medieval Assam" in *Status of Women in Assam,* S.L. Barua (ed.), New Delhi: Omsons Publication.

Misra, Tilottama, 1987, *Literature and Society in Assam: A Study of the Assam Renaissance 1826-1926*, New Delhi: Omsons Publications.

Nath, Rajmohan, 1948, *The Background of Assamese Culture,* Guwahati: Dutta Baruah & Co.

Neog, Dimbeswar, 1982, *New Light in Asamiya Literature*, Guwahati: Suwani Prakashan.

Neog, Maheswar, 1965, *Sankardeva and His Times: Early History of Vaishnava Faith and Movement*, Department of Publication, Gauhati University.

Sarma, Dhiren, 2011, *Brajanath Sarma,* Guwahati: Chandra Prakashan.

Sarma, S. N., 1966, *Neo-Vaishnavaite Movement and the Satra Institution of Assam*, Guwahati: Lawyers Book Stall.

Sharma, Bobbeeta, 2014, *The Moving Image and Assamese Culture Joymoti, Jyotiprasad Agarwala and Assamese Cinema*, New Delhi: Oxford University Press.

Subbiah, M., 2013, "Theatre to Women", *Indian Journal of Arts*, Vol. 2, No. 6: 24-26.

Wijk, Christine Van and Jennifer Francis, *Setting the Stage: Demand Responsive Water Supply, Sanitation and Hygiene,* The Hague, The Netherlands: IRC International Water Sanitation Centre.

www.huffingtonpost.com/entry/theatre-gender-gap-US accessed on 09/05/2016.

ELEVEN

MATRILATERAL CROSS-COUSIN MARRIAGE AMONG THE KOMITI

A Telugu Speaking Caste

S.N. RATHA

I

The role of kinship in regulating sex and marriage is a universal socio-cultural phenomenon. The regulations may be obligatory, permissive or prohibitory (Murdock, 1966: 262). The first leads to a preferential or prescriptive form of marriage with a relative. For a male ego, the most commonly preferred or prescribed relative is the mother's brother's daughter (MoBrDa) or the father's sister's daughter (FaSiDa). Such other relatives like the Mother's sister (MoSi), Father's sister (FaSi), Father's brother's daughter (FaBrDa), Mother's sister's daughter (MoSiDa) and sister's daughter (SiDa) are also found preferred in a limited frequency (*ibid*: 268).

Marital alliance between a man with his MoBrDa or FaSiDa, real or classificatory, is called cross-cousin marriage. The former type is termed as matrilateral and the latter as patrilateral. The practice is widespread. There is considerable ethnographic literature on the subject. In a survey, covering the data available till 1951, Leach (1961) categorized cousin marriages into two types—symmetrical and asymmetrical (*ibid.*: 59). The symmetrical type is characterized by the simultaneous or near simultaneous exchange of women for marriage between two local descent-groups. This is named as the **Karriera type (**Karriera or Kariyarra is an indigenous community of Western Australia). The asymmetrical type is one which precludes exchange of women for marriage between two descent-groups but prefers marriage of a man with his father's sister's daughter (patrilateral cross-cousin) only, or with his mother's brother's daughter (matrilateral cross-cousin) only. The former custom is named as **Trobriand type (**people of Trcbriand islands in the Western Pacific); and the latter is named as **Kachin type** (the Kachin are inhabitants of Kachin Hills in Myanmar).

II

The Komiti, a Telugu speaking South Indian Trading caste (Thurston, 1909:306-348) marry three categories of close relatives—the mother's brother's daughter, the father's sister's daughter and own uterine elder sister's daughter. The first is **prescriptive** resembling the Kachin type. It is called ***mēnārikam.*** This is called *ēduru (*alternative*) mēnārikam* which is preferential. The third is also preferential (the terms—**prescriptive** and **preferential** are coined by Needham, 1962).

Menarikam demands a man to marry his mother's eldest brother's daughter, provided she is within the prescribed age. The ideal is that the bride is younger than the groom and the age difference should not be more than six to eight years. If the eldest uncle does not have a daughter suitable for marriage, the man is allowed a limited preference to marry from among the daughters of his younger uncles, if any. Conversely, a girl is under obligation to marry her father's sister's son. In other words, the families of the procreation of the bother and the sister are under obligation to get their children in wedlock, failing which, the defaulter family has to pay an adequate monetary compensation, commensurate with its economic status and as determined by an *adhoc* body of elderly relatives.

III

The data dealt here relate to 184 marital alliances, entered into over three generations, spread over three lineages, by the Komiti of village Chalakamba, in the Rayagada district of Odisha State, India (Tables 11.1 and 11.2). Among these, only 39 cases (21.20%) were bound by *Mēnārikam.* But five (12.82%) walked out of the *Me¯nārikam* obligations by duly compensating their refusal. Four cases of refusal were from the groom's side; and one from the bride's. Thus, 34 (18.48%) were only *Mēnārikam.*

The refusals are found to be linked to dowry; which is a deciding factor in a Komiti marriage. The demand for dowry is weighed against the economic solvency of the groom's family. Thus, the rich alone can aspire for a fat dowry. When, per chance, there is considerable disparity between the parties, the richer side normally walks out of *Mēnārikam.* Therefore, while entering into a non-*Mēnārikam* alliance that will eventually pave the way to *Mēnārikam;* the Komiti are very meticulous in assessing the economic status of the concerned parties as well as of their near kinsmen, matrilateral as well as patrilateral. MoBrDa marriage, in the apparent absence of FaSiDa marriage, is a one-way flow; which may occasionally reverse with a marriage with a FaSiDa. The brides come from the same lineage in successive generations. Other things remaining as they are, the flow continues, as long as both the parties maintain their economic parity.

Table 11.1: Frequency of marriage with relatives and non-relatives (Figures in side brackets indicate percentage)

	Pre-marriage kinship relationship with spouse	*Ego's own generation*	*First ascending generation*	*Second ascending generation*	*Total*
	MoBrDa	13 (22.03)	6 (40.00)	4 (19.50)	23 (24.21)
	FaSiDa	–	–	1 (4.76)	1 (1.05)
Male spouse	(El)SiDa	4 (6.78)	1 (6.57)	1 (4.76)	6 (6.32)
	Distant relatives *	2 (3.39)	–	2 (9.25)	4 (4.21)
	Non-relatives	40 (67.79)	8 (53.33)	13 (61.91)	61 (64.21)
Total		**59 (100)**	**15 (100)**	**21 (100)**	**95 (100)**
	FaSiSo	8 (11.59)	1 (14.29)	2 (15.38)	11 (12.35)
	MoBrSo	1 (1.45)	1 (14.29)	–	2 (2.25)
Female spouse	MoBr	1 (1.45)	1 (14.29)	—	1 (1.12)
	Distant relatives**	1 (1.45)	1 (14.29)	–	2 (2.25)
	Non-relatives	58 (84.06)	4 (57.13)	11 (84.62)	73 (82.03)
Total		**69 (100)**	**7 (100)**	**13 (100)**	**89 (100)**

* FaBrDaSoDa, FaFaBrDaSoSoDa, (deceased) WiSi, FaBrDaSoDa

** FaFaMoFaSoSo, FaFaDaSo

IV

In the event of non-availability of a suitable marital partner in the *mēnārikam* category, the Komiti prefer marriage of a man with his Elder sister's daughter or that with the FaSiDa. In the sample data, we have 2 FaSiDa/MoBrSo, and 8 (El) Si Da/Mo(Y) Br marriages. Beyond the

Table 11.2: Frequency of Two Types of Cross Cousin Marriage (Figures in side brackets indicate percentage)

Generation	*MoBrDa*	*FaSiDa*	*Others*	*Total*
Ego's generation	21 (16.41)	1 (0.78)	106 (82. 81)	128 (100)
1st ascending	7 (31.81)	1 (4.65)	14 (63.54)	22 (100)
2nd ascending	6 (17.65)	1 (2.94)	27 (79.41)	34 (100)
Total	**34 (18.48)**	**3 (1.63)**	**147 (79.89)**	**184 (100)**

normal prescriptive and the preferential categories, the Komiti still look for marital partners within the wider kinship circle—a distant relative. In our sample. we have 5 such marriages. The rest are between non-relatives—61 (64.21%) for the male ego and 73 (82.03%) for the female ego.

As patrilateral cross-cousin marriage is not overtly discouraged, a possibility exists where the position of the MoBrDa synchronizes with that of the FaSiDa, and that of the FaSiSo with MoBrSo in the succeeding generation. Thus, the Komiti system has a tendency to resemble the 'Kariera type'. This can be illustrated with the help of the structural diagram:

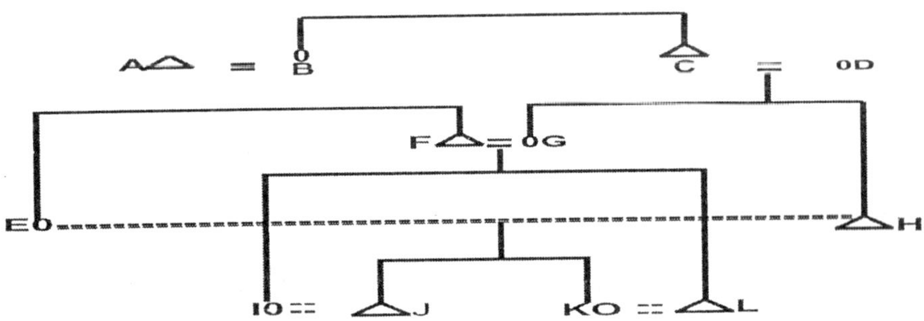

F is under *mēnārikam* obligation to marry **G**. In case, **E** marries **H, I** becomes **J**'s MoBrDa as well as FaSiDa; and **K** becomes **L**'s MoBrDa as well as FaSiDa. In such a situation, the relation on the mother's side overtakes, the cousin is regarded matrilateral to make way for *mēnārikam*. The system reverts back to Kachin type.

V

Kinship terms and marriage types are interrelated. The same kinship terms tend to be applied to MoBrWi and WiMo, to MoBrDa and wife and/or BrWi, and to WiBrDa and SoWi, under a rule of preferential marriage with a MoBrDa (Murdock, 1966:173). The Komiti kinship terms bear testimony to this axiom. The MoBrWi and the WiMoare addressed and referred to as *āttā*. MoBrDa (younger than the ego) and WiSi are referred to as *mārādālu*. *Vadinā* is the term for the (El)BrWi and the MoBrDa (older than the ego). SoWi is referred to as *kodālu*. The WiBrDa is referred to as *mēnākodālu* before her marriage; and when she marries the son of the ego, she is referred to as *Kodalu*.

VI

Typologically, the Komiti type of asymmetrical cross-cousin marriage resembles the Kachin kind. The associated kinship terminology is a function of that marriage type. A marriage type influences the kinship terminology, not so much because it applies to all or most marriages within the society; but, because of the weight of the social prescription and the value attached to such marriages. Among the Komiti, the matrilateral cross-cousin marriage, which is less than 20 per cent in the sample data, is found to influence the kinship terminology.

References

Leach, E.R., 1961, *Rethinking Anthropology*, The Humanities Press (London School of Economics, Monograph in Social Anthropology, No. 22).

Murdock, G.P., 1966. *Social Structure.* MacMillan.

Needham, R., 1962, *Structure and Sentiment—A Test Case in Social Anthropology*, Chicago University Press.

Thurton, E. (Assisted by R. Rangachari). 1909. *Castes and Tribes of Southern India*, Madras: Madras Government Press.

SECTION II

FRIENDS IN THE FIELD

TWELVE

PUBLIC VEGETARIANISM AND PUBLIC MENSTRUATION:

Staging Chastity in a Jain Pilgrim City in Gujarat

ANDREA LUITHLE-HARDENBERG

Introduction

Ascetic values play a vital part in the ethics and religious practice of the Jain religion and its community of Western India. The approximately fourteen thousand wandering ascetics[1] of this ancient religion not only renounce any kind of violence and possessions, but also any sexual relations. This ascetic ideal of *brahmacarya* is also followed by numerous lay adherents[2] when celebrating important events within their community. Thus, celibacy is also of special importance for the context of pilgrimage to one of the most important sacred centres of the Jains, the sacred mountain Shatrunjaya, near Palitana in the Bhavnagar District of Gujarat. During the years 2001 through 2003, I conducted field research of the practice of this pilgrimage, with a methodological focus on participant observation of the pilgrimage rituals.[3] According to the pilgrims, essential conditions for a successful pilgrimage are not only the temporary wandering, but also the strict observance of a vegetarian diet, as well as the observance of sexual abstinence. These forms of renunciation are well known by all cultural anthropologists who have been concerned with ascetic practices in South Asia. The basic principle of this penance is transformation: the sacrifice of physical well-being including sexuality is considered as the fundamental condition for attaining spiritual progress. In addition to that, the physical exertion which is involved in the pilgrim's climb to the top of the sacred mountain Shatrunjaya affords an extra increase of asceticism (*tap* or *tapas*).

Furthermore, in Jainism the fundamental restrictions of pilgrimage, namely vegetarianism and celibacy, are closely interconnected. According to this concept, eating meat corresponds with sexual aggression and demand. In contrast, sexual desires can be kept in check by means of a vegetarian way of life. The restrictive Jain diet even forbids the consumption of certain vegan foods which are considered as life-bearing (such as fruits containing many seeds, root vegetables and yeast bread), which are therefore considered as "hot". Pilgrims also observe extended periods of fasting in order to subdue the sexual drive.

In daily pilgrimage practice, a chaste attitude not only implies abstinence from sexual acts, but it also involves obvious restrictions of conduct, including general rules for conversing with the opposite sex, as well as dress codes. These rules of gender segregation, which apply for all of northern India in general, are considered by the Jain pilgrims with emphasis. Men's sections and women's sections are strictly separated in festival tents, congregation halls and temples.[4] Both parties are protected from each other either by a large gap or by fences in order to avoid intentional or unintentional body contact.

Furthermore, in particular women are expected to dress modestly, which means wearing preferably traditional loose clothing, covering all sexual characteristics, as well as shoulders, upper arms and legs down to the ankles. Clothes should also be inconspicuous and simple. In contrast, eye-catching or body-hugging fashion, as well as short skirts or jeans are associated with "Western" values[5] and practices, which are frequently linked to uncontrolled sexual desires and habits.[6] Women, especially those who are married, preferably wear pastel coloured *saris*, while unmarried girls prefer a *salvar kamis*, a loose dress reaching down to the calves and worn over trousers, which is complemented by a long cloth (*dupatta*) for covering the chest and shoulder and the head, very similar to a veil.[7]

Considering this central and far-reaching significance of celibacy for Jain pilgrimage, an essay on the role of sexuality as an aspect of field research within the orthodox Jain context seems paradox at first sight. However, as perceived during field research in the pilgrim town Palitana, the emphasis on the absolute negation of sexuality during pilgrimage causes a remarkable alertness of the prohibited issue among the pilgrims.

This was noticeable in an increased reflection of the generally tabooed realm of sexuality which was part of a public orchestration of chastity by the pilgrims. To illustrate this correlation, I will exemplify the practical consequences of the strict observances of chastity for my field research by referring to the central impact of vegetarianism, the different attitudes of well-wishers and skeptics towards my reliability, the public display of menstruation rules and intricate encounters with male ascetics.

Vegetarianism and Chastity as Basic Conditions for Pilgrimage and Field Research

From the very beginning of my fieldwork participatory observation of the diverse preparations, rituals and assemblies of the pilgrims formed the centre of my research. During the entire period of my fieldwork, I lived in one of the approximately 120 pilgrim hostels in Palitana, the *dharmashalas*. In my hostel, as well as in many others which I visited, I would join pilgrims in the dining halls, congregation halls and temples, eating with them, listening to sermons of their ascetic leaders and participating in their festivities and rituals. Apart from that, I undertook the pilgrimage to the top of Mount Shatrunjaya for 51 times, together with pilgrims of various local communities and orders.

This intense participation and interaction required ritual purity on my side as a condition *sine qua non*. Consequently, I was forced to adapt to all those rules which the pilgrims impose on themselves, especially dietary restrictions and sexual abstinence. By former visits in Palitana and in other parts of Gujarat, I was prepared to especially consider the ideologies and practices of vegetarianism during my long term fieldwork. Thus, having gained insight in the resulting consequences and conditions of these concepts for a potential research situation I thought I already knew what would be expected of me and was highly motivated to follow all perceivable rules. To prepare myself, I had started to get used to a strictly vegetarian diet even before leaving Germany, and I was also going to follow the dress code of "modest" clothing with determination and without compromise: shortly after my arrival in Mumbai, the womenfolk of my host family helped me to obtain five tailor-made *salvaṛ kamis*.[8] So when I travelled on to the provincial areas in Gujarat, I had already been equipped with appropriate gear.

In addition to that, I had agreed with my husband Roland Hardenberg that he would join me for my first week of field research, in order to establish my status as a married woman. This seemed necessary in order to match the rules of conduct followed by female pilgrims of about my age (20-40 years), who would never have travelled without a male relative at their side. As a woman travelling on her own is considered unprotected, her reputation is at stake as she unnecessarily takes the risk of being sexually molested.

Not only would showing-up with my husband secure my married status which was essential for a good reputation among the pilgrims, but it was also a measure securing my own personal safety. During earlier stays in Gujarat, I had experienced in quite unpleasant ways that in this part of India especially unmarried women without a male escort may be easily exposed to sexual attacks. On several occasions men had come into my room under false pretends and tried to sexually harass me.[9] Sharing these events with Gujarati women in whom I could confide, their response would always be the same: I just had to be more careful—after all, I was unmarried, and Indian girls were having the same problems. This reply was implicitly in agreement with the general notion throughout India that not only is an unmarried woman more vulnerable, but that she is also more *dangerous* due to her attraction of her so far unlived sexuality. Before being controlled and "tamed" by a husband a woman is considered more prone to deceiving a man into violating the rules. Thus, the Jains as well as other Indian communities conceptualise the only legitimate form of female sexuality within a marital relationship exclusively, with the husband acting as the guard of his wife. Under his male authority, the virtue of a married woman is more easily preserved than that of an unmarried one.

So in order to avoid awkward situations and speculations, I decided to involve my husband, even though he soon had to leave for Orissa in East India, where he was doing research himself. This intentional self-portrayal as a married woman appeared to make sense, as it implied a regulated sexuality and would thus point to my readiness for living celibate like any other pilgrim. Taking this measure, I was deliberately playing with the common sense of female sexuality in India. It should be emphasized that even within marriage, female sexuality in general is less associated with sensual pleasure than with the necessary means for begetting children. Moreover, in the pilgrim town Palitana, praiseworthy examples of the present and the past are couples who are appreciated for living together but in celibacy—at least after having begotten descendants, if not before. The most famous of them are the 22nd fordmaker Neminath and his wife Rajimata. Until today, quite a number of couples would formally give a lifelong vow of celibacy in public, as we will learn below.[10]

In this sense, our arrival as a married couple at "my" hostel played a key role and had far reaching consequences, intended as well as unintended: The "watchman" took us to the office of the approximately 60 year-old manager (*munim*), Motilalbhai,[11] who politely greeted my husband while totally ignoring my presence, which was in absolute agreement with the social conventions. So, my husband much to his chagrin had to take on the entire conversation, while my own attempts to communicate were disregarded, and I was not addressed in any way. It was my husband, not I, who negotiated the conditions for my stay: he chose (according to my instructions, admittedly) a small apartment in the rear and thus "safer" part of the building. A carrier boy took our cases to my new abode, distributing our luggage between the two rooms containing a single bed each. This separation of a married couple was one of the few explicit pointers to the actually practised and taken for granted chastity among married pilgrims.

When my husband left after four days, he paid the manager (with my money) for my accommodation, and Motilalbhai involuntarily had to take on the role of my protector. For me as an "emancipated" woman in the Western common sense, this seemed somewhat humiliating, albeit acceptable considering the given situation. Unfortunately, for months I had to suffer the consequences of this transaction which I myself had set in motion: The manager Motilalbhai, whose protection I had been entrusted to, rewarded this burdensome responsibility with an unfriendly demeanour: He obviously was not very interested in guarding my virtues and could foresee trouble—and rightly so, as we were to find out. While my introduction as a married woman might have been a step into the right direction, it turned out that this measure alone was not sufficient proof of my chastity.

Well-wishers and Sceptics

Motilalbhai now had to bear the unquestioned responsibility for my safety. He did this reliably within the compound of the hostel, by instructing the watchman in the courtyard not to let any male pass go to my room, with very few exceptions (see below). I welcomed this regulation (especially on the background of my earlier experience) and received most of my male visitors in the corridor in front of Motilalbhai's office. In the evening, the pilgrims would sit here on long wooden benches, discussing the events of the day. This meeting-point afforded many helpful contacts for me, even though the hallway was open towards the bazar road with all its traffic, and conversations were often difficult to follow due to constant noise.

Much to Motilalbhai's dismay, he repeatedly had to explain to the inquisitive pilgrims on these evening gatherings why "this woman" from Germany was staying in his hostel. Even though he felt obviously flattered when pilgrims from other hostels came to his own, just to meet the woman who had decided to write a book about the sacred mountain Shatrunjaya, he was more often annoyed by the fact that the presence of a woman from the "West" obviously irritated some of his guests. He obviously had to worry that my presence might be of questionable value for the reputation of his hostel. It was in fact unusual, at least during the years of my field research, that a hostel would accept a non-Jain. "Western" tourists for instance were rejected as they were hardly ever acquainted with the communal rules of ritual purity. The major worry, however, concerned my diet, as foreigners' diet is usually considered suspect, i.e. non-vegetarian.

In general, as a "Western" misfit within the close-knit community living together in the pilgrims' hostel, I was given much attention. There were very few Jains who were not interested in my presence. While some welcomed my presence with enthusiasm, it provoked open rejection and scepticism in others. The majority, however, was thrilled by the idea of my project on the sacred mountain of Shatrunjaya and they found it noteworthy that a woman from the "West" should be willing to subject herself to the general rules. These Jains trusted me from the beginning and welcomed me in their group. But even talking to these well-wishers, it became evident that they only accepted me on the basis of my efforts to be an exceptional woman from the "West" and not because they were tolerant towards "Western" values different from their own.

There was, for instance, one of my first longer encounters with a female ascetic (*sadhvi*) who turned out to become one of my strongest supporters. One of my early major interests of research was referred to cosmological concepts of the eternal mountain, and we spent many hours discussing the details. When talking about this subject this *sadhvi* as well as other ascetics repeatedly used the opportunity to explain that the world outside India (Bharat) was called *anarya desh*, a term corresponding to "the country of the Barbaric". Due to the moral decline in that part of the world, where sensual lust and hedonism were paramount in controlling people's actions, true ascetics could not live there, as there would be no admissible food for them to eat. Moral decline was envisaged mainly by notions of consumption: eating meat and drinking alcohol as well as "American" soft-drinks produced by Coca-Cola, using knife and fork, wearing sneakers and lascivious "jeans and tight t-shirts". Many advocates of orthodoxy whom I interviewed or whose sermons I listened to were especially censorious towards unrestricted female sexuality. According to them, it led to love marriages based on emotional cravings, extramarital sexual contacts, and to divorces. Similarly, all the other conversations on sexuality in Palitana (which I had exclusively with women) would point in the same direction: they all ended in fierce criticism of the predominant concepts of sexuality in my "Western" home country where "love", not marriage, is considered the ideal basis for sexual actions, where society provides legitimate options to change sexual partners frequently, and where sexual motives are openly displayed in the media.[12]

These discussions with pilgrims helped me to understand how the scepticism of some Jains towards me was strongly nurtured by cultural concepts. Obviously, my coming from a "Western" culture provoked associations with all that is forbidden not only during pilgrimage, but which is also a deterring counterpart to the Jains' own cultural values concerning vegetarianism and orderly sexuality.

In that sense, there were always some pilgrims who irrespective of my somewhat "illustrious" topic and of my obvious striving to adapt my clothing and diet fundamentally doubted my being acquainted with the code of conduct, and my factual following the rules. As an interesting reversal, this prejudgement might be called exoticisation of the participating observant by my Indian acquaintances. For these sceptics, the signal effect of my origin implied the uncertainty regarding my conformity with their own rules of joined living, especially regarding chastity, and with it the danger of ritual contamination, for example by eating with me. My presence obviously caused a feeling of menace with them, and they openly voiced their worries. Actually, the question asked, usually in English "are you *really* always vegetarian?" conveyed much more than just worries about my diet. Ironically, the sceptic pilgrims were faced with a similar problem as myself. There were in fact many indicators that the pilgrims (including married couples) actually followed the ideal of abstinence, for instance by accommodating family members of the opposite sex in separate rooms, and by formally demonstrating temporary celibacy while sleeping on the floor (*bhumi santhari*). However, especially the latter was not practised by all pilgrims and I occasionally met couples who spent the night alone in one room. Therefore, I would have liked to check out whether there were conditions justifying sex during pilgrimage. Much to my regret, there was no way for me to find out without myself breaking the vow of chastity as it implies the prohibition to even talk about sexuality. In the same way, the sceptical pilgrims could not seriously ask me to the face: "Do you have sex while you are in Palitana?", without bearing the harmful consequences to the spiritual success of their pilgrimages.

Some of the sceptical pilgrims avoided contact with me if I was unable to disperse their unvoiced doubts. Even though this had no serious impact on my research as there were enough well-disposed pilgrims willing to help me, the latent scepticism regarding my "chastity" resulted in a strong sense of being continuously and thoroughly observed. First of all, this was frustrating as I felt my attempts to adapt were not appreciated, and I remained a "foreign body". Furthermore, it was a nuisance to find many sceptic pilgrims taking their first opportunity to put me through their paces and to check me out personally by indirect questions. To make matters worse, there was the exceptional context of pilgrimage. Usually, a cultural anthropologist is likely to leave this basic question-and-answer-game behind after a couple of weeks living and participating in daily activities. However, it was necessary to make numerous new contacts as part of my daily work. Especially during the high season for pilgrimage lasting from November through March, pilgrims would stay in Palitana only for a few days. So, the guests in the pilgrims' hostels, too, were changing almost daily, and I often had to stand this testing of my person a couple of times a day, leaving me with the sensation of being stuck in a time warp, similar to the meteorologist Phil Connors in the movie "Groundhog Day": only if I had managed to perfectly master the same situation in a moral sense each and every time I would have been able to draw closer to my long-desired goal of being able to have informative conversations with pilgrims about their pilgrimages.

By and by, however, I learnt that being observed constantly offered the great chance to regularly prove my adaptability, and to disperse the scepticism by means of culture-specific trust-building measures. While my attempts towards this end were successful at times, I was not doing so well on other occasions. Generally, it appeared right to me to not only answer questions patiently, but to also exhibit my correct behaviour as much as possible in order to prove I was following the rules. This, of course, was possible only indirectly as far as chastity was concerned: after all, chastity is defined by abstinence from intimacy, which in the Indian context would not be noticeable in public anyway.

Public Vegetarianism and Public Celibacy

Very early during my fieldwork in Palitana, I had decided that only by becoming one of the pilgrims myself I would be able to raise the data which should form the groundwork of my research. This implied to keep to the rules of conduct as fixed during pilgrimage, including vegetarianism, not eating during the night, the regularly partaking in ritual penances and celibacy. In order to deliberately counteract the general dietary scepticism toward "Westerners", I made it a point to openly display my eating habits. Compared to other aspects of daily conduct this was quite an easy task: I just had all meals together with other pilgrims in the hostel's dining room (later also in other pilgrims' hostels), and only within the permitted times, i.e. after sunrise and before sunset. In addition, I would show Motilalbhai[13]—often in the presence of the other guests at the hostel—the contents of my shopping bags each time I had been at the bazaar, so as to demonstrate that they did not contain any impure items, but only permitted fruit, such as bananas. In the few cases, he found something prohibited—once there was a loaf of toast, and another time there was an aubergine—he just took them out and handed it to the non-Jain maids, who were allowed to eat them.

I was rewarded for this intentional behaviour with additional appreciation by many pilgrims and Jains living in Palitana (as well as a satisfied nod from Motilalbhai). If not before, shared vegetarian meals proved to the "well-wishers" my trustworthiness, and they welcomed me warmly into their community. Clearly, however, this group of "well-wishers" almost exclusively consisted of individuals who might take a certain risk ritually by trusting me and keeping contact with me, but not much of a risk in social respect. This group included a large number of pilgrims whom I had either met in my hostel, or during our ascent to the temple city on the top of Shatrunjaya. As the pilgrims themselves were away from home for some time, and thus also from their daily context of a mostly urban neighbourhood, misjudgement of my person would have hardly had any consequences for their lives at home. This group of pilgrims consisted of any kind of people, ranging from very young to very old, married, unmarried, widowed and celibate. However, among the Jains living in Palitana permanently or at least for an extended period only those considered marginalised or even peculiar kept contact with me during the entire time of my field research. Remarkably, nearly all members of this group of friends and acquaintances were living an institutionalised or a habitual life of celibacy, thereby leaving their own reputation unquestioned: Bina, my best friend in Palitana, was an unmarried woman in her mid 40s, who at our very first meeting told me she had taken a public vow of celibacy. We regularly met in her little house which she only reluctantly left for extended periods of time in order to nurse her father who was terminally ill (and who had come from Jamnagar to Palitana, where he wanted to die). She was also a lay follower of a group of six female ascetics within the order of Tapa Gaccha (Ramcandrasuri Samuday). As their leader was too weak to go on the prescribed itineraries this group of nuns (*sadhvis*) was staying in Palitana during the entire time I was there to do research. Mina also initiated a long lasting relation between this group of *sadhvis* and myself. Over the months, a growing friendship developed between me and three of the younger ascetics in this group, women of approximately the same age as myself, around 30. I was allowed to see them in their temporary residences at any time day or night. This relationship was exemplary for other short acquaintances with female ascetics of the same and other orders who in a similar way welcomed me warmly. Besides them, I had another beneficial contact with two unmarried men in their 60s, whose family treasure enabled them to do unsalaried work for various pilgrim organisations. Arvindbhai and Hasmukhbhai were the only men allowed by Motilalbhai to visit me in my room for interviews. This fact led me to the conclusion that they must be "harmless". They would also escort me in public, and by their role as grandfatherly friends and "protectors" they granted me a glance into the male world on occasions. They also brought me in contact with Jain families living in Palitana, including the family of a retired and liberal high-school teacher, consisting of himself and his wife (who was in her late 50s) and their two unmarried children in their 20s (son and daughter). Apart from this family however, it was difficult to make contact with families and married couples. This kind of acquaintances might have been easier to establish had my husband been there with me. There was, however, a friendly relationship with a couple based in Pune (Maharashtra), aged around 30. Both of them had taken the vow of celibacy together—after the birth of their son five years ago.

The three of them were staying in Palitana for extended periods of time while I was in Palitana.

These and other well-disposed individuals who had already been convinced of my benevolent intentions often remarked at our very first appointment that besides my vegetarian diet I was "even" appropriately dressed. To my relief, all these well-wishers also welcomed that I was riding my bike when I had to get somewhere on my own, as this kind of transport made it difficult for "trouble makers" to molest me. Usually, however, especially during pilgrims' processions and meetings, there were immediately several women who would take me into their midst in such a way that an accidental meeting with a man would have been impossible.

Regarding my sexual virtue, these "well-wishers" were content to conclude that in accordance with my clothing and diet, my sexual behaviour, too, would be in agreement with the pilgrims' code of conduct, and that I was celibate during the absence of my husband. The conceptual interrelation between vegetarianism and sexual abstinence helped me enormously in this respect. It was especially my "public" vegetarianism that was considered a formative value by these pilgrims, and it was also seen as an indicator of my sexual abstinence which they were not able to monitor as such. For this reason, I was welcomed into the group of the other celibates, even if this was not verbalised.

The strong association of my person with the status of a celibate pilgrim became especially obvious when my husband whom I had not seen for five months announced his visit to Palitana. Even though my new friends were keen to see my "Mister", as none of them had met him at my arrival, one of the older female ascetics took me aside one evening and counselled me towards a very good opportunity for another display of my chastity. She suggested I had better not meet my husband in Palitana, as after such a long time of separation the mere sight of him might trigger feelings and thoughts of a passionate kind in myself. Though these feelings were otherwise legitimate for a married woman towards her husband, they would certainly be an obstacle (*antaray*) for my spiritual progress, and were therefore unwelcome in a sacred place like Palitana and during my current project on the sacred mountain. Following her advice, I first met my husband in nearby Bhavnagar. When I came back to Palitana, the same ascetic praised me saying I had proved my earnest striving to practice the rules (*niyam*) of the Jain pilgrims.

Even though the well-wishers appreciated my displayed virtue they were constantly concerned about me, providing me regularly with more or less discrete advice in order to complement my "safety", which I myself would *de facto* call my chaste habitus. On the one hand there were general recommendations like the one that I should always return to "my" hostel before darkness (or to be escorted home by a trustworthy person), that I should keep the door to my room firmly closed while being alone, and that I should not let any men come inside (which would have been impossible anyway, due to Motilalbhai's supervision); I should address men only if unavoidable, if at all possible, and when doing so never look them into the eyes. Talking to men, I should never speak out loud, and leave to the man the task of promoting the conversation.

On the other hand, I was on occasions provided with matter of fact advice which surprised me by its bluntness judged by my own "Western" standards. The central issue of this forthright advice addressed that part of female sexuality which in its conception differs most of all from "Western" concepts: menstruation.

Public Menstruation

In spite of being acquainted with the literature on the concepts of menstruation based on the Jain doctrine, I was still surprised to see how ever-present they were in the daily life of my female friends and acquaintances in Palitana. According to those concepts, the monthly bleeding is considered deeply polluting in a ritual respect.[14] The ritual impurity of a menstruating woman is not only caused by the abominable substance, namely the menstrual blood, but also by the emotional involvement of the menstruating woman. Menstruation is not just considered an involuntary process, but the result of conscious or unconscious sexual desires comparable to male ejaculation during sleep. Consequently, menstruation is seen as direct proof of a woman not being free of sexual desires. This awareness causes shame in every woman, but also fear of sexual assault both of which constantly latently govern their general emotions. Furthermore, due to menstrual blood loss, every woman destroys a huge number of minimal creatures living as parasites in every human or animal body. Owing to this offence against the superior principle of non-violence, every woman is prone to additional negative karmic influences, causing her emotions to be unstable. Menstrual bleeding is thus considered accountable for women's general tendency towards emotional outbreaks and other negative expressions of uncontrolled passions such as fearfulness and mental restlessness.

This kind of substantial and emotional defilement prevents a woman from participating in religious actions during this time of her cycle, and even from mentally reflecting on spiritual issues. Consequently, all menstruating women are strictly forbidden to visit a temple, touch or see sacred objects, or even recite religious texts. For the same reason, menstruating women by all means have to stay away from the sacred mountain Shatrunjaya, e.g. they are strictly suspended from pilgrimage. A prohibition sign in English even informs female tourists about this necessity.[15]

Only very few women are able to suppress menstruation (and with it all aspects of their sexuality) by rigorous fasting, thus relieving themselves at least temporarily from this burden. Without menstruating for a longer period they are able to devote themselves to their own spiritual progress without monthly interruptions. In the same way, not suffering the defilement of monthly bleeding, girls who have not yet menstruated and post-menopausal women are considered to have much greater potential for spiritual progress.[16]

While in the urban context, these concepts only prevent Jain women from going to the temple during their menstruation. Consequently in the beginning of my fieldwork, I only had a vague idea about the far-reaching consequences of these concepts for female pilgrims, and thus also for my research in Palitana. In this context, too, it was the female ascetics who pointed out the necessities. As soon as I would enter the living quarters of female ascetics, I was reminded on an almost daily basis who was menstruating at the moment and therefore was not to be greeted referentially (as this act would have involved touching the nun's feet). Doing so the female ascetics effectively protected me from contamination which is spread by any menstruating woman, including nuns, and for which there is only one remedy: to take an elaborate ritual bath, including washing and changing all clothes. Similarly, all menstruating lay women openly announced their own impure state, warning me not to draw too close. All of them were very conscientiously concerned not to touch any other person by chance during their menstruation. Even all profane utensils touched by a menstruating woman including not only her underwear but also her upper clothing and crockery, have to be thoroughly cleaned after her menstruation is over and are kept in a separated place afterwards.[17]

These interrelations directed my conversation towards menstruation rules at the very beginning of my research, as the female ascetics and other female pilgrims repeatedly discussed them at length. At first they did so because they correctly realised that I was not familiar with them, and later quite a few new acquaintances repeated the instructions because they were of the opinion that a woman from the "West" just could not be familiar with them. On the one hand, they wanted to make sure that I should not be a source of ritual hazard. Therefore, I realised from the beginning that violating the rules of menstruation could lead to my exclusion from the pilgrims' community at any time, because I would only be admitted to the rituals if I closely followed the prescribed seclusion and avoidance. On the other hand, at least the well-wishers were also concerned to protect me from unpleasant consequences of potential violations of the rules. According to the Jain concepts, violating the menstruation rules would have negative consequences for my *karma* in the long-term. In order to avoid these, several female pilgrims who unexpectedly got their period during her sojourn on the sacred mountain were advised to fast for three days in a row without drinking any water in order to compensate for the adverse consequences they would otherwise suffer regarding their *karma* as they had contaminated the sacred mountain. Most of the pilgrims were convinced that the woman concerned might otherwise suffer from infertility or other gynaecological diseases, or her conjugal relationship might seriously be impaired. In the case of unmarried women, they might remain unmarried for the rest of their lives.

To be honest, I found these concepts and regulations irritating at first as they were obviously contradicting all emancipated ideas. Nevertheless, I did not want to waste precious time and energy only to face the predictable consequences of my refusal to comply. So in the second month of my research, I followed the example of the other female pilgrims, openly displaying my three-day menstrual seclusion. How else could I prove that I was familiar with these rules? Consequently, I stayed in my room for the first three days of my period (to be exact: for the first 72 hours) and ate my meals on my own only there.

On the very first morning, I would inform one of the servant girls that I would not have my meals in the dining room "for three days", but would be eating on my own in my room. Consequently, all the guests of the hostel knew what was going on. The tray with my meals would be left outside my door on the floor as no one working in the kitchen dared entering my room. During this period, I hardly ever left my room, but more or less "enjoyed" a three days' break every month. As I had to stay away from all sacred places and objects, not only physically but also mentally, the female ascetics advised me to also stop working during this time, as the topic of my research was the sacred mountain. To be on the safe side, I had rather not even use my notebook where all the data were stored. Therefore, I could not do much more than look out of my window (but not facing the sacred mountain, or the pilgrims' processions!), sleep, or write letters home to Germany. The latter, strictly seen, might also be considered an offence according to the pilgrims' standard, as the individuals receiving these letters would be contaminated. By and by, however, the pilgrims accepted my explanation that the recipients of these letters would not mind, as on the long distance the letters had to travel, they would "lose" their contamination.[18]

Interestingly, all the women with whom I was in close contact over an extended period of time noticed the days on which I had menstruated. They were pointing out to me immediately who else was at the same time affected by the same "hindrance" (*antaray*)[19]—the usual circumscription for the menstruation period in Gujarati. I thus found myself integrated in a supportive network: first, women who were not menstruating at the same time as myself would come to my hostel and provide me with fruits, sweets and sanitary articles—without touching me, of course. Second, other women who also had "it" came, and we would talk for hours as a pastime; we would even eat sweets together from a plate which I kept separate from my other crockery. So to my relief I was not fully banned to doing nothing, and was almost automatically supplied with interesting data. It was on one of these occasions that someone explained to me in detail the proper way of how to dispose of the lost menstrual blood[20], and how to clean clothing from ritual contamination.[21]

Seventy two hours later, i.e. usually on the morning of the fourth day, I would take an extended bath and ostentatiously hang up to dry the things I had been wearing for the last three days. I also never missed roaming around in the hostel's yard and talking to other pilgrims with my hair still damp, so as to show that I had indeed washed it—as washing one's hair is an important aspect of the ritual bath.[22] After my hair was fully dried I also paid a visit to the hostel's kitchen in order to show that I was now ritually pure and thus touchable again. After this period of three days, visiting the sacred mountain Shatrunjaya would have been allowed as well: like the other female pilgrims, however, I would wait for another four days before participating in those temple rituals which generally include direct contact with images of the fordmakers (*tirthankara*), the Jains' holiest beings.

The counsel and support of my well-disposed friends concerning menstruation also made me aware of the fact that this intimate process was much more exposed to public control than I would have expected in a context where sexual issues are usually taboo. While the practice of menstrual seclusion appeared somewhat strange but still quite easily acceptable to me, the real shock came when one late afternoon during the third month of my field research, I met a bunch of rather sceptical pilgrims. One man aged around 30, who had come in the company of his wife, two sons in pre-school age, and his parents, greeted me politely albeit seriously, introduced himself as Sāmit from Vadodara, and then bombarded me in English language with the usual questions I had already become familiar with (What's your name? What are you doing here? Are you vegetarian?·Are you married?). It was burdensome for me to patiently answer even Samit's general questions, as I had had a tiring day returning from the temple city on the mountaintop, and all I wanted was to go to my room and sort through my notes while the impressions were still fresh. Finally, after reassuring Samit that I had indeed "always" been a vegetarian, he abruptly came right to the point: "Yes, but, well… do you know about the menstruation rules?" This upfront question indeed struck me as extremely impolite; and rightly so—as I could hardly imagine a female Gujarati pilgrim having to explain herself in such a way to a male stranger. For a moment, I had to turn aside and take a deep breath. To my relief, my spontaneous reaction later proved to be culturally quite acceptable. Instead of answering his question, I told the "inquisitor" he was very impolite, and would he please ask the manager Motilalbhai for further information. Then I left him standing there. When later whispering with one of the older female pilgrims about the event (with Samit watching), she padded my hand reassuringly and told me I had done the right thing, and I had nothing to fear. Afterwards, the "inquisitor" Samit even came over to me personally and formally apologised for his outspoken bluntness, claiming he had not intended to hurt my feelings.[23] My sensitivity had obviously taken him by surprise. I had stood another test, though it would not be the last one.

Intricate Encounters with Male Ascetics

As a result of the strict segregation of sexes, I spent long periods of my research in groups of females only. It was especially complicated to make contacts with male ascetics. Due to their life-long vow of celibacy they are extremely conscious regarding a possible contamination by women, or rather by female sexuality. However, after I had convincingly displayed myself as a strict vegetarian and as being familiar with the menstruation rules, I was also admitted to the proximity of male ascetics. These meetings, were even pushed by female ascetics, because male ascetics were considered authorities in spiritual matters, including questions regarding my subject of study, the pilgrimagc to the sacred mountain. Consequently, male ascetics were regarded most appropriate for answering all those of my questions concerning pilgrimage which no-one else had been able to answer to my satisfaction. In order to prepare me for my first meetings, the female ascetics taught me the formal ritual of greeting the male ascetics. This ritual of *guru vandana* is considered to be essential for approaching the ascetic in an appropriate manner. As this expression of reverence also includes a ritual prostration (at a decent distance) a clear hierarchy is established, and an explicit submission under the ascetic authority is demonstrated.

Remarkably, my well-intentioned friends always arranged meetings with pronouncedly charismatic ascetics of my own age who were considered especially educated and who had "taken over the mantle" from their ascetic leaders, the *Acaryas*. The dignified *Acaryas* in turn were content to express their benevolence at my audiences, and to bless me. The suitability of the younger ascetics was on the one hand based on the fact that they spoke English, which facilitated communication. On the other hand, older ascetics holding important offices were too busy within their orders to answer my beginner's questions. Looking back however, it appears obvious that these meetings were following a pre-set cultural pattern, and at the same time served as a test of chastity for everyone involved.

During my 16 months of field research, I met four male ascetics, aged between 38 and 42, who were considered hopeful up-and-coming *Acaryas*.[24] All of these meetings went on for several weeks, and usually followed a similar dramaturgy: After a female ascetic or a male lay person had arranged the first meeting, I would visit my "teacher" in his living quarters at the appointed time, always escorted by another person—never alone. After performing the greeting ritual and after having received his blessing, I would place a piece of paper on the floor in front of him on which I had written all my pre-formulated questions. Then I would withdraw and take a seat at a certain distance. This measure of carefulness was necessary as male ascetics not only have to avoid physical contact with females, but must also not touch any item at the same time as a woman or girl. If they fail to follow this measure, their penance will be a full day of fasting without drinking. Often, the circumstances of these meetings were so tiring for both parties that especially during the first meetings I did not really get any information from the ascetics. While our focus was fully taken-up by following the rules of avoidance, I would only receive standardised answers, while I was looking down modestly. These meetings would always take place under the close observation of other ascetics. Also, there were mostly some other lay pilgrims waiting for their audience. Often, these were small groups of very attractive young women who had chosen this particular charismatic ascetic as their personal "Guruji" and would approach him with almost quixotic but shy devotion, while he in turn would treat them with a pronounced matter-of-factly demeanour. In three cases, I witnessed the decisive development of young women who under the influence of a young male ascetic decided to become ascetics themselves, and who consequently took the vow of life-long celibacy.

Finally, after I had endured a fourth or fifth formally immaculate meeting, a meaningful conversation would ensue in all cases. Mostly, the ascetic himself would also take the opportunity to question me about the "customs" in my own home country. Usually with increasing intercommunication, the meetings became more and more beneficial for the research task, as the ascetic opened-up. Surprisingly, however, each of these lively discussions were followed by a clear withdrawal at the following arranged meeting, when I would be publicly greeted rather briefly by a different ascetic, and then refused an audience on the grounds of various excuses: either the ascetic in question was "busy" doing other things, or he was weakened from fasting and unable to talk. In one case, he had even made a vow of several days of silence.

At first, I got the clear impression of being held at arms' length, possibly after unwittingly having trespassed a rule at the previous meeting. Only after the same sequence had been repeated for several times and with at least four male ascetics, I finally realised that this withdrawal was orchestrated in order to establish a clear boundary for the ascetic who had to prove his unswerving chastity. There were, in fact, rumours during my time of research about younger ascetics between 25 and 35 who had drawn too close emotionally to young women in similar settings, and who after that had to submit themselves to rigorous vows of fasting. Others even left the order and opted for marriage. Even though in my own perception no such situation arose that I myself might have considered "dangerous" for overstepping a vow of chastity, the ascetics concerned staged their rejection as a public statement of his unswerving steadfastness. As I was received kindly on the visits thereafter and my questions were taken seriously and answered politely, I felt right to conclude that there was indeed no serious problem and I was not considered dangerous for the respective ascetic.

Conclusion

In summary, during my field research in the Jain pilgrim town of Palitana, I realised that the issue of sexuality is unusually often discussed in order to ascertain its very opposite, namely chastity. These discussions include rules for the time of menstruation, as this physical process is considered an active aspect of female sexuality. Moreover, especially extramarital sexuality was portrayed as an extreme counterpart to chastity. This kind of opposition is comparable to the enhancement of a strict vegetarian diet by regular references to the repulsiveness of eating meat. My presence reinforced this polarity in a double way: Firstly, I was a newcomer whom the well-disposed friends and informants were keen to introduce to the rules of communal living among the pilgrims. Therefore, it was required to address the issue of sexuality at least indirectly, while it is generally considered strictly taboo. Secondly, the less well-disposed individuals perceived my coming from a "Western" country as a hazard, as this part of the globe is associated with unrestrained sexuality. Therefore, the sceptics felt it sometimes necessary to allude to sexuality in more drastic ways than they would have done otherwise. At the same time, I contributed my own sensitivity regarding this issue, as during earlier stays in India, I had learnt that a woman has to live with the daily possibility of being sexually molested and can only protect herself by using cultural signals which are understood. These signals gradually became matter-of-fact behaviour during my fieldwork in Palitana, albeit in the beginning I was frequently annoyed by the necessity to consciously act them out. With this in mind, I would like to conclude, adding the observation that the constantly required staging of chastity for the 16 months of my field research had such a strong impact on my daily conduct that it surfaced even after returning home to Berlin. So, firmly had I internalised the appropriate ways for the Jain context that I finally felt it was inappropriate to sit beside males in the Berlin underground. Also, several male acquaintances would ask me whether I was annoyed with them, as I avoided their eye-contact!

Notes

1. Flügel 2006 / Conquering the Self, *Ahimsa Times,* 2009, No. 108, online Version: http://www.jainsamaj.org/magazines/ahimsatimesshow.php?id=161
2. Approximately 8.5 million people in India are Jains, at least according to the last census (Distribution of Population by Religions *Drop-in-Article on Census—No.4*). http://censusindia.gov.in/Ad_Campaign/drop_in_articles/04-Distribution_by_Religion.pdf, 03.06.2012 However, some representatives of the Jain-community claim, that the Jains are underrepresented in these statistics and they estimate the actual number of Jains as large as 35 million (Parshvanath, 2010).
3. Luithle-Hardenberg, 2011.
4. From the perspective of the sanctum or of a preaching ascetic, the men are always sitting or standing on the "pure" right side or at the front, while the ladies are to the left, or behind the men.
5. This vague category includes countries located to the West of India, as well as to the East: Europe, USA, and Australia.
6. Consequently, during pilgrimage the clothing is usually different from everyday dress, especially in the case of younger pilgrims below the age of 30. Most Jains dress in their residential urban places according to the Indian variation of "globalised" fashion: men are wearing Jeans and T-Shirt or shirt and trousers, while women are wearing Jeans and T-Shirt or fashionable tightly cut leg wear combined with a close-fitting dress, an outfit which hardly resembles the traditional *salvar kamis* (see below). Married women, too, do usually not wear a *sari* for everyday life nowadays.
7. Only girls who have not yet reached puberty may wear short dresses or trousers. Anyone else who does not follow this basic dress code is called to order by other pilgrims in Palitana. Even men prefer a white *kesh dhoti* for pilgrimage (two cloths, one of which is wrapped around the hips and between the legs, while the other covers the upper body), or a white or beige coloured *salvar kurta*, which is a shirt reaching down to one's knees with a stand-up collar and worn above trousers, often in combination with a sleeveless waist.
8. Fortunately for myself, the *salvar kamis* has become acceptable even for Hindu and Jain ritual contexts especially during the recent decades, as the *sari* is difficult to wear for the unpractised. Anne Grodzins Gold (1988:13) however, describes that for her own field research situation in Rajasthan, she could not wear a *salvar kamis* on a daily basis as this outfit was still clearly associated with Muslim habitus in the 1970s, and wearing it regularly might have had unfavourably affected her work on Hindu pilgrimage.
9. In each case none of the attackers had expected my dauntless defence by which I was able to drive the intruders away.
10. This ideal spiritual partnership is not limited to the Jain community, but Hindu traditions also have many examples of it, e.g. Ramakrishna and Sarada Devi.
11. This as well as other personal names are changed in order to make the data anonymous.
12. It is questionable, whether these oppositions are *really* as characteristic for the

two different cultures ("Western" and Indian) as usually depicted by my informants, but this issue has to be discussed elsewhere.

13. This as well as other personal names are changed in order to guarantee my friends' anonymity.
14. Cp. Jaini, 1991: 13-14.
15. The strong inhibitions imposed on a menstruating woman render menstruation a significant and often problematic issue for any female pilgrim. During my research in Palitana, it often happened that to their great disappointment, women were unable to participate in certain religious events as they were menstruating. In order to guarantee their participation in a long planned pilgrimage or in other important rituals, many female pilgrims take hormones in order to postpone their menstruation.
16. Following the same logic, most female ascetics are incapable of reading the longer sacred texts of the Jain Canon, as their study has to be performed without interruption. One month is not enough to study the longer texts of the Canon.
17. In case of minor violations of this rule of avoidance, for instance the case of touching an item which had before been touched by the menstruating woman, it may be enough to touch gold (e.g. ornaments) and recite a *mantra* as a rectification.
18. During the period of my fieldwork, it was not possible yet to establish a permanent access to the internet. It is an interesting question if an e-mail, written during the menstruation, would be considered as contaminating.
19. The same term is used for contaminated food, cp. Cort, 2001:224.
20. One may, for instance, carefully wash the menstrual pads and pour the water in a spot where no-one steps on. Never, however, should the water be poured down the drain. Another option is to burn them – which, however, is difficult to do in town. Pads that are carelessly thrown in the garbage pose a special risk as in India the garbage is often left in the road for weeks. One lay person explained that when the protecting spirit of a certain area (*kshetra pala*) or a snake god (*naga deva*) noticed the menstrual blood, he would curse the woman and punish her by life-long infertility and other gynaecological diseases for contaminating his land. The danger is the greater the holier the place is, as many protecting gods are accumulated there.
21. The clothing has to be washed during the woman's own ritual bath; but not until it has completely dried is it considered "cleansed".
22. For hair as a metaphor of sexuality, see Hershman, 1974; Obeyesekere, 1981; Pfeffer, 1997.
23. Pilgrims are concerned not to let any friction arise among themselves, as this would have negative consequences for their *karma* and would impair the spiritual success of their pilgrimage.
24. While usually anthropological literature on the Jains mentions the ascetics' actual names and do not give them a pseudonym, I will make no allusions to the actual person in consideration of the touchy subject of this chapter.

References

Flügel, Peter, 2006. "Demographic Trends in Jaina Monasticism" (pp. 312-398) in Flügel, Peter (ed.), *Studies in Jaina History and Culture: Disputes and Dialogues.* London and New York: Routledge (Taylor & Francis Group).

Gold, Ann Grodzins, 1988. *Fruitful Journeys: The Ways of Rajasthani Pilgrims*, Berkeley: University of California Press.

Hershman, Paul, 1974. "Hair, Sex and Dirt", *Man*, 9(1): 174-189.

Jaini, Padmanabh S., 1991. *Gender and Salvation: Jaina Debates on the Spiritual Liberation of Women*, Berkeley/Los Angeles/London: University of California Press.

Luithle-Hardenberg, Andrea, 2011. *Die Reise zum Ursprung. Die Pilgerschaft der Shvetambara-Jaina zum Berg Shatrunjaya in Gujarat, Indien*, München: Manya.

Obeyesekere, Gananath, 1981. *Medusa's Hair. An Essay on Personal Symbols and Religious Experience*, Chicago/London: University of Chicago Press.

Parshwanath, H.A., 2010. Jain Census, in: *Jain Voice*, February 2010, http://www.jainheritagecentres.com/News/Jaina_Voice/Feb-2010/Editorial.htm, 11.06.2012.

Pfeffer, Georg, 1997. "Die Haardebatte: Gender, Glatzen und Gewalt der Bondo," *Zeitschrift für Ethnologie*, 122: 183-208.

THIRTEEN

NARRATIONS OF COMMITMENT: FRIENDS IN THE FIELD

EVA REICHEL

Introduction

This chapter is intended to shed light on a few crucial and sensitive moments in December 2005/January 2006 when I was in search of a suitable field site to do fieldwork among the Ho, a tribal community in Central Eastern India. Close Indian friends from Delhi, educated university people who have been extensively travelling in India and the world could not offer any assistance as they were unaware of an *adivasi* population of around one hundred million people in that part of their country and had not heard of Ho, Santal, Munda, Kharia and Oraon. I will focus here on some of those who due to their commitment and local knowledge contributed to making the project of fieldwork in that early stage materialize. They paved the way for us[1] to spot 'the field', to enter it and eventually settle down in a concrete house. Our collaboration was such that I keep thinking of them as my "friends in the field". As a consequence, the narrations here are written from a more personal angle and do not attempt to hide a certain subjective bias.

Paving the Way into the Field

The first of the three persons to mention in this context is Deepak Behera, then from the Department of Anthropology at Sambalpur University,

Orissa, now Vice Chancellor at Berhampur University, Odisha. Our dependence on his assistance in search of a suitable field site was considerable, and it was utterly one-sided, for we had nothing to offer but ignorance, passionate curiosity and determination. All we knew, though, was where we did not want to go and that was anywhere close to or within the christianized stronghold in the larger Chaibasa area in the state of Jharkhand.[2] Deepak was the only contact we had in the region at that time, but the district of Sambalpur was not Ho country—if there was anything like Ho country at all—and not even close to it. Much was at stake for us when we decided to address him, since on top of there being no alternative of which we were aware of Deepak had made it very clear that his daily duties would not allow him to spend more than a day to help us make an informed decision.

In a busy week, on a busy day, he suggested to meet at his private place in the town of Sambalpur where we were allowed to browse through his rich library. Together we consulted maps, discussed the project of doing fieldwork among Ho people and brainstormed ideas how best to locate *Ho disum* (the country of the Ho) and a suitable field site, while his wife Rita was preparing a lovely meal for all of us. At that time, in 2006, there were only two internet entries on the Ho, as far as I recollect, so little orientation was to be gained from there. One of the two entries concerned the Koel-Karo dam project, the ecological catastrophe to be expected from it and international protests against it, the other one was about radio-active nuclear waste being dumped into the open fields in East Singhbhum/Jharkhand causing drinking water to become polluted and babies to be born deformed by parents left uninformed about the dangers by disinterested companies and a state indifferent towards tribal people's well-being. Also, Ho people though constituting a population of more than one million, did not figure at all in the Census of India for Odisha then and they still do not to this day. So, the Census of India carried through once every decade, also failed to be a source of orientation. Looking back in 2016 at the beginnings of our endeavour 10 years ago and the fieldwork 'completed' in the meantime, we realize how much we drew from Deepak's expertise. Without being aware of it at the time, we were in the middle of doing fieldwork—as yet from outside the field. Officially Odisha's Ho tribal population appeared to be a non-existent category, but, of course, Deepak knew better, as he had done fieldwork among a tribal community of middle India, the Kisan, himself. Eventually, it was Deepak who had the idea to get in touch with P., a former student of his living in the proximity of what would later become the research area. After enquiries into the composition of the tribal population in the area, especially about a larger Ho population there, Deepak obliged P. on the phone to assist us in finding a proper field site. I was quite impressed by Deepak's far-reaching authority. Perhaps this was my first encounter with the principle of seniority and its very practical consequences.

P. lives in R., a town in district Mayurbhanj, Odisha as a lecturer of anthropology at a college there. The textbooks that he uses in his anthropology classes focus on aspects of physical anthropology and methods of how to collect data in the field. In 2005, he had a Hero bike and lived in a small house, looking very much like an IB, a governmental inspection bungalow and situated on the campus of the school where his wife worked as a teacher. In 2012, he had moved into a two-storeyed, airy *pakka* house whose construction was not yet completed. In 2016, P. had moved-up and rented out the basement. We were proudly shown on the top floor first the toilet facilities and afterwards a carefully decorated and meticulously clean separate room full of paraphernalia and Hindu deities to protect P., his wife and their two children. In front of the house, there was now a well-kept garden, his Hero bike, a Tata car and a tall fence.

P. is a non-tribal person. He stays away from the tribal area as much as he can. But he knows about the region and its people, as the world of the tribals is part of his professional curriculum, as many of his students have a tribal background and as his brother-in-law works at the local school in M. as a teacher. The villagers of M. treated P. with respect and cautious reservation, and he addressed them with an air of polite distance and authority, but on par with them. He clearly came from outside, but did not behave and speak like a *diku* (foreigner) although he conversed with them in Odiya, his mother-tongue, and one of the meanings of *diku* is "to speak Hindi or Odiya". For many of the villagers, we learnt later, it is an ideological barrier rather than a technical problem to switch from their indigenous languages Ho and Santali to Hindi or Odiya as many tribals are bi-or multilingual. P., in the course of our fieldwork, would later often announce to come and visit us, but in fact he never came—only once to attend the last of our *saki* (ritual friendship; namesake) ceremonies. Sitting on one of the two chairs of the house he politely, but determined avoided the meat, the water and the rice beer that he was offered. On the other hand, he bitterly complained about our not visiting him regularly in R. Towards others, however, who did not know better, he claimed that we would stay overnight at his home, whenever we were in R. It seemed that being acquainted with us was about to transform into some kind of symbolic capital.

P. was loyal to Deepak, his teacher. He took us around in a hired car-*cum*-driver (he absolutely refused the degradation in status by getting on a bicycle as we would have preferred), showed us the vicinity, enquired about empty houses and talked to people without any patronizing note in his voice. This surely invited people's cooperation. He explained to them our project and eventually found us a house in a village at the foot of *Parwa Buru*, a holy mountain to the villagers in that area. The house was right in the centre of the village. In front of it was one of the two community wells which was a busy site especially early in the mornings and again towards the evening, while in the day time it was used by elderly people who took their bath there. Plenty opportunities and plenty people waiting to communicate with us—or so we thought. The *diuri* (ritual guide) had his residence right opposite our front door. We could observe agricultural activities inside his huge courtyard or rituals starting off from there first hand, when those who had promised to inform us in time, continuously 'forgot' to do so. The information was given that 80 per cent of the population were Ho, 20 per cent Santal. This sounded like the ideal research site, but needed to be corrected later, when we found that there are no Santal at all in that particular village, a considerable number of diverse servicing castes, *Gau* (cowherder) households and just over 50 per cent Ho, but Ho is the dominant language spoken also by those who are non-Ho just as our neighbours. But all of that was not P.'s responsibility. As correct census figures have never been published for that region, nobody could have a detailed knowledge of the situation on the ground. It was up to us to explore it, if we considered it part of our fieldwork which we did, but which was also highly problematic. P. had completed his job and left. The only way for us of giving back a little was giving a lecture at P.'s college which he arranged for his students. P. had provided us with a place to stay, even if there were holes in the walls and parts of the roof missing. It was a *diku* building for *diku* people like us, but in a Ho environment. P. had also provided us with a young assistant, S.

As P. was a former student of Deepak's, S. was P.'s former student. P. had initially introduced to us two young students of his who were prepared to work for us as assistants, a girl and a boy, both very pleasant youngsters, both Santal. Should we ask the girl or the boy or both?

When I decided on the girl to introduce me into the female universe of the Ho, she all of a sudden was no more available. Explanations were not given. I kept waiting, insisting, but to no avail. She was gone for good. Male conspiracy? P. shrugged his shoulders, S. would not comment. I was grumbling, but we agreed on working with S. In the discussions concerning payment and working conditions P. did most of the talking, while S. contributed his cheerful mood and nodded his head. He seemed too excited, we thought, to join in the talk in English. P. and S. were quite unhappy that they could not talk us into providing bikes for all of us and bought two bicycles instead. This construction taught us a lesson in terms of status distinctions and classification: while I was safe on my lady-bicycle, because S. would refuse to use it at all, S. would also refuse to sit at the back of the bicycle with my husband riding it. However, he minded less riding the bicycle with my husband at the back, but he was not really strong enough for that. His favourite option was to take the bicycle, ride it himself and forget about us. We became his first employers.

S. came from Bhubaneswar where he had been in touch with anthropologists from abroad, he said. Later he would confide in us that it was there where he had experienced discrimination because of his tribal background. He stayed together with us in the one-room IB with attached tiny kitchen for the first month. He was supposed to guarantee our linguistic and gustatory survival in the field the latter of which worked out really fine.

S. was a charming, self-confident and polite young Santal, a good dancer and a good cook and very proud of both. He was impressed by how different and more sophisticated Ho dances were. It had been his suggestion to be both our assistant and our cook. Of course, this could not work out and did not work out, but S. was so confident that we gave it a try. I hoped that by accompanying him to the markets and gardens I would learn about the region and its horticulture, meet people, find out about 'events' and get into the language with his assistance. But this kind of cooperation never happened. This was not part of fieldwork in his understanding and hence not his job. A young man with a bachelor degree in anthropology he knew what fieldwork was about: "data collecting", filling in questionnaires, doing a census, and our approach of entering the field must have been deeply irritating for him and a complete waste of time. So instead of taking us to 'the field' he used to vanish all by himself with one of our bicycles and often came back only many hours later—with fresh vegetables for our lunch or dinner and always in high spirits. The Ho villagers, especially the young girls, liked him a lot and invited him for a chat or two and a good long rest in their courtyards. There was a lot of giggling. Having read elsewhere about ethnographers' assistants from the coastal plains who were unable to cope with the situation in the tribal environment of middle India and who fled/quit after a short while, S. seemed to love it, he loved being there, he loved socializing with the villagers, he surely loved his warm non-prejudiced overall reception also by non-tribals. Perhaps with the experience of discrimination on his mind—this is my speculation—he said that he did not feel any of this here, but unfortunately his command of English was so limited that he was unable to explain what this "any of this here" was. Maybe that he was allowed to hang his wet clothes on the washing line of our neighbours who were members of the cow herders' category, and to lie down on their cots anytime? This and the cooking he did so extensively that little time was left for us. Tensions came up when we insisted on his accompanying us and translating for us as our assistant in the field, as was our arrangement. Maybe we were too inexperienced in guiding him, too impatient with him and ourselves, maybe our voice was not gentle enough or too gentle, maybe he shied away from situations in which it would become too obvious that his English was too limited to converse with us? Could we be sure that our demands were culturally adequate to him? Towards the end of the month he complained about tensions in his head and bad dreams both of which seriously troubled him. He wanted to go back to his parents. I was wondering if the villagers of M. put the blame on us for making one of 'them' leave the village and did not rule out there might be consequences for us which there were. Before he left he asked if I would consider in my thesis the map of M. that he had drawn in collaboration with my husband and put his name on it. I promised.

Deepak and his anthropological descendants had paved the way for us to enter the field and to get going. The 'project' was on the way and we were exactly where we wanted to be. Despite irritations and occasional moments of frustration and despair we were about to understand frictions and misunderstandings as expressions of a collision of underlying divergent cultural assumptions. While we have been in touch and on visiting terms with both Deepak and P. ever since, we have never again seen S.P. has not either and does not know of his whereabouts. I still feel about S. as our young friend, almost our son, and every once in a while I keep wondering if we have been fair enough with him.

Notes

1. Whenever I write 'we' or 'us' I refer to those periods when my husband was able to accompany me to middle India.
2. The reasons why we had decided against doing fieldwork in the Chaibasa area, especially in the Jesuit stronghold of Lupungutu are given in the paper on John Deeney.

FOURTEEN

SCHOLARLY COMMITMENT:
John Deeney and the Ho of Kolhan

E. REICHEL

Introduction

More than one million Ho people constitute a tribal community in Central Eastern India, where they make a living on the plateaux and hills alongside non-tribal and other tribal categories of which there are officially 62 different Mundari and Dravidian speaking ones alone in Odisha. Not too much is known as yet about the multicultural composition and conviviality of these tribal societies, little fieldwork has been done on the south-eastern fringes of the Chota Nagpur Plateau, even less is to be expected in future as tribal issues have been disappearing from anthropology's and anthropologists' agendas, and Majumdar's comprehensive book on the Ho was published in 1937/1950.

When considering in faraway Europe research on the Ho in 2005 for the first time Deeney was pointed out to me as a Ho scholar and Jesuit of American origin living in Lupungutu (LPG) near Chaibasa in the state of Jharkhand right in the heart of Ho country in a community of Jesuits for more than sixty years. I thought this might be a good starting point, and I did not have any other. My dependence on gaining "friends in the field" was total and, of course, at that initial stage I could not have the faintest clue that it would be the Jesuit John Deeney to introduce me, an atheist anthropologist, into the poetics of the Ho language and the intricacies of the Ho's universe.

My husband was able to accompany me. We had never been to this particular region so far, we had never before entered tribal middle India. We were informed that the nights at the beginning of the year can be chilly and that the area is infested with cerebral malaria, that people die from it so we better take care. In a brochure with facts and figures of Mayurbhanj we later read that the region has been made out as one of many tribal-infested districts which, however, was fine with us. We were told that there is a good library at the Tribal Research and Training Centre (TRTC), that Deeney was a very busy man and that we needed to respect that by all means.

Deeney and the Jesuit Setting of Lupungutu

Nobody expected us, when we arrived in Lupungutu, but Deeney and other members of the Jesuit community were around. They were polite and friendly and busy as all of them were involved in some Ho related project or the other. They had a tight schedule everyday leaving no spare time for two curious elderly Europeans to be looked after. Deeney himself was the most outspoken of all. "I have no time for you. I once allowed myself to become distracted from my work, so I better tell you straight away", he said when we met for the first time. He had just completed the revised and enlarged edition of the Ho-English Dictionary from 1978 whose publication was to be expected by autumn that year. His days now were completely absorbed by translating the Old Testament into Ho. He did this in collaboration with D.S. Purty, a Ho graduate and his co-worker for over 40 years about whose poor health he seemed more worried than about his own. He felt he could not afford to miss out on a single day's cooperation with his Ho *pandit*, as he called him. Of course, we accepted all of that. We were happy enough to be allowed to stay there, to be offered the safety of an ascetically furnished room with a mosquito net, three meals a day and the key to the library. At that time Deeney was 84.

So, at the beginning of our stay we spent a lot of time in the library in the daytime because most Fathers left in the morning and returned only for dinner. They worked in the vicinity and in what they call 'the interior' as priests, teachers, social workers, lawyers. Some were busy planning a scheme of night schools to be installed in villages in the jungle for Ho girls and boys who should be taught there in their mother tongue Ho, others were supervising the construction of a new TRTC complex offering non-formal and adult education programmes, computer cabinets and computer classes for *Adivasi* of the surrounding and more remote villages in West Singhbhum district. A garden was to be attached to provide the vegetables, a hostel for tribal boys and one for tribal girls, and a repair shop for jeeps, bikes and bicycles. The new site was in Guira, in walking distance from LPG. While Deeney was not part of the outdoor activities of his Jesuit colleagues, he was part of much of it due to his published work on the Ho and his extensive research into the life of the Ho.

Over breakfast the Fathers talked about their plans for the day, over dinner they shared the experience of their days and discussed news. They did not mind us joining them for the meals, listening to their reports and eventually getting involved in the discussions. And they seemed not to mind that we were not affiliated to the catholic church although this was one of the first questions that we were asked. All were non-Ho, but fluent in the Ho language. They came from different parts of India, many from Kerala or from Tamil Nadu. All treated Deeney with that extra note of respect when he was around or when he was talking. There was an overall appreciative, undogmatic and non-patronizing atmosphere towards the Ho community and among each other. The Fathers were concerned about the Ho community's fate in particular, informed about tribal issues in contemporary India in general and argued not only from a humanitarian, but from a political perspective. They criticize the Indian Governments' policy of attempting to 'advance' tribals into the Indian mainstream as a strategy of assimilation contributing eventually to the loss of their tribal identity and their distinct ways of being in the world. This strategy, they say, they attempt to counteract in their day-to-day interactions thus safeguarding and paying tribute to the specific values prevailing in the Ho's universe. It is an expression of this attitude that in parish services Jesus is addressed as Sinbonga, the Ho's creator god (an affair that required negotiations with Rome and a battle that was won), that sermons are regularly held in Ho and that Jesuit trainees in the area have to acquire fluency and precision in the Ho language. In 2008, when I attended a Ho language course for future Jesuit priests, use was made of the language material that Deeney had developed for grown-ups in which Ho is rendered in a modified Devanagari script. By then the construction work for the new TRTC in Guira was completed and the site had turned into a bustling place. The only place that was almost always deserted was the wonderful library that had been transferred from LPG.

The Fathers usually conversed in a mix of Hindi, English and Ho. But for the occasional female guest from outside and the (Ho) cook's wife it was an all-male lot. Almost all of them had been suffering from malaria more than once. One of them had caught the disease twelve times, but this may be no exception. They lived with it and kept going. As priests Jesuits live, often for decades, in remote tribal villages. When they catch malaria there, they sometimes go to Lupungutu to rest and recover, before they go back to their 'field'. These were no-nonsense people. Their days began with Mass at five.

Deeney concentrated on his work and confined himself to his study. He was given a tiny room at the back of the refectory hall where he could work quite undisturbed or sit outside on the porch next to a garden with flowers which he was very fond of. He was usually present in the day-time, as he seldom left the compound. One day he joined us for a cup of coffee after lunch, gradually we began to sit together, have our meals together, discuss Ho issues which we had read about in the library. Quite of his own accord and contrary to his professed intention he eventually gave us some of his time and a number of articles written by him that had not yet been published and that dealt with different aspects of the Ho such as their spirit world, the relationship with their dead, their creation myths, their clan (*kili*) and totemic sub-clan nomenclature, their language and a comparison with the Munda's language. He entrusted us with the only type-written copies he had and confessed that he had taken his baby steps in computer lore only in his late seventies. It seemed that he began to enjoy our get togethers. His academic and personal commitment, his genuine respect for Ho people, their sincerity, diligence, and their worldview certainly inspired us. Maybe he realized that I was serious about doing fieldwork and about learning their language. When we left Lupungutu after about ten days in early 2005 planning to return roughly a year later, he offered, in case his health and his time allowed, to be our teacher for a three-day crash course into the Ho language. He gave us his email address to stay in touch.

When we returned the following year, the crash course was cut down to one and a half days. Deeney was busy and above all impatient and we were too slow. But otherwise we continued to discuss Ho kinship matters and the Ho system of relationship terms of which he had collected 56 encompassing altogether five generations and brought into a graphic grid differentiating between the relationships of a man and a woman. Deeney introduced me into playing a game of Solitaire on the computer ("just a little distraction!"), he remembered Serge Bouez and Michael Yorke and his wife ("she had learned to prepare rice-beer and sold it in the market, and she got involved in silkworm breeding"), he talked about his Irish roots which had made him study Gaelic as a young man. We continued to meet also in later years, when I paid him (and the library) a visit from my field site in nearby far-away Odisha. He never questioned my decision of doing my long-term fieldwork among Ho (and Santal) people in a non-Christianized region of Mayurbhanj in Odisha. In the course of time not only my husband and I had begun to consider Deeney our friend, but Deeney himself did so by introducing us to others as his friends. Of this we are really proud. We remained friends for the following five years. When eventually Deeney's health grew so weak that he needed to be transferred to Jamshedpur, I paid him a last visit. Give me a hug, he said before I left. A week later, in January 2010, he died.

He had wished to be given a Ho burial in a Ho environment which he was promised. Also, a John Deeney Memorial Centre was to be erected in Chaibasa.

John Deeney: The Scholar

"If anything is going to be remembered about me after death, it will be the Ho-English dictionary" (personal communication 2010). Between its publication in its revised and enlarged form in 2005 and Deeney's first appearance in the Chaibasa scene half a century had passed.

Deeney was born in Philadelphia, USA in 1921. He joined the Society of Jesus when he was 18. He came to India in 1949. He stayed on and lived in the Jesuit community of Lupungutu most of the time. He was ordained a catholic priest in 1952 and received Indian citizenship in 1991. After having been denied it before, this really meant a lot to him and he was sure that his publications helped in this. Before going to India, he had acquired a thorough knowledge of the grammar of English, Latin, Greek, French and Gaelic. After his arrival in India, he studied Hindi whose script he later modified to spell Ho words. He was not in favour of promoting and spreading a distinctive Ho script such as *Warang Chiti* which already at Deeney's time had turned into a political issue. In 1952, he came to Chaibasa for a month and immediately began to learn Ho. When he was appointed headmaster of St. Xavier's High School/Chaibasa in 1955, he already knew much Ho. He continued studying the language while he was headmaster of St. Xavier's High School/Lupungutu from 1957 until 1962. It was in the course of these seven years that he developed the habit of riding by bicycle to visit most of his pupils and their parents in their villages, one by one, to learn about their lives, their culture, their language. Initially meant for his own benefit he began to have index cards with him on these excursions on which he not only noted down Ho words and their denotations in English, but added other useful information in connection with that word (personal communication). The vocabulary collected on these cards plus the added notes containing information from the indigenous point of view constituted the foundation of the Ho-English dictionary to be published 50 years later. Maybe Deeney was inspired in his approach by Hoffman's *Encylopaedia Mundarica* all the 16 volumes of which he had in his study in LPG, as the added data turn the Ho-English dictionary into an ethnological encyclopaedia of the socio-cosmic universe of the Ho in many respects. In it any references to sickness, spirits, rituals, 'folk beliefs' etc. are expressed as seen through the eyes of a Ho without Deeney himself holding such views as he points out in the introduction to the dictionary. After all, he is a scholar, not a 'going native' person.

Deeney began publishing on the world of the Ho and their language in the mid-seventies after an extended period of extensive research. After hosting an anthropologist in LPG and observing him interview elderly Ho informants while tape-recording their talks Deeney approached Dhanur Singh Purty, a Ho graduate and former student of his. Their collaboration began in the early sixties by Dhanur interviewing and tape-recording his own father. Deeney recollects how amazed Dhanur was about his father's memory and knowledge. The recordings plus Dhanur's follow-up research in a number of villages in the heart of Kolhan plus Deeney's own research led to the publication between 1978 and 1982 of a seven volume encyclopaedia of more than 1000 pages on Ho village life, customs and culture entitled "The Ho of the Ho Country" (*Ho disum Ho honko*). The process of writing up took almost twenty years. D.S. Purty is given as the author, Deeney writes the introduction. The text is written in the Ho language making use of the Devanagari script. Simultaneously, Deeney and Dhanur began preparing the Ho-English dictionary containing the denotations in English of all Ho words that appear in the books of the series (*see* Reichel, 2009 for the content of the seven volumes) enriched by detailed ethnographic information. The first edition of the Ho-English dictionary came out in 1978, the same year when the publication of the seven volumes began. Deeney claims that all 12,000 entries of the dictionary plus those 900 added in the 2nd edition 2005 have been filtered through Dhanur. I do not know any of Deeney's publications in which he does not emphasize his complete dependence on Dhanur at every stage of their work. Also, when I sometimes got stuck at home while writing up my thesis and I consulted him *via* e-mail, his answers were always carefully argued and would usually begin by: "I have discussed your mail with Dhanur".

Dhanur also collaborated in the preparation of the "Ho Grammar and Vocabulary" which was published in 1975. Deeney hoped that everybody who is familiar with the Devanagari script will be able to read and understand the seven volumes written by Dhanur by making use of the Ho-English dictionary and the Ho grammar. When the Jesuit language instructors realized that for teaching purposes there should be a faster, more effective and less theoretical approach than that conveyed in the "Ho Grammar and Vocabulary", Deeney wrote a condensed "Introduction to the Ho Language" which was published in 1991. This booklet is a jewel, a survival kit of no more than 50 pages. Although all of the language materials have been accompanying me throughout my fieldwork it was the "Introduction" of which I needed a second copy since my sweaty fingers due to the daily use in tropical climate had eaten-up the letters. I still remember the first sentences: I drank rice-beer. She made/built a house. We ate cooked rice. They sowed the seed. You ploughed the field.

Deeney's latest publication from 2008 is "The Spirit world of the Ho Tribals and other glimpses into the Ho world." It is a revised and updated collection of those hitherto unpublished essays that he had given to us in 2005 when we met for the first time (see above). This publication written in English draws heavily from the seven volumes written by Dhanur. Deeney had originally considered to translate these volumes into English or to have them translated with Dhanur's help, but they never found the time. Also, Dhanur had fallen victim to moneylenders in the meantime and did only irregularly turn-up for work in LPG, as he felt the lives of his wife and his ten children to be threatened in his village. Deeney himself was 87 years now and getting weaker. Before running the risk of the contents of the seven volumes getting lost to many because they are written in Ho, this publication from 2008 then is the condensed result of Deeney's effort to make available in English to others in one book the Ho's relationship towards their deities, their *bongas* (the body of tutelary and malignant spirits), their ancestors—and other glimpses. Deeney calls it a book about the Ho's religious attitudes representing their own perspectives. As all the books have been regionally published with Xavier Ho Publications in LPG, Chaibasa and Ranchi, they unfortunately may be known and accessible only to a limited number of scholars dealing with tribal issues in middle India. In my book "The Dead in Tribal Middle India" (Manohar/New Delhi, 2009) there is a chapter on the Ho and the concept of their ancestry and Deeney's/Purty's contribution and research into that field. When I gave a copy to Deeney he was embarrassed and moved at the same time. "You know", he said, "no one beyond our region has so far paid published tribute to our work. Little is known about the world of the Ho in the academic world outside." Maybe he was right at that time. He had met and discussed with Serge Bouez, who published his book on Ho and Santal in 1985 without reference to Deeney's material. He had enjoyed, he said, sitting with Michael Yorke and discuss aspects related to the Ho's *miyad mandi chaturenko*. In fact, Yorke quotes him and lists him in his references, but then his thesis has never been published and at that time, in 1976, only Deeney's Ho grammar had been out. Barbara Verardo did long term fieldwork among Ho and Munda people in the Ranchi area and was in touch with Yorke and M. Areeparampil from the TRTC in LPG. There is no reference to Deeney's material in her thesis, but they met, if only briefly (personal communication). Had he greeted her the way he greeted us when we met for the first time: "Good afternoon. I have no time for you?" Eventually, Deeney's language books are listed in the bibliography of D.S. Anderson's "The Munda Languages" (2008), but in the part introducing relevant publications on Munda languages all through the 20th century, Deeney's works are missing. While Das Gupta (2011) in her book on the Ho lists Deeney's "Ho-English Dictionary" from 1978(!), in her glossary of Ho terms she does not stick with Deeney's transliteration. Pucilowski (2013), on the other hand, for her linguistic study in Ho morphophonology and morphosyntax makes extensive use of Deeney's grammar (2nd edition from 2002), but that was three years after his death.

EPILOGUE

Had Deeney been given a Ho burial as he had wished? I was wondering. My question was confirmed, though, even a film of the burial procedure had been made entitled "Fr John Deeney, S.J., The Apostle of the Hos", a copy of which I was given. It was irritating, then, to see that the stone to cover the grave was not a *sasan diri* which is one chosen and transported from the jungle as would have been the Ho tradition. It was polished granite instead engraved with a large cross. It lay in an East-West and not in a North-South direction as is customary with Ho people. D.S. Purty who I met in 2012 called it a *diku diri* (alien/ foreign stone) and complained about the burial site. When digging the grave, he said, water flushed inside and could not be redirected. Ho people always offer their dead a good site, he continued, which by all means is a dry grave. He and his wife would be quite unhappy to know Deeney to be exposed to such humidity for good. Those in charge of the burial site just would not listen when they were informed about the water leakage inside the grave. He and his wife could live with this knowledge only as they had done everything to prevent this from happening.

The John Deeney Memorial Centre in Chaibasa had been erected soon after Deeney's death. It had a library consisting of a few shelves with Deeney's and Dhanur's books that had been transferred from Deeney's study in LPG, and a larger room for seminars. When I was there in 2013 the place did not look used, some of the books and shelves were covered by cobwebs, others had been damaged by water or gnawed at by rats—an altogether poor sight as it conveyed the impression that there was no demand for the intellectual passion encapsulated in Deeney's and Dhanur's material. Obviously, the wonderful library at the TRTC in Guira was suffering a similar fate. It was closed and locked most of the time when I went there in 2013. So many books had been stolen in the course of the years that this seemed the most effective way of rescuing the rest. A charming, polite and educated Ho girl from the vicinity was in charge of the key, had regular office hours which, of course, were not kept, and books could only be read under her constant supervision. Unaccompanied individual entry was disallowed. She had learnt how to use a computer in one of the courses run by the TRTC especially for the advancement of tribal girls and had produced a modern, computer-typed inventory of the books.

In my interpretation the active role that Deeney played within the community of the Jesuits and the way he was included in their day-to-day activities very much revolved around Deeney's personne and his scholarly commitment. Although, a Jesuit and as such a member of a large community and a world-wide social net, as a scholar of the writing profession he at the same time was an isolated single individual, especially when Dhanur withdrew from the scene. The Jesuits of LPG and Chaibasa were working hard, disciplined and efficiently in order to advance the Ho tribals' material and spiritual well-being. This to them spells constructing and running Hindi medium schools and colleges, initiating a number of agricultural development projects and irrigation schemes in the 'jungly' villages, and defending as lawyers free of charge Ho women and men when these are taken to court in cases of impending land dispossession. In my understanding Deeney's perspective on the Ho was different from that of his fellow Jesuits. He did not want to improve their lot, but to understand what constituted their Ho-ness and write about it, document it. He unconditionally respected Ho people, their tribalness, their religious beliefs, their tribal values for what they were, the way they were. He did not have this hidden developmental agenda.

Despite all the support I have received over the years from the LPG community for which I am very grateful, I have in the end decided against doing fieldwork in this environment. In the course of the discussions I had with Deeney over five years, I realized that my focus should be on locally defined Ho priorities and local Ho perspectives. I became interested in observing how Ho communities, how Ho people are faring without the assistance of Catholic Church, social activists, Chaibasa academia, disciplined formal education, proselytizing activities of sorts and Non-Governmental Organizations.

Eventually, a suitable site less than 40 kilometres away from Chaibasa was found where these requirements were met. The chapter in this book "Narrations of Commitment: Friends in the Field" is about how this was accomplished. The relative spatial distance from the Chaibasa area meant the possibility of an alternative and rather unveiled entry into the Ho's universe, its relative closeness to the Chaibasa area meant that once in a while I could meet Deeney there by taking the public bus, the Chaibasa *gari*, which, however, always implied a horrible ride on horrible 'roads' and a constant fear of the bus overturning.

References

Areeparampil, Mathew, 2002. *Struggle for Swaraj*. Lupungutu: Tribal Research and Training Centre.

Bouez, Serge, 1985. *Réciprocité et Hiérarchie. L'AQlliance Chez Les Ho Et Les Santal De L'Inde*. Paris: Société D'Ethnographie.

Das Gupta, Sanjukta, 2011. *Adivasis and the Raj: Socio-economic Transition of the Hos, 1820-1932*. New Delhi: Orient Black Swan.

Deeney, John, 2002. *Ho Grammar and Vocabulary* (2nd Edition). Lupungutu: Xavier Ho Publications.

——. 1991. *An Introduction to the Ho Language*. Chaibasa: Xavier Ho Publications.

——. 2005. *Ho-English Dictionary*. Ranchi: Xavier Ho Publications.

——. 2008. *The Spirit World of the Ho Tribals*. Ranchi: Xavier Ho Publications.

Majumdar, Dhirendra Nath, 1950. *The Affairs of a Tribe: A Study in Tribal Dynamics*, Lucknow: Universal Publishers.

Pucilowski, Anna, 2013. *Topics in Morphology and Morphosyntax*. University of Oregon, (Unpublished dissertation).

Purty, Dhanur Singh. 1978 – 1982. *Ho Disum Ho Honko*. A series of 7 books in Ho language. Chaibasa: Xavier Ho Publishers.

Reichel, Eva, 2009. *Notions of Life in Death and Dying: The Dead in Tribal Middle India*. New Delhi: Manohar Publishers.

Verardo, Barbara, 2003. *Rebels and Devotees of Jharkhand: Social, Religious and Political Transformations among the Adivasis of Northern India*. London: London School of Economics and Political Science (Unpublished dissertation).

Yorke, Michael, 1976. *Decisions and Analogy: Political Structure and Discourse among the Ho Tribals of India*. London: School of Oriental and African Studies (Unpublished dissertation).

FIFTEEN

THE FIELD, THE ANTHROPOLOGIST, AND THE RESEARCHER'S SPOUSE

JURGEN WOLF

Introduction

On completing her professional life, my wife decides to study socio-cultural anthropology at the university. Right in the middle of her studies she finally wants to observe with her own eyes whatever she hears or reads, or be a part of it. At her initiative the opportunity she obtains an opportunity to conduct field research among members of a numerically rather small tribe.[1] Instantly, I am as keen as mustard and offer to accompany her. In fact, when studying physics, I had already been concerned with the question, how humans of different cultures view the world, describe it, and live in it. Here I see the opportunity to approach these topics in empirical reality beyond the tracks of tourism and the selectiveness of books. More than a year ago I had applied for a sabbatical and was quite prepared to spend it for this purpose.

We decide to approach the fieldwork project as a joint venture. I read a considerable amount of anthropological literature and, as a basic principle, try to learn to question any established conviction. A three week tour to India is to prepare our long-term stay by exploring the region, approaching the language, and getting to know the people over there. We are satisfied with the results of the journey and have another six months to prepare our 'expedition'. How much of technical equipment are we to take? Not much. Do we want a car at the site? No. What about a water filter? Yes. A number of such queries are being answered.

The First Contact: We Meet People

We start without knowing, where exactly we are going to settle down. We do, however, have the addresses of some persons to contact. One source turns out to be very rich indeed: Deepak Kumar Behera, then at Sambalpur University, is putting us onto proper track by mediating the decisive contact. We travel to R, a small town, in the vicinity of which several villages with a majority population of 'our' tribe may be found. The situation over there is to be explored and we are advised to meet P who is teaching anthropology at the local college. He may be helpful in our search for some kind of a shelter and an assistant.

Finally, we are in a village, have a place to stay, the required equipment and an assistant named S who is a student of anthropology. He speaks tolerable English, or so we think initially, and the language of the tribe. He is to help us survive in the village. He offers his services as cook-*cum*-interpreter and is confident to carry out both functions. I like him. He could be my son or even my grandson. He calls us by the English terms "uncle" and "aunty". We share with him our "one-room apartment", though a sheet of cloth, hung-up provisionally, separates our places to sleep.

S likes to cook, is communicative and has his own ideas what we should do: We should proceed with 'data-collection'. I too can think of nothing better. What am I to do? We live next to the villagers and try to convey to them that we want to live as they themselves conduct their lives. We are here to study their culture they are quoting us after some time. We request them to inform us when important things are happening, such as deaths, births, or marriages but, with rare exceptions, if at all we get to know that something had been 'going on' it is after the event.

Should I remain in our little hut idling away my time? L, a young man of the village speaking some rudimentary English, helps us frequently during the initial period. The two of us make-up our minds to record, who is living in which one of the houses of 'our' village. S decides to cover hamlets of the neighbourhood and, with my help, works on a map of the village and the surroundings.

Meanwhile, I take note of my wife's growing dissatisfaction. One point relates to the data-collection which she observes with almost demonstrative dislike. I fail to understand this. I want to know who among the villagers happens to be a member of 'our' tribe at all and where exactly they live within the settlement; I would have even preferred to inquire about who owned how much and what kind of land.

Yet another point is the fact that she is dissatisfied with our assistant, a feeling, which initially I do not want to share. Admittedly, his English is definitely limited. Often his translations contain a single sentence only, ending in the less than precise observation "and this like" or "and that like". Also, he likes his sleep and likes it long. Consequently, A does get very impatient in the mornings, later asking him, if she may wake him up. Of course, she may. If, however, she does so early in the morning to obtain translations of female talk at the village well and the like, he turns around to sleep as soon as he hears that 'data-collection' is not on the agenda. At that time, or between four and five o'clock in the morning, I too am awfully tired myself.

His conceptions of time and priorities of the day are different from ours. He likes to cook, and cook well, but this takes ages and ages and then, of course, he must always take a bath before lunch, of course. This plays havoc to our schedule. Often he is simply gone and we find him after some time at some neighbour's or the other. In short, he rarely does, what we had earlier discussed, but likes to do what he enjoys for the moment.

Thus it is a relief, to have G appear in front of our hut one day, offering his services. He is an adult man from a neighbouring hamlet, married, father of two sons, good in English and educated. His father had been a steelworker providing the son with decent schooling. However, G had given-up his job as a teacher at the government school, since, as a member of an ST (Scheduled Tribe) he felt discriminated against. He married—it was a "run-away marriage"—a woman of his tribe and now lives in the village and the house of his forefathers on the returns of his farm which, however, he has to share with others, i.e. brothers of his father and their relatives. His agricultural property is big enough to permit a modest existence.

However, he is not personally involved in agricultural work. He offers his services to others as a reader, a writer and by doing accounts. At times he is provided with small government contracts. Furthermore, he had, along with other members of his tribe, founded a private elementary school with the idea of teaching children in their mother-tongue rather than in the official language of the land, as is done in government schools, but unfortunately the institution was short-lived. The way he carries himself when he moves or when he speaks always has the air of some theatrical dignity. He is, as far as I can see, respected by the locals.

Now, we have two assistants. Both G and S belong to a tribe that is culturally and linguistically related to 'ours'. Whereas S thinks he knows all about our tribe and is thus more interested in 'data-collection' or substantial facts of our village, G may be convinced that we want to experience everything on our own, first-hand as it were, even though he finds it difficult to comply and must be reminded of the notion again and again. Being a local person, he has the advantage of multiple contacts.

G seems to have understood us. He volunteers with information on deaths, births, and marriages that have just occurred or are forthcoming. He does accompany us and is translating, though out of some hundred words we hear at the most ten are reaching us. Evidently, he himself is also forwarding questions. Are they still our own ones for which we are receiving answers? It seems to me that he enjoys his role as an intellectual in the village gaining additional renown by performing on behalf of us by this important task.

Isn't it amazing? We are entering the villages as complete strangers, have nothing but ignorance to display and the fact that we have come here from afar, yet we experience friendliness, respect, courtesy, or at the worst neutrality. All the same, the days are strenuous: watching G with full attention, having an eye for the informants and for what is going on, managing one's own behaviour in an adequate style, being very well aware of the fact that I can make a fool of myself at any moment. Taking photographs after asking for permission is another issue, or writing down the regular report just as the coming to terms with the day-by-day physical intake and disposal.

Quickly I learn to trust G and enjoy conversing with him about anything under the sun. He is introducing his wife and children to us and whenever we are near his house, or some kilometres away from our hut, he invites us for a meal. Insisting that he offers his services due to his genuine interest in our work, G is instantly attempting to push aside S. The latter, evidently following the principle of seniority, is submitting himself. I think G wants to reduce S' function to that of cooking. This is hardly acceptable for us, though it may appear to be practicable at first sight. He had been employed by us as an assistant "also cooking".

Suffering in the Field

Unfortunately, G too is causing us some headache. He loves *diyan*, or rice-beer, and more so *rasi*, some kind of rice-liquor. Thus, we frequently wait for him in vain, or he is late, but fully turned on and hardly helpful. Thereafter, he likes to tell us, how he had been away exploring where something has been happening and what he had found out. He is recalling his observations and we have to tell him that the information is of little value for us. We hope to see and witness almost everything. In several cases, our presence, on the other hand, has in a way been announced by him in advance. We are being invited then which is really good and helpful for us.

We try to soften the status rivalry of our two assistants by assigning them to each one of us separately. This is always a balancing act and cannot continue. A is highly dissatisfied. The extent of her discontent makes me fear that she would want to give-up. The two of us join in talking on many extended walks. The locals are quite concerned. Who on earth would simply choose to walk without a definite destination? As an optimal solution A would want to get rid of both assistants and I do understand her discontent, as she rather existentially depends upon reasonable results within a limited period. However, without help we might face the danger of making no progress at all. The only person of our village, of whom we know that he possibly might qualify as an assistant, never seems to be sober at all, being even more addicted to alcohol than G. Finally, we agree upon the following: Since S himself has been dropping hints about our asking too much of him, we will let go of him to work on with G, provided a formal agreement can be reached. He is to work for us and be compensated in monetary and material terms.

Do relations between us change by this? So far G had conveyed the impression of being personally interested in our work, accordingly supporting us. Even more so he conceives of himself as researcher of an equal standing, a point which happens to agree with me, but not at all with A. I realize after all, that basic issues arise out of this. About G's agenda we are certainly in the dark. Occasionally, he talks about members of the *ST* (i.e. *Scheduled Tribes*), to which his own tribe and 'ours' belong, being characterized and discriminated against by the government and the mainstream society as backward and uncivilized and accordingly he finds it important to fight against these prejudices with a more informed opinion in a publicized form. For our stay to make sense we must clarify our own agenda.[2] At the same time, we do not want to exploit him. He has his own life and his own work. Devoting time to us means that he cannot look after himself and his family. Such are the thoughts going through our minds.

What—in this case—could be an appropriate agreement, since occasionally he disappears for days, just as he is frequently missing appointments. An additional aspect is S' absence (we have, so I hope, parted on good terms) and the fact that I do not conceive my role as a cook. How are we going to feed ourselves? Far and wide no restaurant is in sight. Moreover, cooking ourselves would cost too much time. G's wife is agreeing to supply us with a warm meal a day and with the fact that we give her something for it. She is a clear and steadfast person. When A raises the issue of her husband's liquor problem, my heartbeat is about to halt. As she is unable to understand a word of English and our linguistic competence in the local tongue is as yet too limited, G must translate.

I am flabbergasted. No trouble whatsoever follows. She simply suggests cashing the money for her husband's work herself with G agreeing without the slightest protest. He says, she can better handle it. The modalities of accounting, i.e. half-time as well as full-time payment once a week, are also agreed upon by both. Following this halfway clear pronouncement, A and I hope to find an easier way to relax when confronted with what we conceive as a lack of dependability.

Not always can we manage. An event, meaningful for the entire village, is to take place. G has promised to appear in time. A and I sit and wait in front of our hut. On the other side of the street, within the courtyard, people are gradually assembling. We are invited. A does not want to go without G. For her it makes no sense to observe something and understand nothing. Time is passing. Finally, only I walk across. In the yard the rituals are commencing. Two chairs, the only ones of the house, have been placed at an exposed site. I am made to sit on one of them, feel left alone or like counterfeit money, exposed with the empty chair next to me. Do not understand A.

Living in a geographical zone classified as tropical, we are not yet entirely able to manage the issue of hygiene. Every day the villagers take a bath in artificially constructed ponds which are filled by the monsoon and rather empty at this time. Cows share these 'bathing' facilities. We do not dare to follow suit, given the fact that all travel-guides warn of the grave diseases due to a sweet water bath in these regions, not to mention stagnant sweet water. Though I tend to look for special signs of such infections among the locals, I cannot detect any. Perhaps I am unable to recognize the signs properly. Daily the neighbours ask us, whether we have taken a bath. Embarrassing! A is the first to dare go bathing with the other women, while it takes at least another two weeks for me to act alike. Until then I was washing myself alone in our house at night. Against our expectations, we remain healthy.

A and I continue to reach our limits, including those of partnership. What could be the reasons, A is asking me during a walk at the end of our first stay in the village. Within the course of ten years, a further six visits to the place, shorter or longer ones, are to follow.

My role within a 'ladies programme'? On Finding a Role in the Field

I admire A's determination to gain contact with the women of the village.

She is quite successful: When a group of women asks her to join in collecting firewood from the jungle, or clay to mend the facades of the houses, she goes along spontaneously and courageously. She is also to join for cleansing by the daily bath or road-works for a day with other women. The men, as it appears to me, happen to be less involved in such undertakings. Am I more inhibited, or do I conceive myself not quite equal and my role rather that of company and support?

At that time I understand myself as an—almost—equal partner of A and want to share all of her experiences. I am curious. Furthermore, I seem to notice that people are rather happy to accept us, because both A and I are of the elderly kind having children and grandchildren. Belonging to the grandparental generation and proceeding together on equal footing indicates that I am not an attachment of A, or *vice versa*. I conceive us to be a good team. But I have to watch out. Again and again it happens, in conversation for example, that I have it my way and ask informants one question after the other. This, at least, is the echo I receive from A, along with her profound disagreement. Naturally, she too is asking questions, though following up with further enquiries less frequently. She rather wants to listen, to wait, and to find out what is important to the speakers themselves. This is the way she explains her point and, given these priorities, I interfere with my questions.

I do manage to understand this position, though frequently I fail to see the point in what I hear. Whether, for example, I am confronted with a banal statement or, hidden behind it, some deeper meaning, simply escapes me. Moreover, I catch myself ever so often in finding life over here rather similar to our conditions at home, say some 150 years ago. What is being said I classify within the framework of my own world-view, my own hypotheses. Having come to know the tendency of humans to forward replies of the kind, they think, are the ones expected by their opposites, I must be more skilful in my questions to avoid this trap. Since we do not really participate in their everyday lives, initially at least hardly more than in bits and pieces of what goes on in the village. I cannot test my hypotheses through own experience. This is how I argue, or like this. I cannot convince A. Thus, she frequently steps on my foot to remind me not to ask too many questions. I feel ordered about. Am I, after all, nothing but the attached programme, as is often the fate of wives accompanying 'important' husbands when attending cultural highlights[3] ? Indeed it is correct: A—not I—will report on her/our happenings and experiences in scholarly style. She is the 'expert', I the amateur. However, if I do not join the venture in a manner that agrees with me, I will cut a pale figure and be bored to death.

In fact, I do take a major interest in relations of kinship and descent among our informants in the village. On preparing our journey, I had read an article of A's professor on relations of kinship and marriage which I found exciting but also hard to comprehend. Now, in the midst of practitioners, I see the possibility to understand more. After initial researches I presume that cross-cousin marriage does happen among our tribal neighbours. I want to find this out and for hours ponder over diagrams which I design after enquiring about the ancestors not just of men but of their wives as well. I think I occupy myself with genealogies and learn, back in Germany, that they are pedigrees instead. Such a difference had simply not been known to me. A continues to ask me: "What are you doing over there?" However, she does not want to be concerned with my thoughts.[4] I am unable to advance, feel left alone. Only much later I sense, why I have failed.

What role am I to play over here? Am I myself a researcher in this village, only A's company, or even a millstone around the researcher's neck? At times, I have the feeling not to be able to cultivate the carefree company of the people we meet. Naturally A and I have, before starting our journey, talked about how to deal with the people we were going to meet, and I have read some literature on this subject as well. What are my intentions? What requirements do I want to meet? Firstly, wanting to come across the people at eye level is not difficult, I think. Secondly, finding the right relationship between proximity and distance to my subject of research, as is required by anthropologists and thirdly: With whom should we cultivate closer contacts? Would they not prevent relationships to other important people in the village?

Thus, there is G. Spontaneously I developed friendly feelings towards him, and *vice versa*, as it appears to me. His forefathers have all been *munda*, or what used to be the hereditary title of a kind of village headman, an office of the honourary kind and not related to material privileges. In one part of the hamlet he continues to be looked upon and respected as the real *munda*, though in the larger portion of the village there is an elected *munda* who later on will become my *Saki*, or some kind of a ritual friend. We observe tensions between the different sections of the village. What will be the consequences, if I very visually befriend one of the two more than the other? Are we then perhaps going to be avoided by a part of the population, thereby losing access to important information?

How to Continue?

I continue to find us to be a good team. We must have been able to manage some things quite well. We are still alive[5] and have only once been seriously ill with a nasty diarrhea lasting for three days. Neither, the police nor the Naxalites[6] have threatened us. Only once a policeman, meeting us on the weekly market, wants to see our papers which we do not carry along. He says, he is responsible for our safety and wants us to accompany him to the police station. Suddenly at this point, innumerable inhabitants of our village encircle us, push away the policeman and make him understand that they themselves will be looking after our security. Furthermore, again and again we manage to discuss our difficulties, including the mutual ones.

Over the period of ten years, we have been visiting the village again and again. With every additional arrival I notice, how my role has been changing in the course of this time. I enjoy the stay there in the strange environment which is no longer quite as strange. I happily leave the role of the researcher to A, who is professionally concerned with 'our' tribe all year long.

It is a relief to be no longer concerned about that balance of proximity and distance to the people in the way I had earlier attempted to, especially at the beginning of our stay. Sure enough caution is still advisable with the many sand traps one might hit. And yet I have the feeling I can carry on with people in a more spontaneous and carefree manner. Now-a-days, on meeting our acquaintances and friends, we are greeted kindly, as is customary over there, by regular kinship terms, though I still find it difficult to offer the adequate reply in spite of the fact that I have really tried to learn the local language. It is simply damn difficult.

At every visit our friends and acquaintances expressed their amazement of seeing us once more. During our last one, I had the impression of real joy. Meanwhile, the children have almost become adults, the adults, like us, have been aging. My *Saki*, or ritual friend, is concerned about the idea of what will happen, once he and his wife are no longer able to work. Who is to look after them. They do not have a son.

G has moved to R because of the schooling for his children. He and his wife accompany us to his village. It goes without saying that we live in his house. They call A "ma" (mother) and me "babu" (father) and supply us with all we need.

Notes

1. Within anthropology, I am told, such a tribe (numbering a bit more than a million people) is considered to be large.
2. For me, the most important difference compared to G's agenda is the fact that we do not pursue political aims and that direct information and experience is the focus of our work which of course, has quite a different quality for him. The quotidian for him for us amounts to observing life of a different planet.
3. As may be seen by the prominent example – Mrs. Merkel on a state visit—or a case of the opposite gender assignments.
4. Only later and on an entirely different route, A is approaching the same concern.
5. I have read reports from British colonial times according to which travellers would not dare to trespass into the country of 'our tribe' for fear of their lives. From my experience I can confirm that these people are excellent archers, also at night. Only recently, not too far away from the area, an Australian family (missionaries) were killed. They fell victim to Hindu-nationalist agitation, however. What happened to them, is unrelated to tribal people's everyday lives. Today people are peace-loving and not aggressive.
6. A militant left extremist underground organization fighting, by their own account, for the rights of tribal people.

SIXTEEN

RESEARCHER AND ASSISTANT ENTERING THE FIELD

On Becoming Friends and Kin

TINA OTTEN AND SUNITA SUNA

Anthropological research in the 'field' involves different levels of relationships between the actors, thus influencing directly or indirectly immediate and subsequent commitments. Such levels will primarily identify the ethnographer's hosts whose culture is under study, but may also involve contacts between academic colleagues as well as those with assistants, the close and permanent companions within the research venture, who at the same time are contractual partners of the researcher. The following contribution will consider these relationships during their initial stage. Continuing our earlier collaboration in the field, it has been written by two authors, with Tina Otten being responsible for the introduction, the conclusion and the first part whereas Sunita Suna has written the second part.[1]

Introduction

Entering the ethnographic 'field' is a unique experience for any researcher and the local counterparts. The memories of the first days and weeks are likely to last, but even though such an entry is distinctive, certain steps and features will be of the general kind, or faced and experienced by every professional. William F. Whyte, a Chicago sociologist, has written a methodological study on this topic, the pioneer work in the 1940s.

During the late 1930s, she had been living for three and a half years in a borough of Boston which was known to be poor and also distinctive by its Italian community. After extended preparations and considerable problems he managed to live with an Italian family for 18 months.

This initial duration was emphacised by the author along with the importance of learning the language and being part of a group. In order to be accepted, time was required. Thereafter, he was assigned a specific social role, or culturally given rights and duties. As a general priority, Whyte noticed the relevance of finding a "gatekeeper" (1984:35), or a person to open-up the community for the new entry. In an organization this task could be assigned to an official position, whereas in an ordinary community, the gatekeeper will usually be an informal broker. At the same time, every community will offer leadership roles (*ibid.*, 37), so one's research effort amounts to finding the gatekeeper and the leader of a group, who may be one and the same person.

Moreover, C.W. Watson (1999) and others have ordered fieldwork into three phases, preparations, "the time in the field", and the post-fieldwork period. The questions raised in the initial phase may, at a later stage, turn out to be irrelevant but, reflecting theoretical concepts of the discipline at the given time, serve as a guideline for the researcher. During the fieldwork phase, she tries to obtain a deeper understanding of the people. In this rather intense and at the same time limited period, every researcher has physical, emotional and psychological experiences which will leave their impression. It is closely connected with the period of post-fieldwork, when the researcher, within a given distance of time and space, is engaged in reflecting in an altogether different cognitive and experiential environment. In the same vein, the following report will contain memories of our first entry into the field and its impact upon the involved persons with a special emphasis on the friendships that developed.

Tina Otten's Entry

In 1999, I approached my 'field', the Koraput district in the Indian province of Odisha, as a member of a small research group. Three of us had just graduated and our supervisor was Professor Georg Pfeffer. Earlier Roland Hardenberg had taught us a course in Oriya, the provincial language, so we were prepared to manage basic communication on site.

However, it soon became obvious that some knowledge of the official language and being understood by the local people were not the same cup of tea.

Our first destination had been the University of Sambalpur to which the project was affiliated. Professor Deepak Kumar Behera, the academic counterpart in India, had made extensive preparations for our research, but initially his house and family became our safe haven where we tried out our Oriya sentences, an exercise received which enthusiasm though not always understood. During our stay there, we met most of the staff of the anthropology department and related subjects, just as we came into contact with students of whom two would accompany us to the field sites. They spoke Oriya and English and were to translate for us while also helping us to learn the language.

A female researcher was to be accompanied by a female student and a male one by a male person of the department. Any other arrangement was out of question. The distinction and separation of gender was most important[2] in both the field and the University of Sambalpur. Some of the male staff members there would not greet or address my female colleagues and me, ignoring us out of politeness, while vividly conversing with the men of our German team. Similarly, our academic status meant that we had to behave appropriately and ignore unknown men trying to speak to us. As women we were to dress properly. Accordingly Rita, Professor Behera's wife, personally took all of the female guests from Germany to the market to choose suitable Indian clothes for us. In the year 1999 women appearing in jeans would have been out of place in the countryside of Odisha. Our male team members never faced such difficulties, jeans and shirt being their suitable dress.

Another logistic job on behalf of the project was the purchase of a jeep, which was arranged by R. Hardenberg and facilitated by the newly introduced intercontinental communication *via* electronic mail. Thus, the paperwork was conducted within a comparatively short period. At that time, I learned that any bureaucratic work could be completed without delays, if the officers in charge would be provided with a little extra money. They had to be given "something for tea".

After a period of networking with our Indian colleagues, we left Sambalpur for our field sites some 500 km away. We were planning to establish a centre for the regular conferences of the group[3] in a nearby market place, while living separately in various villages for most of the time. After renting an old go-down, G. Pfeffer had given adequate amount of money to a contractor who should renovate the building, repair the roof so that it would at least be waterproof and construct a latrine along with a simple shower facility. However, on our arrival during the rainy season, we were made to understand that no worker had ever lifted a finger. The house was in a deplorable condition, since the entire money given to the contractor had been spent on the marriage of his sister. This had implied a prestigious wedding leaving him indebted to the local money-lenders. We thus received a befitting introduction into the anthropological relevance of family and marriage in India.

In this market place, we met several kind of persons who helped us learning the local language, since the Oriya we had been taught was not spoken here, and even the students from Sambalpur had difficulties to understand the Desia dialect of the Koraput district. Bidyut Takri, nicknamed Tuna, a young man of our age living next to the market, was of special help, learning English from us in return. He was—and still is—our gatekeeper even for the subsequent projects conducted in recent years, just as in return he might agree that the foundations for his later governmental employment to work among the tribal people were laid by the training he had received in our project.

Another gatekeeper was Hussain, the local police officer, who died some years ago. For a police officer Hussain was an astonishing personality. He had migrated some twenty years ago from Gujarat and was one of the very few Muslims in this area. Most of the time he refused to wear a uniform just as he treated the tribal population of the area with respect. Obviously, this was not the rule for other inhabitants of that small market place, consisting mostly of Hindu worker sailing from different provinces.[4] Hussain liked to dance the tribal dances and to drink the local liquor. He was well-known and respected in tribal villages and thus a perfect gatekeeper in Whyte's sense. In addition he was generously explaining the particular social rules and sanctions of the region, just as he knew about the activities of the Naxalite groups nearby. He also became the driver of our jeep.

Soon the members of our research group departed to different villages, with each one being at least 20 miles away from the other and in some cases almost 200 miles.[5] My first village of about 30 houses was called M, an hour's foot walk up the hill away from the market place. The founders of the village were Kond who had migrated from the Kondmals some generations ago. Many of the women spoke only Kui, their Dravidian tribal language, but their friendly attitude helped in building relations.

I was accompanied by Ruby, a young Brahmin graduate from Sambalpur University who was simultaneously conducting her own research in the village and had agreed to help with Desia and Kui. After a while we found out that for her too communication was difficult. Among her fellow students Ruby had the air of a heroine. At the end of the old millennium, it was extremely unusual for a graduate to go off to a field site for months. Anthropological research in the universities of Odisha was conducted by joint study groups and limited to a period of two weeks.[6] Given these regularities it was far from easy to find a female student or graduate willing and being allowed to accompany a foreigner on a long-term stay in a tribal village of an "interior" area on the highlands. The region was so remote, that next to no one had been engaged in long-term fieldwork there since the days of Christoph Fürer-Haimendorf and Verrier Elwin who had had separate research sprees among the tribal Bondo and Gadaba during the first half of the last century.

Ruby and I were to live with one of the leading families of the village of the Pangi or vulture clan. The only problem was a lack of space in the house of our hosts which, like all the others, was very small, being designed to provide sleeping place and not much more. At the same time, I was keen to live in a house in the centre of the village in order to be able observe what was going on. Accordingly, a solution was found in the shape of an abandoned goat shed just in front of the house of the Pangi family. It provided enough space for two persons, being 2.5 m long and 1.30 m wide. In the middle of the thatched gable I could almost stand in an upright position.

It was agreed that Ruby and I should live as daughters of the family, and we would address Mrs. Pangi as mother and Mr. Pangi as father just as their children were our siblings. Being co-residents, we were bound to be adopted into the local kinship system. Irrespective of all 'blood' relationships, the terminology implied that we had to address any other villager systematically by the appropriate kinship term and be addressed likewise. The system provided social order to the village. Later, I understood the overall importance of kinship in this kind of society.[7] Even when somebody was involved in the causes or the treatment of an illness, which was my particular subject of research, the kinship system was of the utmost importance.[8]

During the first weeks we were trying to learn Desia, the *lingua franca* of the region, without textbook as goes without saying. Simultaneously we tried to catch some words of the Kui language. Children often facilitate the learning process for a fieldworker. They use simple sentences and adults speak to them slowly, so we could train our competence of comprehension. In addition, we were soon part of a group of girls who met at night. Ruby and I were unmarried and thus belonged to the age-set of the unmarried girls for the people in the village. Though we were 25 years old, we found ourselves spending the nights with the other unmarried females of the village, aged between eight and twelve. Kond girls marry at the age of thirteen or fourteen, and from seven onwards are encouraged to spend their nights within their age set sleeping in groups on the verandas, a custom reflecting the tradition of dormitories for the young. The girls taught us the local songs and talked about their daily work and duties. Occasionally, and with considerable shyness, they also mentioned their prospective husbands and in the course of the months we were also guests of some weddings or witnessed formally arranged or unexpected elopements.

Ruby and I accompanied the girls to their work in the fields and followed our new mother completing her chores. I contacted the local healers and Ruby inquired about nutrition which was her own particular research. One highlight was the weekly market, called *hāt*. On the *hāt* many aspects of economic and social life were negotiated. The villagers, especially the women of the *Mali* or Gardener tribe, sold a wide variety of vegetables. In particular, I remember the vendors behind heaps of dried fish, the dish relished in the region and the major source of protein for the people. The girls of the village dress up for such an event, expecting to meet their friends and prospective husbands. Everyone comes together from the nearby villages to exchange news and invitations and, of course, the local healers make appointments for treatments. Bondo women sell liquor and their men tend to fight when drunk.

Ruby and I used to purchase our weekiy groceries, meet people for tea and sometimes the German colleagues, before heading back to the village. Another weekly highlight were the ceremonies at the shrine in Bairipada on Mondays, where Gurumai Guru Darli treated people of the region. Sometimes nearly a hundred persons had assembled, most of them needing treatment by the gods. For me it was a good occasion to contact women of different villages and tribes and these new friendships later facilitated my acceptance in a second settlement, where I subsequently stayed along with Sunita, as described below. The women there had seen me at the healer's and conversed with me at length, thereby obtaining a fairly good idea of my work before I ever thought of staying in their village.

After the first few weeks, I became ill with dysentery and accepted it as an opportunity to learn more about the local healing methods. I followed the villagers' diet regimen and took some herbal medicine, before I was treated with a broom against the evil eye. Our mother massaged my belly with her special technique instantly helping me to understand, why people moaned when getting such a treatment. It pained rather intensely and I had the impression of her fingers working their way through my stomach up to my spine. Ruby could not understand why had I agreed to undergo this treatment, but after ten days I was well again, having learned a lot about the local healing methods. By that time, I was in a position to talk about its details.

The experience proved to be of value in the Kond community and also when meeting the other inhabitants of the village known as *Mali*, or gardeners, who carried on like any tribal unit of the region and were definitely a part of the indigenous population. I was now in a position to witness many healing rituals of Kond and *Mali* and their interaction with the healing experts of the Rona, the third indigenous community inhabiting villages of the vicinity. Having met Rona women at the shrine, I was later able to spend the longest fieldwork stint with them. Earlier, individual *Mali* women contracted bonds of ritual friendship with me, known as *mafsad* or *mapuru sad*[9] in the regional version of the Oriya language, which would allow me to enter their houses as a—sibling-like—guest and witness the domestic rituals. The fact, that I was already the daughter of a Kond family was irrelevant in this context.[10] Later, when I had moved to other villages under different circumstances, I contracted similar bonds of ritual friendship which would guarantee a certain proximity without including the obligations of a very close friendship. Like the *bāliphul* friendship[11], they would also be gender-open.

In view of all these ritual ties my life in any of the tribal villages implied that research was only possible after having been made a social person, or assigned a social role as a daughter or a sister. What outsiders define as 'ritual friendship' in tribal Odisha is in fact deliberately created *relatedness* (*see* Carsten, 2000), or the introduction into the kinship universe which orders society. People expect you to act according to the norms of your social role, which at times makes it slightly difficult to obtain different viewpoints, visit other family members who are not on talking terms with your 'sibling', or be familiar with outsiders.[12] A healer, for example, might not appreciate my visit to his rival right after having witnessed his particular rituals. At the same time these complications provide valuable data for the researcher.

Gender roles also apply to the researcher, though perhaps not as strictly as to others. Accordingly, the women appreciated my wearing the *sari* in their particular tribal style. It was, I felt, something like a statement towards the village community, since none of the town women would ever have worn a *sari* in the tribal manner of the Kond, the *Mali* and the Rona. Similarly, I would wear my hair in the Desia[13] style. Every morning, I met with women to chat while they enjoyed doing my hair. This, of course, was a good time to learn about their personal and village matters.

Once a researcher is settled in the field, days go by very quickly and not so much later the departure has to be prepared. After a stay of more than a few months at least three to four weeks were required to prepare my farewell, thus making sure that everybody could be met again on a later occasion. The pressure of leaving is often a vehicle of communication; often people would like to convey some views to you which they treasure. I found that some of these "last minute messages" have to a considerable extent broadened my understanding of the messengers' world.

Part of the farewell ceremonies is the art of gift-giving. The hosts expect a decent present of the kind they themselves would give in a comparable situation, but at the same time, finding out what is decent may be rather difficult. Another question concerns publicity, or what—and what not—is to be given openly. Some cultures have even standardized the parting gifts. When Ruby and I left the village, we had, of course, left our household items and several newly bought tools and implements to our family and friends and also, at the advice of the latter, a little something to everybody in the village. A little farewell feast for the people we lived with went without saying. However, when the hour of departure arrived and nearly half of the village had assembled for the occasion, our 'mother' had a fit of anger. Finding out the reason took us another hour before we learn that a *sari* was an indispensable farewell gift for a mother. She felt disgraced by the omission. The norm of *sari*-giving went without saying. Nobody could image us not to know this simple act of courtesy. The moment I had settled the misunderstanding, my 'mother' put on a smile. The crowd, so far uneasy at the public scene, visibly relaxed the moment the 'daughters' could demonstrate that they had learn their lesson.

A few months later, I returned to the area. Since the subject of my research was studying local concepts of illness, another village had to be found which would have to be larger and include esteemed healing experts. I also wanted it to be situated near the only hospital worth its name in the entire area which, being a charitable institution, was offering treatment almost free of charges or only for nominal fees. The idea was to observe when and why people would choose the free services of the hospital or, alternatively, would prefer the more expensive services of a local healer.

Meanwhile, Ruby from far-away Sambalpur decided to terminate her engagement, so I had to search for a new assistant. Professor S.N. Ratha, Deepak Kumar Behera's teacher and a general well-wisher of our project, lived in Koraput town and could recommend Sunita Sunato me, an urban educated young woman of the area who spoke and understood the regional variation of the Oriya language. Hussain took the two of us to a suitable village within a walking distance of twenty minutes away from the hospital. Several female inhabitants had known me from extended conversations during the Monday sessions of the prestigious healer at Bairipada and, in fact, invited me to live with them. Coming from another village of the area, my new hosts adopted me as 'daughter-in-law' in their home, whereas Sunita, arriving without such a background, became their 'daughter'.

Our new village was inhabited by Rona, the traditional warriors of the local king. In spite of their migration legends they were very much a part of the Desia or indigenous population, though their relatively high status was emphacised by a strongly expressed avoidance of beef. For Sunita, the stay was her first experience of an intimate long-term interaction with tribal people, just as she had never before been employed at all, not to speak of the foreign employer. All of these reasons suffice to let us share her impressions of this initial phase.

Sunita Suna's Entry

I still have vivid memories of my stay in the village P, in Koraput district of Odisha, while working as an interpreter to assist my dear colleague and friend, Dr. Tina Otten, in the years 2000-2001. Indeed, this was a unique experience of my life, to witness many interesting things which were new to me, learning about tribal lives, their beliefs, culture, religion, tradition, listening to interesting stories, and meeting many people who became my friends, brothers, sisters, mother, father—a family. These fond memories will remain treasured with me forever.

It was the perfect time for me when I applied to work for Tina, since I was looking for a job to engage myself soon after my graduation from the Bachelor of Education programme. After having a brief face-to-face interview, I received the good news that I was selected to assist Tina as an interpreter in her research work. Obviously, I was excited to hear the news, but more excited about the kind of job I was going to do while living in a village.

I vividly remember the day I travelled to the village Pwith Tina, to look for a new place for us to live. The villagers both young and old, women and children surrounded us as we approached the village. It is common that visitors draw a crowd in the village, especially if the visitor is a white person. We told them that we were looking for a house to live in their village. The villagers did not take our request seriously and they were more interested to know about Tina. While I was explaining about Tina and the reason to live among them to the head of the village, the kids came closer giggling at us, and some of them quietly went closer to Tina touching her clothes, her fingers, and then there was a loud giggle by all the children and women when Tina greeted them. Interestingly, Tina was more familiar with the villagers' behaviour than myself since she had lived in other villages prior to coming to P. Though I am from Koraput, Odisha, I never had a chance to live in a village.

We had to talk to the head of the village and explain in detail, why we wanted to live in there. Most of the villagers in P belong to the Rona tribe, and they were hesitant to allow the foreigners to live among them who are not from their community. Finally, they agreed and when we convinced them that Tina and I do not eat meat (beef) we were guided to see a house. Surprisingly, we were offered to live in one of the vacant thatched houses of the head of the village located in the centre of the village community.

This was the first time for me to live in a village and that too with a white woman. I was happy that it did not take long for me and Tina to get along and become friends. Though, it surprised me to see Tina, who had adopted the village lifestyle—with no toilet and proper bathroom and living among a completely new community. My main tasks were to interpret our conversations and interviews with the villagers for Tina and prepare transcripts of the recorded interviews with her. Everyday we both went to different places to meet people in the village and to talk to them.

Gradually, the villagers became friendly and we started gaining their trust. The house owner was our neighbour—a joint family. The elders in the family became Tina's and my *baba* (father) and *mā* (mother). We found a family, who took care of us and was concerned about us, despite hardly knowing us. As I spent more time with Tina, I came to know her better. We called each other by our first name, which is not common in Indian culture—particularly in Koraput, Odisha. Tina used to call me by my nickname "Suni"—the name used by my family members. This also helped us to be more like friends, rather than employer and employee. We lived together like a family; with Tina even going to the open fields in the morning to answer nature's call. At night we had supper together and slept in the same room.

I had an insightful and enriching experience to learn about different tribes' views and perception of life and death. I came to know, how they welcome and celebrate life, perform rituals to avoid any mishappening, how they mourn their deaths and connect with nature and earth. We met many *disaris* (male healers) and *gurumais* (female healers) to interview on these topics; who were key persons to guide the villagers. *Disari* Kotelel was the oldest *disari* in our village P, and people still go to him with their problems to seek advice.

One of the festivals I liked most is *Bāli Jātrā*—a thanks giving or fertility ritual to the earth—praying to God for a good harvest. The assigned people in the village would bring sand from the riverbank to the *bāli ghar* and the villagers collect and use this sand to germinate paddy and grow their sprouts at home. This is also considered a prediction about a good harvest based on the looks of the sprouts so all of them would take extra care to sprout it well. On the final day, all would bring their sprouts in baskets, mostly women in colourful clothes walking in a line carrying it on their heads and marching to the river. This was indeed a beautiful sight. The interesting part is at the riverbank, where they symbolically harvest their crops and exchange that with another person and that person becomes his or her *bāli phul*. And these two become friends and remain friends forever! Thereafter, they call each other not by their names, but *bāli phul*. I too had my *bāli phul* during this ceremony.

One of the interesting things, which I also treasured most, is talking to the women at night. Our veranda became the meeting place of women at night. The women used to wait for us to return home after our visits to other villages for work. Once we finished our dinner, we all used to sit on our veranda and talk. This was the time I enjoyed the most, because all the women—married, or unmarried, shared their stories, incidents, sang songs and many more. Some of their sharing is quite amusing. We talked on many issues, topics—like their understanding of life, the universe, beliefs, family, and relationship and also about sex! I was surprised to know that women in the village were quite comfortable talking about sex. The funny part was how they communicate with signs and symbols of sexual activities. Some of the stories were so interesting that I would forget to interpret for Tina. Some of their views and understanding of the universe are extremely fascinating. I remember one woman shared about why we have an earthquake? She said, "the *Dhartimā* (mother earth) is carrying the earth on her head, and when she is tired, she shifts the position of the earth, hence we experience an earthquake". They also wanted to know about Tina's personal life and mine, our families back home etc.

The *hāt*

One of the main attractions of the village life was the *hāt* (weekly open market), which we both loved to visit. We bought nearly all our provisions from the weekly *hāt*. Once Tina dressed up like a tribal woman for the *hāt*, so our women friends came home to help her to drape the *sari* in the tribal style and then did a beautiful *khosa* (side bun hairstyle) with her hair. Tina looked beautiful with her tribal costume and it was impossible for her to be unnoticed—a white tall woman in a tribal dress in a *hāt*! Almost everyone giggled at Tina with a sign of appreciation and admiration.

I had the opportunity to visit different *hāt* in different villages. This was an amazing place to see the variety of things that are sold in a huge open area. One can get almost everything in a *hāt*. The villagers bring their produce, cattle, clothes, and many more to sell in the *hāt* and they buy their daily needs from the *hāt*. Women carry baskets on their heads and men on their shoulders with two baskets, like a balance, known as (*kaudi*) walking to the *hāt*—a beautiful view indeed. In no time, the *hāt* becomes a riot of colours with fresh vegetables, 100 per cent organic, traditional snacks, candies, food, clothes, beautiful baskets, lots of country liquor and what not! Children in bright clothes running around with parents and relatives with their own demands to buy; cockfights drawing a huge cheering crowd in another section, it was indeed an intense and happy experience. *Hāt* becomes a real busy place with so many different activities. We enjoyed spending time in the *hāt*. Our friend Hussein used to drive us to different *hāts* nearby in a vehicle. One thing that used to irritate me at the *hāt*, was to see urban men, or people coming from "outside" the region, and living in the village who came to the *hāt* too, as they got everything cheaper. Some of them bargained aggressively and some even grabbed vegetables from the women, in spite of their shouting and resisting, and end up taking more than what they had paid for!

Hāt was also a meeting place for families, relatives, friends and unmarried couples (lovers). The young men were trying to impress their women friends by buying things for them. The most interesting thing, I came to know is that *hāt* is also an important meeting place for young lovers to meet and elope. If a young woman does not return home from the hāt, then it is understood by the family members, that she has eloped with someone she loved. But, scary things do happen for young women at the *hāt,* as men hatch plans to even abduct young women they are obsessed with, or if the girls' family has refused to give their daughter in marriage.

Each *hāt* was unique in its own way. It was fascinating to see the Bondo tribe at the Chatamput *hāt*, especially the Bondo women who covered their body with colourful beads, huge bangles, earrings, and necklaces and a small loincloth! From top to bottom their body was covered with tribal tatoos. Some of them enjoyed sipping country liquor and smoking while they were waiting for people to buy their stuff. It felt like they were the freest women, doing what they pleased because I cannot imagine women, in Koraput town for instance, drinking liquor or smoking in public, or even privately, as drinking and smoking are considered to be immoral habits in urban surroundings or in general among the so-called "civilized" people, at least in India.

This also helped me to understand the role and status of tribal women in private and public spheres and the norms, culture, tradition that is very different from people living in towns. I find the tribal woman quite independent, including economically to some extent. She also has the power and space to do business like a man—when she decides to come out from her home and participate in a public market place—*hāt* with other men. This also gives her freedom of mobility to interact with a wider community. Overall, for me the *hāt* is not only a marketplace, but it's a vibrant space for tribal people for a variety of activities that sustains the tribal economy and enhances the beauty and meaning of village life![14]

Later in life when I became a global coordinator for Women's concerns of a global organization, these experiences in my formative years helped me a lot to understand issues around women's empowerment with a feminist perspective. Though I might not be able to meet again some people who have passed away, but I would definitely love to go back to the village once again to meet those, who once became mine and Tina's friends and family!

Conclusion

The entry into the field is unique for every researcher, though the structure of the fieldwork process as described by Whyte and Watson is similar in every research experience. Memories of the entry and friendship in the field have led to the theme of the volume and our article. Friendship in the field is a personal experience and distinct from working relations, although overlapping sometimes. A researcher might form bonds of friendship with people in the field on different levels, as mentioned above:

(a) On a academic level,
(b) With the people met in the field,
(c) With the research assistant as the daily companion.

Every community has specific normative ideas on friendship which may only partially coincide with the researcher's concepts. For Sunita it was unusual that a person who is a few years older and from a different cultural setting would address her, and be addressed, as a friend. The use of first names, indicating friendly equality, deviated from her own social norms that drew regarding hierarchy based upon age and status.

In the village we were incorporated into the kinship system which is the general method of assigning a social position. In addition, different forms of amity structure benefits and obligations. We were able to construct formal as well as informal forms of friendship with girls and women, whereas those with men were to remain on a formal basis. At the same time, the closest of all bonds was out of question for us, the one known as *moitr.*

The formal ties that enhanced our research began in M, when we became members of the age-set of unmarried Kond girls. A second link of this sort was the *mafsad* bond of the *Mali* community in M, the only possible door-opener in the local concepts of hospitality. In P and other villages, where we observed the Bāli Jātrā, a month-long ritual and epic conducted by women, we became *bāliphul*-partners of some selected households, and this 'flower-bond' implied being hosted and fed at anytime. Within the household we were living, we became kin. The same form of integration applied to the old *disaris* (healers) we had been visiting. After some time, when being invited into their houses on a regular basis, they would address us as daughters or granddaughters.

Through Sunita her German employer became a friend of all of her family members. The others have also been involved in my work and their house has become a home for me. After fieldwork with Sunita, her sister Sushmita substituted her and her brother Sunny cooperated with me for almost fifteen years involving different projects in various parts of Odisha. The family members were a part of any regular research activity. Their friendship, along with that of Deepak Kumar Behera as a general guide, has been invaluable.

Notes

1. The authors would like to thank the entire Suna family as well as Bidyut Tuna Takri and family who have always helped in various ways. M. D. Hussain facilitated the entry into the field. Many villagers of the Koraput district have been very helpful. We thank our friends in Satsemli, Lamada, Hanjar, Bardel, Burdiput, Jeypore and Koraput and Disari Kotelel, Disari Guru Maji and Somari Maji, Guru Darli and Disari Mangala Pujari. We are especially grateful to the families we lived with: family Guru Maji and family Guru Pangi.
2. *Vide* for gender issues in field research Warren (1988).
3. The members of the research group in this place we call Chatamput were Peter Berger, Elisabeth Conzelmann, Lidia Guzy and Tina Otten. Later Uwe Skoda and Christian Struempell joined, just as Ulrike Blindt and Roland Hardenberg of associated projects turned up occasionally.
4. *Vide* Struempell (2008) on the Chatamput relations.
5. Many of us were involved in research for their Ph.D. theses which were later published in English such as Peter Berger (2007), Lidia Guzy (2004), Tina Otten (2007), Uwe Skoda (2005) and Christian Struempell (2008).
6. *Vide* Tanka Subha (2009) on this subject.
7. *Vide* in this context the work of Pfeffer (e.g. 1996, 1997, 2004).
8. Otten (2007, 2009, 2010).
9. The word is derived from *mahāprasād*, the sacred food of Jagannath, who is the "Lord of the Universe," in the huge temple of coastal Puri.
10. The most valued ritual friendship is called *moitr*. A *moitr* is a person of one's own sex but of a different community, having distinct social and financial obligations at life cycle rituals and on other occasions.

11. This form of friendship is connected to a ritual, described by Sunita Suna below. The text of a similar ritual is jointly published by Chris Gregory and Harihar Vaishnava (2003).
12. On a broader scale, Adams (1999) deals with the role of the mascot researcher and the effect this role had on her access to information.
13. This is the general term for the indigenous population.
14. *Vide* Gell (1992) describing a tribal market in neighbouring Bastar.

References

Adams, Laura L., 1999. "The Mascot Researcher: Identity, Power, and Knowledge in Fieldwork", *Journal of Contemporary Ethnography,* 28: 331-363.

Berger, Peter, 2007. "Sacrificial Food, the Person and the Gadaba Ritual System", (pp. 199-221) In G. Pfeffer (Ed.), *Periphery and Centre: Studies in Orissan History, Religion and Anthropology.* New Delhi: Manohar Publishers.

Carsten, Janet (ed.) 2000. *Cultures of Relatedness: New Approaches to the Study of Kinship.* Cambridge: Cambridge University Press.

Gell, Alfred. 1982. "The Market Wheel: Symbolic Aspects of an Indian Tribal Market", *Man, 17* (3): 470-491.

Gregory, Chris and HariharVaishnava, 2003. *Lachmi Jagaar.* Kondagaon: Kaksad Publications.

Guzy, Lidia, 2004. "Babas and Alekhs—A Religion in Its Making", *Journal of Social Science, 8* (2): 105-111.

Hardenberg, Roland, 2005. *Children of the Earth Goddess: Society, Marriage, and Sacrifice in the highlands of Orissa (India).* Post-doctoral Dissertation. Münster: Westfälische Wilhelms-Universität.

Otten, Tina, 2007. "Given from God and Come in its Own Will: The Hierarchy of Illness Causes among the Rona of Tribal Orissa", (pp. 173-197). In G. Pfeffer (Ed.), *Periphery and Centre Studies in Orissan History, Religion and Anthropology.* New Delhi: Manohar Publishers.

——2009. "King, Tribal Society and Fertility in Koraput: Different Aspects of the Ritual *Bāli Jātrā*", (pp. 33-51). In Georg Pfeffer and Deepak Kumar Behera (Eds.),*Structure and Exchange in Tribal India and Beyond.* New Delhi: Concept Publishing Company (P) Ltd.

——. 2010. "The Concept of *Biba* among the Rona of Highland Orissa: Wedding Rituals to Ensure Health", (pp. 143-161). In Berger, Peter and Roland Hardenberg (Eds.), *The Anthropology of Values. Essays in Honour of Georg Pfeffer.* Delhi: Pearson.

Pfeffer, Georg, 1996. "The Young and the Junior Set in Tribal Middle India: On the Category of Age", (pp. 98-109). In Georg Pfeffer and Deepak Kumar Behera (eds.) *Contemporary Society: Childhood and Complex Order.* New Delhi: Concept Publishing Company.

——. 1997. "The Scheduled Tribes of Middle India as a Unit: Problems of Internal and External Comparison" (pp. 3-27). In Georg Pfeffer and Deepak Kumar Behera (eds.) *Contemporary Society: Tribal Studies.* New Delhi: Concept Publishing Comapny.

——. 2004. "Order in Tribal Middle Indian 'Kinship'", *Anthropos*, 381-409.

Skoda, U., 2005. *The Aghria: A Peasant Caste on a Tribal Frontier*. Delhi: Manohar Publishers.

Strümpell, C., 2008. "We Work Together, We Eat Together: Conviviality and Modernity in a Company Settlement in South Orissa", *Contributions to Indian Sociology*, 42(3): 351-381.

Subha, Tanka, 2009. "Group Fieldwork. Revisiting an Old Anthropological Practice in India", (pp. 487-506). In Berger, P., Berrenberg, J., Fuhrmann, B., Seebode, J., & Strümpell, C. (Eds.), *Feldforschung. Ethnologische Zugänge zu sozialen Wirklichkeiten. Berlin: Weißensee.*

Warren, C.A., 1988. *Gender Issues in Field Research* (Vol. 9). Newbury Park, CA: Sage Publications.

Watson, C.W., 1999. "Introduction: The Quality of Being There", (pp. 1-14). In: Watson, C.W. (ed.) *Being There: Fieldwork in Anthropology*. London: Pluto Press.

Whyte, William Foote, 1984. "Planning the Project and Entering the Field" (pp. 35-63). In Whyte, W.F. (Ed.), *Learning from the Field: A Guide from Experience*. Beverly Hills: Sage Publications.

SEVENTEEN

CLOSENESS AND DISJUNCTURE:
On Friendship in the Field

(FOR ORI, JOMNA AND SAMO)

PRTER BERGER

Introduction

In May 2001, shortly after I had completed the main part of my fieldwork and returned to Germany, I visited a friend and his partner in Berlin. I had spent 21 months in the field studying the rituals and society of the Gadaba of Odisha in India. I was still immersed in the impressions and experiences I had undergone there and was perhaps, mentally, still in the field rather than back in Germany. My friend's partner was a determined and outspoken woman, and as is common shortly after my return, I narrated some events related to my fieldwork and described some experiences with my Gadaba 'friends'. My friend's partner commented, somewhat ironically, how I could call them friends, based on the nature of our encounter they hardly could be that. My friend rebuked her for what he probably considered to be rude behaviour and the issue was not discussed any further at that time.

Although, I probably would not have acknowledged it then, this comment hurt me. After having invested so much time and energy in the establishment of social relationships, after living with the Gadaba for so many months, this was not what I wanted to hear. At the same time, in the very moment she said it, I also felt sure that she was right, at least in a way. The aim of this contribution is, therefore, to unearth and spell out these ambiguities concerning the possibility of making friends in the field. It is written to pay tribute to Deepak Kumar Behera, a true friend of us all who work in Odisha.

Friendship in Western Cultures

As I was writing this paper while travelling in Odisha and was offline for most of the time, I asked my friend and colleague Sarbeswar Sahoo in New Delhi to check the definition of 'friendship' and 'friends' for me in Webster's Dictionary. 'Friendship', he read to me from the website, "would entail friendly feelings or attitude, kindness or help given to someone, acting like a friend, showing interest and goodwill, serving a beneficial purpose".

This characterization of 'friendship' instantly struck me as poor. What about loyalty, trust, love, a history of shared experiences, what about mutuality? After all, as Sahlins (1965) reminds us, friendship is as much the product of gift-giving, as gift-giving is a consequence of being friends. This bloodless Webster's definition did not mirror the relevance and value of friendship in contemporary European societies (and elsewhere). Popular culture and literature are full of accounts that testify to the idea of friendship as a relationship which is pure and uncorrupted. The story of Harry Potter, to name just one well-known example, is to a significant degree about the power of friendship. Lord Voldemort is powerful and feared but he is without love and without friends.

I would argue that the sanctity of friendship in Western societies is derived, to a large extent, from individualism as a value, with the notions of freedom and agency being derivatives of the value of the individual (Dumont, 1986). From this perspective, friendship is more important than kinship, because friendships are entered into voluntarily rather than being the result of prescribed relationships. Unlike filiations and siblingship, friendship is based on choice, and it is also different from matrimonial relationships insofar as friendship is not formalized and is without legal implications. Of course, we are supposed to and usually do love our parents, siblings, spouses and children, however, the value of friendship is based on the notion of a 'free gift' and thus beyond the networks of social obligations and rights. The notion of *communitas* may also entail some aspects of what we consider relevant in friendship; that is, a social space where human beings meet as humans and equals outside the ascriptions of social status and roles (Turner, 1969: 94-130; 1974: 274).

Of course, this is an ideal and one which regularly leads to disappointment. As Mauss (1990) has shown, the notion of the free gift is a cherished illusion, and gift-giving is never completely free of mutual obligation. Similarly, friendship does not exclude expectations of reciprocity and personal interest and may also involve asymmetry. However, even though reality does not always live up to the ideal, this does not reduce its power.

Although, there may be a certain agreement in European societies as to what friendship is, there are certainly variations and differences in emphasis. Without doubt, we cannot expect 'friendship' to be a universal category or have a constant meaning through time and space. In highland Odisha, for example, I found friendship, but little 'friendship'.

Friendship among the Gadaba

Among the Gadaba of south Odisha, where I have conducted a total of more than two years of fieldwork since 1996, friendship is not elaborately conceptualized. In order to show this it may be compared to the concept of brotherhood. Every individual is part of a multilayered agnatic network, a network of brothers (*bai*). Each member of a village is part of one of the unit of 'four brothers' (*chari bai*)—the four agnatic groups that constitute the village—but is also one of the 'twelve brothers', primarily an idea of the totality of Gadaba society. Furthermore, every person, as part of a local group is related to another collective as sacrificial food brothers (*tsorubai*). In addition, one's local group engages in a specific relationship with another one, a relationship called *panjabai* (meaning of *panja* unclear). While the former brothers reciprocally cook and feed sacrificial food, the latter, also reciprocally, at different times, eat the spirits of the dead in the form of water buffaloes during death rituals. Moreover, such relationships *between* villages are considered to be senior, while those *within* a village are regarded as junior. Therefore, brotherhood is a complex cultural idea that structures social relationships prescribes forms of social interaction and exchange depending on the context, is the key to ritual practice and is constantly a topic for discussion. 'Friends', on the other hand, are simply called *sango*, they are ritually invisible, socially irrelevant and rarely the topic of discourse.[1]

In the literature, an institutionalized relationship that is found in many Central Indian societies has frequently been called ritual 'friendship' (e.g. Mohanty 1973, 1974 for the Gadaba). Perhaps these relationships are called this because they usually exist outside or beyond structures of affinity and descent and may also involve members of different communities. However, the Gadaba do not refer to these relationships as *sango* but as *moitor* and they do not relate *sango* and *moitor* in any way. Consequently, I find the designation of 'friendship' in this context to be unhelpful for the reasons outlined below.

The Gadaba distinguish between *sada moitor*, *bai moitor* and *koloj moitor* and they have only one Gutob word that designates the latter and most important relationship, *dissel*. The 'plain' (*sada*) *moitor* refers to a relationship between households of different communities. For example, the Gadaba household in which I lived maintained such a relationship with a family of horticulturalists (Mali) from a different village. Once a year the Mali would visit the Gadaba and exchange, next to general courtesies, some vegetables for rice. On this basis, the Gadaba referred to this relationship as *dalsag isap*, "about lentils and vegetables". 'Brother' (*bai*) *moitor*, also generally have little significance, although such brothers are eligible to receive some of the buffaloes in a *goter*, when (as mentioned above) these animals represent the dead and are distributed amongst external agnates (*see* Pfeffer, 2001; Berger, 2010).

The concept of 'liver' (*koloj*) *moitor*, finally, designates a relationship that the Gadaba consider 'most senior' (*sobutu boro*). This relationship permanently connects local Gadaba groups that belong to different clans (*bonso*). The 'liver' *moitor* do not exchange brides and cattle, as affines do, nor buffaloes and stone plates, as agnates would. Instead, they revere each other. One of the many rules that regulate such a relationship is that one should always give to a 'liver' *moitor* and should never demand anything. This comes close to the ideal of the 'free gift' as discussed previously. A local story (*katani*) narrating how one village of the cobra clan and a village of the tiger clan (to be more specific, segments of these villages) became *koloj moitor*, illustrates this dimension. The cobra went to the river and drank all the water that was there. After a while the tiger came along and found the river empty. The cobra noticed the distress of the tiger and vomited up some of the water so that the tiger could drink. In that way they became 'liver' *moitor*. 'Liver' is the organ that (along with lungs and blood) is associated with the life-force of animate beings. *Koloj moitor*, this story shows, are a matter of life and survival—the cobra saved the life of the tiger by giving it water without being asked.

From our perspective, the idea of the 'free gift' implied in the story, one without any expectation of a return, fits with our notion of friendship.

However, the other aspect—that one should never ask the *moitor* for anything—rather does not. Surely friends can be asked for a favour without feeling shame. In practice, this rule of excessive free giving/not demanding leads to a situation whereby the 'liver' *moitor* avoid visiting each other's villages because such visits can cause stress for the hosting party and are potentially embarrassing, for example, if the beer is not ready or liquor is nowhere to be found. While there are some elements that may qualify this *moitor* relationship as friendship from our perspective (being outside the kinship structure of agnation and affinity, or generalized reciprocity), others clearly contradict our view of friendship, particularly the high degree of formality (not mentioning each other's names and not demanding anything, for example).

In sum, firstly, it is the question if, or to what degree, our understanding of friendship corresponds to the Gadaba view. Secondly, the local notion of 'friendship' is probably hardly related to, certainly not the same as, the idea of *moitor*; finally, I would argue that while the Gadaba maintain a concept of friendship (as the linguistic categories surely indicate) it is not of great social or cultural relevance as almost every kind of social relationship between the Gadaba is conceptualized with in the framework of brothers (*bai*) and affines (*bondu*).

Becoming Friends not 'Friends'

As everyone knows, going into the field means beginning socially as a *tabula rasa*. Integration into the community in which the anthropologist lives usually follows a series of similar stages. My Indian colleagues have told me that when they go into the field they are often initially classified as a tax collector, a government agent (e.g. from the forestry department, *foresti*), or a member of an NGO. Most anthropologists from Western countries are at the beginning perceived as tourists or missionaries—it was the former in my case. Of course, these representations soon prove to be inadequate when the ethnographer stays on and shows an interest in things that no tourist or government employee (but probably some missionaries) would ever care about. I have described elsewhere (Berger, 2015: 531f) how my status changed and with it the ways I was addressed: from *foren*, *agiya*, *sir*, *saibo* to the rather vague notion of *bai* (which indicated a certain common ground in this case) and then in the framework of kinship terminology after my partner arrived.

We were married in the village and our social positions subsequently became very specific. Once again, the notion of '*sango*' or 'friend' never became relevant. Although I made friends, the idiom of the relationships was provided by the kinship structure, with its fundamental division into agnates and affines. The following section is about these friends and the qualities of the relationships concerned. How can we possibly identify and grasp that one person or another has become a friend?

On Closeness

I would argue that the initial situation of an ethnographer in a new field is very fertile ground for friendship. The complete lack of local knowledge, language, social identity and the level of dependence make the ethnographer a kind of nascent being who has the potential to develop a new kind of sociality.[2] Even if an adult, you are a person in the making. Given this situation, I think it is the process of mutual learning that makes friends. Although, this is not the only ingredient needed to develop friendship, it is, however, a crucial one. In certain field situations, there are particular individuals who dedicate themselves to helping the newcomer understand things and who are willing to share something of their world. Often they become the closest friends.

Samo Sisa of Gudapada was such a person. Although, I did not live as part of his household initially—I first lived in the house of one of the two Gadaba villagers who were involved in a small-scale local tourist business—Samo was seriously interested in 'the foreigner' from the start, not as a trophy, like my first host, but as a kind of teacher. We were about the same age (I was 29), although he already had four children, the youngest of which was perhaps three years old when I first came to Gudapada in early 1999. In those first months, it was mainly Samo who showed me the sacred places in the hills and in the village, explained the different kinds of fields and the history of leasing them to one house and then another, and he also taught me how to participate in the death rituals properly (and in other rituals). Samo also pointed out the practical things I needed to know in a place without electricity and toilets. He also convinced his father—a widower living alone in a house close to Samo's—to share his house with me when I returned for a second time and stayed in Gudapada for a year. His father, Rogu, agreed and we became house mates. I moved into the small mud house, Rogu slept on the veranda (covered by the low roof).

In addition to the experience of mutual learning, two key aspects necessary for friendship to develop are commensality and conviviality. When I returned to the field after that first brief stay, I found myself at Samo's house, sharing the food his wife Jomna prepared day in and day out for 19 months in total. I believe that eating everything that was offered to me and not looking down on their culinary practices of consuming beef and alcohol (as outsiders usually do), created its own kind of intimacy. Sharing all of those meals, as well as drinks, chatting, joking, laughing, listening to the neighbours fighting and witnessing local domestic conflicts in turn, all contributed to the developing friendship.

My relationship with Samo started to change at some point, which I cannot clearly determine, it was a gradual process. He increasingly drew away from me and began answering my questions with 'How do I know?' more and more often. Perhaps he was bored with answering all of my questions (and the longer I stayed the more I had), or perhaps he had expected something else from our relationship that did not materialize (perhaps financially or otherwise). Surely he had also noticed that my relationship to Jomna had also changed and that we had become friends as well.

Friendship is, of course, gendered. Standardized joking is part of the relationship between eBW and HyB—the way our relationships was classified as—, and Jomna and I joked a lot. During the transplantation of the wet rice, for instance, it is customary to engage in a mud fight. Potentially, everyone can be a victim, although some people are usually avoided—for example, the MB (*mamu*), while others are especially targeted, such as the HyB/eBW. Hence, Jomna sought to plaster me in mud and *vice versa*. She also often made fun of me due to one or another of my many inabilities, such as being slow to learn Gutob, the Munda language (which only the Gadaba speak, next to the ubiquitous Desia, a dialect of Oriya).

After I had been in the village for a year, Jomna squeezed my arm and said: "There is much love between us, is not there?"(*Amor bitre besi premo, ki nai?*). She was right, although I only became fully aware of it once she had said it. In contrast to her husband, Jomna was not the teacher-friend Samo had been. In fact, I learned very little of Jomna in any explicit way. I never conducted an interview with her; she did not tell me Gadaba stories (*katani*); and I do not recall asking her to do so. However, the countless comments on village affairs and our conversations while sitting close the hearth were invaluable in a different way. In Jomna's case, these exchanges of a quotidian nature became the basis of our friendship.

In addition to Jomna and Samo, I made other friends in Gudapada, the closest, however, being Ori. He was about the same age as Samo, also had four children, and his house was located between mine and that of Samo and Jomna. Shortly after I had settled into Rogu's house, Rogu was Samo's father and Jomna's actual mother's brother), the relationship between Ori and myself developed quickly. While I have mentioned learning, commensality and conviviality as important aspects of friendship in the field, in discussing my relationship with Ori I will now focus on understanding, events (i.e. shared experiences) and trust.

Ori was an ideal partner in the field because he liked to roam around and had a genuine curiosity. Moreover, he liked to socialize and have a drink. We went to countless villages together on all kinds of occasions, and wherever we went there was some kind of affinal or agnatic connection that could be established with our village. "My *ata* (FZ) lives in that village", or "let's have a drink in my *banja's* (ZS) house" he would say. Significantly, he never mentioned to have any 'friend' in a village. I can still hear his voice, as he regularly stood outside my house in the early mornings shouting: "Get-up, we have work to do" (*ut, kam ochi*). Gradually, he came to understand what I was doing like no-one else. He knew what I was at during a conversation with another informant, noticed when I had misunderstood something or my interlocutor did not grasp what I was trying to say. Different aspects of social structure are, for example, a matter of practice for the Gadaba, and when talking about these matters abstractly many interlocutors confused different levels of social organization. In contrast, during the process of our interaction, Ori began to see the institutions and practices of his own culture with different eyes, as if he were observing them for the first time. Therefore, he was developing an analytical eye himself. In fact, several times I had to stop him during conversations with other Gadaba, as he was too quick to steer them in the 'right' direction. We became a perfect match.

This mutual fine-tuning of our perceptions occasionally turned into a complicit experience shared only between us. For example, we had been staying in a village where a secondary funeral (*goter*) was being held. Ori had brought my binoculars along, which I hardly ever used—in contrast to my camera, which was a constant companion. At that time, there were still many people who could not recognize someone's face in a photograph; sometimes when I showed them photographs people held them the wrong way up without noticing. In short, most were unaccustomed to photography and therefore could not tell the difference between binoculars and a camera. Being aware of this, Ori organized a fake group photograph session, holding the binoculars in his hand. For ten minutes or so, peering through the binoculars, he ordered people around, "stand here", "get closer to her", and so forth, and people would follow his orders. He was hilarious, glancing at me every now and then. He concluded the performance with the comment: "Oh, I'm sorry *reel sorigola*", "the roll is finished".

Events are very important in ethnographic fieldwork. Certain events which I have called Key Emotional Episodes (KEE, Berger, 2010) involve the loss of behavioural control on the side of the ethnographer and, instead, entail spontaneous action, as well as an emotional interaction between him/her and the social environment. KEEs, I argued, have effects on the level of social relationships. Depending on the situation, KEEs can lead to a further social integration but also to the social exclusion of the ethnographer. If reflected upon they provide important insights into the position of the field worker in the local community. Moreover, they can point out (or confirm) important themes and values of the community concerned, that is they also can be important tools for understanding. Strangers can play important roles in such KEEs, but certainly friends can and do so regularly, on the one hand because one simply spends so much time with them, on the other hand because the relationship is already emotionally marked and intense situations are likely to occur (including conflicts). In the episode, I discussed in detail in the contribution on KEEs, when I pushed a crowd of villagers out of my house, at least Jomna, perhaps also Ori and Samo had been involved. My marriage in Gudapada was certainly an event; however, it was not a KEE, as everything was controlled and highly regulated (I have written about this elsewhere, *see* Berger, 2015: 531f). All three, Ori, Samo and Jomna, were, I assume, vital in initiating the marriage and they were among the key figures who organized the ritual process. However, no one danced as enthusiastically as Ori.

Many other important moments occurred during our trip to what the Gadaba still call 'Assam'. I had heard a lot about the teagardens, where Gadaba have been working since the early years of the twentieth century. Many had gone to Assam as young men and later returned home, some had stayed, and some had been born there and had never visited Koraput. Those who had returned home could be recognized by their command of some Hindi or English orders, for example, rhythmically shouting "one-two, one-two". After I had completed the research for my Ph.D., I wanted to visit the area to learn about the life of the Gadaba in the plantations. Of course, I wanted to take Ori along, as his older brother had been living there for at least fifteen years and still does. As well as Ori, I also asked Samo to come along and, together with my field assistant, Manto Pradhan, we embarked on the long train journey towards the north of West Bengal, at the foot of the Himalayas. On the train, an incident occurred, which all of us referred to many times afterwards.

We were in the second-class sleeper compartment—I sat next to the aisle, Manto was beside me and Ori and Samo were at the far end on both sides of the window—when some *Hijras* entered the carriage. Ori and Samo had never seen *Hijras* before and were probably a little scared but, of course, also curious. In any case, they did not know how to handle them. They pretended to stare out of the window, while keeping one eye on what was going on inside the carriage, noting the obscene gestures and speech of the *Hijras*. Manto had encountered them before and pretended to be asleep. Consequently, I became their main target. The *Hijras* approached me in the usual way, though gradually they became more persistent. For some reason, I did not feel like giving them money and the more they pressured me the less willing I became. Finally, I pushed a *Hijra* sitting next to me with my leg so that she fell into the aisle. She jumped to her feet again and I closed my eyes just in time, avoiding seeing what she revealed as she lifted her *sari*. By that time Ori and Samo had both eyes turned towards the scene. Later on, Ori clapped his hands in the *Hijra* way over and over, rocking with laughter while recalling the event. For me, the situation had some long-term effects that I have discussed briefly elsewhere (Berger, 2014).

Finally, trust is the basis of many kinds of relationships, but certainly of friendship. Ori came to trust me and *vice versa*. For example, after I had lived in Gudapada for many months, Dalima, a woman with whom I had a very friendly relationship too, asked me if I was aware that the whole village was talking about my presumed affair with Ori's wife. I told her truthfully that I had not heard about this and that it was ridiculous. She said she had assumed that this was the case, however, she thought that I should know about it. After that conversation I was seriously alarmed and I feared this rumour could ruin my relationship with Ori. How should I discuss this with him? What evidence did I have to prove these allegations false? Who was the source of these rumours? (I had some suspicions, though I never found out). I decided that the best thing was to talk to him directly. Nervously, I told him that I had to talk to him and called him into my house. He sat down and listened to what I had to say. At the end he merely said, "Ah, that's nothing, just gossip" (*gopo sopo, au kichi nai*), and that was the end of the story.

Overall, given the parameters I have discussed above, I think that Ori, Jomna and Samo truly became my friends. However, the relationships were all very different and they developed and changed over time. All three were very close to me, although, after I left there was a radical disjuncture and our lives developed very differently, and at different speeds, or so it seemed. In contrast to the aspects of closeness and friendship, I have discussed thus far, I will, therefore, in the following attempt to explore the aspects of distance and disjuncture that also characterized these relationships.

Disjunctures

Making friends is one thing, maintaining friendship quite another. There are some obvious differences in the life-worlds of ethnographers and their friends in the field, or, between the people of a place and their ethnographer-friends. For example, in my case, these differences included language, formal education, physical skills and economic status. These can all be overcome in a process that involves mutual learning, commensality and conviviality, trust and shared experiences, as I have mentioned. There are, however, some severe challenges to the possibility of remaining friends. Among these are asymmetry in the participation in each other's lives, muteness and different temporalities. I will address these dimensions in turn.

Since the beginning of my fieldwork—and I am sure this is an experience shared by many ethnographers—I have suffered from the inability to properly explain my life-world to my friends, which to a large extent was beyond their comprehension. It was like attempting to explain what water is to someone who has never seen, touched or tasted water—it remains pure theory. At the beginning, almost everyone was interested in the price of all kinds of things in Germany, a kilo of rice, a *lungi* ('Ah, you don't wear *lungis*?') and of my personal belongings, like my watch. Those who became my friends were usually much more curious, so they would try to imagine the nature of water nonetheless. They asked about marriage, relationships between men and women, marriage, about house construction and agriculture. Earlier in this chapter, I mentioned Ori's objectification of his culture as we increasingly interacted in my attempt to understand Gadaba society. In turn, his questions about my culture also became increasingly specific. However, explaining my world remained a task I felt I did only accomplish poorly. When my daughter was born and later my sons, I had a strong desire to take them to Gudabada. On reflection, my desire to introduce my children to the Gadaba (and *vice versa*) was partly due to compensate for the asymmetry in my relationships with them. Thus far, for various reasons, the visit has not eventuated.

This asymmetry in actually participating in each other's lives became more reciprocal as the intervals between my visits became longer. I had been visiting the village in all the years between 1999 and 2004. However, there was a six-year gap before my next visit in 2010 and then another six years passed before my visit in 2016 (two weeks ago as I write). Therefore, important changes occurred without me being present and which I only found out about later.

What exacerbated the lack of participation in each other's lives was the impossibility of communicating during the periods of my absence. Most Gadaba men and women of my age cannot write, and those who could (like Samo) were not in the habit of writing letters. Even if they would have been, it would have been difficult for me to decipher their hand-written letters (which would have been written in Oriya script). Today, telecommunication would be an option, but not so then. During most of my research, I had to drive for almost an hour to get to the next town to call my family and spend astronomical amounts of money (by local standards) to do so. I can still envisage the stunned faces pressed up against the window of the telephone shop, watching the cost of the call (electronically displayed for all to see) rise higher and higher. For a short period before mobile phones made them superfluous, STD/ISD telephone shops emerged in the small administrative town only a few kilometres away from the village—I had seen the Gadaba and other locals digging the trenches for the cables. The place where the telephone booths were located was also the location of the Saturday market (*hāt*) that the people of Gudapada visited regularly. So after my return to Germany, I called the man in the telephone shop and asked him to find Ori or Samo, saying I would call back in ten minutes. If he could not find them, he would bring someone else from the village to talk to me. These conversations turned out to be rather disappointing, for both parties I guess. Everyone knows it is difficult to start a conversation after a time of absence. Moreover, my friends had no experience at all with making phone calls—they would hardly say anything and I would constantly have to reassure myself that they were still on the line. To make matters worse, my Desia conversation skills were not improved by speaking on the phone and after long times of not talking in that language. In short, I quickly abandoned these attempts as they only testified to muteness in the presence of a friend. Consequently, we remained silent for years.

This muteness led to very mixed feelings when returning to Gudapada. I expected that some things would have changed, and they had. Both times that I visited after a long absence, in 2010 and 2016, I found a local community in fast-forward mode, at least in certain obvious ways, such as house and road construction, the material culture of everyday life, electricity and school education. Also, I became aware of the fact that there is a certain lack of synchronicity in the development of life-cycles. As I mentioned above, Samo, Jomna and Ori were approximately my age, although much further advanced in their lives, in terms of having a house, children and a life filled with responsibilities. When I first lived with them as a Ph.D. student, I had little else on my mind (and on my shoulders, I now realize) other than research. Moreover, due to the hard physical work Gadaba engage in everyday, as well as bad or non-existent healthcare and considerable consumption of alcohol they age quickly. A man or woman of 45 is old, one of 60 ancient. What added most to my anxiety, of course, was the fear that someone very close to me might die. Sadly, my worst fears always came true.

Upon my arrival in the village in 2010, just ten metres from her house, I was confronted with the news that Jomna had poisoned herself. This was a blow that made me feel numb for the whole day. With Jomna's death, the whole domestic situation had changed. The former kitchen was no longer used in that function, it then (in 2010) served as a kind of lounge for the youth of the household and now (in 2016) as a garage and storeroom. This was because Jomna's daughter, who had taken on the duty of cooking for everyone, refused to do so on the old fireplace her mother had used (*see* Berger, 2015: xiii f). For her children, and for Samo (who had lost his mother under similar circumstances, i.e. suicide), Jomna's death must have been traumatic. For me, it meant a certain sense of dislocation in the village, which has never been the same since. In many ways, the kitchen, more than my own (read Rogu's) house next door, was the nodal point of Gudapada.

Unfortunately, female suicide in this region is an all too common phenomenon—Dalima had poisoned herself as well, and we also witnessed another case in the village—and in attempting to understand it, I was reminded of Renato Rosaldo's (Rosaldo, 1984) efforts to unravel the meanings of headhunting among the Ilongot. I came to understand that it essentially amounted to an ultimate act of revenge in the context of a domestic conflict, which in most cases was between a husband and wife. The only explanation I ever was provided with was that the women had been angry and then killed themselves. This seems to be a very drastic step to take, particularly given the agonizing way the death usually takes place (by drinking insecticide) and the fact that marriages can be easily dissolved and new partners sought (in comparison to the Hindu context, in any case).

Another six years later, in 2016, I was standing in almost the same place after entering the village, as Ori's and Samo's sons came to greet me. Within a few seconds all was said."Is Ori at home?", I asked—it was after the harvest time, when the men often went on labour trips for a few weeks. "He died", his younger son replied. In 2010, Samo had gone to Bhubaneswar to prepare the Adivasi Mela, so I asked, "Is Samo here?" His son replied—"He too has died".

Samo had been diagnosed with tuberculosis at the hospital and—partly a result of his constant alcohol consumption, people said—he never recovered. The circumstances of Ori's death, however, are unclear. He had gone to cut wood with another Gadaba from the village and most people said the trunk they were cutting must have slipped and hit Ori in the chest. However, the person who accompanied him, denied this version, suggesting that after eating something, Ori laid down to rest and simply died in his sleep. As with Jomna, he had died outside the village—this was thus a 'bad death' that required the sacrifice of twelve animals in order to prevent the enraged spirit from attacking family members. Although, the people in Gudabada have stopped sacrificing cattle in the context of death and marriage generally, and now rarely eat beef, such a bad death makes the sacrificing of cattle still necessary.

At the time the sons were telling me about their fathers'death—just as, six years earlier, when I had heard about Jomna's suicide—I felt an acute need to mourn, although I had no means to do so. All the death rituals, which occur within a year after a death, had been completed. I had attended many death rituals, but had missed those of my three friends. I did not even know that they had died. What kind of friendship could that possibly be? Sometimes, when people are away from the village or are not able to attend the death rituals, upon their first visit to the village they will go to the cremation ground. Women will mourn loudly, while men will just quietly leave some rice and beer for the spirit. In both cases, in 2010 and 2016, this did not occur to me. Perhaps this was because there are no reminders of the people cremated there—de-individualization is part of the process of death—just a heap of white ashes and the remains of former rituals. Moreover, no one reminded me to do so either. Perhaps, one day, a *goter* will be held in the village and Samo, Jomna and Ori will be given away as living buffaloes to agnatic groups from a different village. If I am lucky and can be present, this could be a moment of final farewell and closure.

There are still many people in Gudapada with whom I can share memories of past events, and whenever I visit this inevitably happens. Just this year, the *pujari* of the village showed me a scar on his thumb—*china*, meaning significantly both 'scar' and 'memory'. "Do you remember?" he asked. I did not, although I had treated his wound sixteen years earlier after he had chopped his thumb with an axe. However, the three people with whom I had spent most of my time are no longer there to share memories. This produces something like a compound past. Not only are the events a thing of the past, the people I experienced them with have passed away too. Memories are thus no longer part of an active discourse and have become something like artefacts. The past becomes a foreign country one can no longer travel in. Certainly, this is not specific to friends in the field. However, the nature of the life-world of the Gadaba and the various twists of fate that occurred in the lives of Ori, Samo and Jomna, created a situation whereby this disjuncture opened up all too early.

***

Perhaps making friends in the field is no imperative: one can imagine ethnographic contexts in which friendships are absent. Good ethnographies could be written that are based on research in which friendships played no role. However, it is certainly possible that relationships in the field can be based on real sympathy and love, as anyone can learn by reading Piers Vitebsky's wonderful new book on 40 years of engagement between the ethnographer and his Sora friends (Vitebsky, forthcoming). More than being merely a possibility, making friends in the field is highly likely because of the nature of the ethnographic encounter and the anthropological project in general.

For our first-year students in Groningen, I regularly summarize my view of what anthropology is about in three words—*understanding through difference*. Anthropology challenges the general assumption that the different is difficult and the familiar is easy to understand. The initial impulse behind understanding through difference is curiosity—to encounter something 'strange' or 'exotic'. Usually, the common response is to leave it at that, which may lead to prejudice, racism and xenophobia. Anthropologists take this initial moment of not-understanding further. Based on the assumption that, when a real effort is made, and only then, the long-term and systematic encounter with cultural difference called ethnographic fieldwork can produce significant insights into the relative position of one's own 'common sense' and partial comprehension of another life-world.

Making friends in the field is, I think, an almost necessary result of this sustained effort and is probably due to the initial situation in which ethnographers, new to the field, will find themselves. Some of these conditions are quite profane and surely selfish. One wants to discover something that is not self-evident and for which one has to build relationships based on trust. One wants a degree, to write a book or find a job—not really altruistic motives. During the process, however, the curiosity I mentioned above resonates with a few individuals in the new social environment. They then take-up the challenge of mutual learning, which inevitably means spending a lot of time together, doing things together, participating in different kinds of events together and jointly transforming these into shared stories afterwards. The result is friendship; not a free, disinterested gift, but a gift nevertheless. This friendship, the product of constructive difference, moreover, entails *likeness*, with the word 'like' significantly entailing both resemblance and affection. While Ori and I liked each other, during the process of fine-tuning our perceptions and partially synchronizing our ways of thinking, we were not only representatives of our different cultures, we also became more like each other.[3]

Furthermore, I have shown here that the relationships we would categorize as 'friendship' are in fact quite different—depending on the personalities involved, the gender of the participants and on the contingencies of the situations. The ways in which my friendships with Ori, Jomna and Samo were initiated, the features they developed and how they evolved through time were very different. I could add another friend here, Domru (who figures prominently on the cover of a book, Berger *et al.*, 2010), whose friendship with me was, yet again, different. He was much less of a roamer than Ori, less of a drinker than both Samo and Ori, and he engaged less intensively in the project of mutual learning, yet we still became friends. In 2010, I had found him in an awful health condition, whereby he could no longer use his arms. Attempted ritual healings had produced no improvement, so I took him to Koraput town, where they gave him medicine and also demanded that he stay for two to three weeks of physiotherapy. I knew he would not stay, and he did not, partly, I think, because of the condescending way he was treated there. When I came back to Gudapada after a few days away from the village, he was back sitting on his veranda, unable to do anything and somewhat remorseful as he had fled from the treatment. This was how I left him in 2010. I was much relieved to find that by 2016 he had recovered and I watched with delight as he climbed his sago palm tree.

Ambivalence is the predicament of ethnography and anthropology in general—perhaps stemming from the fundamental and creative tension between oneself and the other. The encounter with difference not only produces closeness, it also produces disjunctures. Here, I have focused on three aspects of disjuncture: asymmetry in participating in each other's lives, muteness, and distinctive temporalities in the way life-cycles develop. The premature deaths of my three friends and the fact that I did not know about their fates and could not attend their funerals, emphasizes all three of these aspects.

Why write about all this? Should one write about all this? Demystifying ethnographic fieldwork and understanding the processes that are involved in this very particular kind of academic activity is a process that is going on for decades and is likely to be with us as long as there are anthropologists engaging in these kinds of encounters. I think that discussing features of friendship in the field can be an important contribution to the aim of "participant objectivation" (Bourdieu, 2003). Fieldworkers should be honest to themselves, to their readers and the people they write about (who more and more often are their readers as well).

Perhaps the tone of this contribution has been a bit bleak due to the recent news of Ori's and Samo's deaths. I am, however, very grateful for the friendships that I 'found' in the field.[4]

Notes

1. There are other words in the languages of the region that designate friendship, although I did not personally come across these to any relevant extent. Dictionaries translate *moitor* or *mahāprasād* (*maphsad*) (see the discussion that follows) as 'friend' and lists *mit* or *mitro* (*mintana, mintani* being the male and female forms respectively), *ikala, songita* (*song lok*), *sneho, soina*, as denoting 'friend' or 'friendship'. The term *got* is also mentioned, but in my experience *got* refers to 'relatives' only (see Gustafsson, 1989; Mahapatra 1985; Malten n.d.). Goud's *Gutob Dictionary* (Goud, 1991) lists *bulon* as 'friend', and Battacharya's *Remo, Dictionary* (Remo being the language the Bonda speak, which is very close to the Gutob of the Gadaba) lists the terms *banai lok* for 'two friends' and *moitor* and *bai lok* for 'friend'. The latter in my view rather literally means 'brother people' or agnates.
2. As I mostly speak of my experiences in this contribution I will often use the male form and only will be gender neutral in some places.
3. Ori's mother once made a comment in this regard after I had behaved in a way her son sometimes did (*see* Berger, 2010).
4. I want to mention two more non-Gadaba friends I made in the field. M.D. Hussain was a local village guard in a township on the border between the Bonda and Gadaba areas. He was there to greet me when I first arrived at Koraput as student in 1996, and he later became the driver in the Orissa Research Project. He was a complete exception in that township as he had intimate and regular contact with people from the tribal villages that surrounded the place, with nearly all other inhabitants being ignorant about or arrogant towards (mostly both) the tribal people at the fringes of their settlement. Hussain's great interest in and deep sympathy for the tribal people inevitably led him to meet Georg Pfeffer—in the context of a *goter*, I think it was—who was visiting the area before anyone else among the contributors to this volume. Without the culture-broker Hussain all of us working in Koraput would have had a much more difficult start. He also died too early. My other friend, Manto Pradhan, has already been mentioned above. We lived together for more than a year in Rogu's house and he shared many of the experiences mentioned in this contribution (and many more). He too became a general supporter of all those ethnographers who work in and around Sambalpur.

References

Berger, P., 2015. *Feeding, Sharing and Devouring: Ritual and Society in Highland Odisha, India*. Boston & Berlin: De Gruyter.

Berger, P., 2014. *Moving Encounters, Shifting Doubts*. Contribution on occasion of the retirement of Yme Kuiper. Unpublished.

Berger, P., 2010. "Assessing the Relevance and Effects of Key Emotional Episodes for the Fieldwork Process", (pp. 119-43). In: D. Spencer and J. Davies (eds.) *Anthropological Fieldwork: A Relational Process*. Newcastle upon Tyne. Cambridge Scholars Publishing.

Berger, P., R. Hardenberg, E. Kattner, and M. Prager, 2010. (eds.) *The Anthropology of Values: Essays in Honour of Georg Pfeffer*. New Delhi: Pearson.

Bourdieu, P., 2003. "Participant Objectivation", *Journal of the Royal Anthropological Institute*, 9: 281-94.

Dumont, L., 1986. *Essays on Individualism: Modern Ideology in Anthropological Perspective*. Chicago: University of Chicago Press.

Gustafsson, U., 1989. *An Adiwasi Oriya-Telegu-English Dictionary*. Mysore: Central Institute of Indian Languages.

Mahapatra, K., 1985. "Desia—A Tribal Oriya Dialect of Koraput Orissa", *Adivasi*, 25: 1-304.

Malten, T., n.d. *Desia Dictionary* (complipation of Gustafsson, 1989, Mahapatra, 1985 and own data). Unpublished.

Mauss, M., 1990. [1925] *The Gift: The Form and Reason for Exchange in Archaic Societies*. London: Routledge Publications.

Mohanti, U. Ch., 1973/4. "Bond-Friendship among the Gadaba," *Man in Society*, 1: 130-55.

Pfeffer, G., 2001. "A Ritual of Revival Among the Gadaba of Koraput," (pp. 99-124). In H. Kulke and B. Schnepel (eds.), *Jagannath Revisited: Studying Society, Religion and the State in Orissa*. New Delhi: Manohar.

Rosaldo, R., 1984. "Grief and a Headhunter's Rage: On the Cultural Force of Emotions." In E.M. Bruner (ed.), *Text, Play, and Story: The Construction and Reconstruction of Self and Society*. Washington DC.: American Ethnological Society.

Sahlins, M.D., 1965. "On the Sociology of Primitive Exchange", In: Banton, M. (ed.): *The Relevance of Models for Social Anthropology*. London: Tavistock.

Turner, V., 1974. *Dramas, Fields and Metaphors: Symbolic Action in Human Society*. Ithaca: Cornell University Press.

Turner, V., 1969. *The Ritual Process: Structure and Anti-structure*. Chicago: Aldine.

Vitebsky, 2016. *Loving and Forgetting: Changing Forms of Loss and Redemption in Tribal India*. Chicago: University of Chicago Press.

EIGHTEEN

GETTING BYE WITH A LITTLE HELP OF A FRIEND

The Ethnographer's Dependence

GEORG PFEFFER

I

Special courses teach anthropology students to enter and cultivate a 'field', as if standardized methods, comparable to laboratory procedures, could be executed in a social context. The point is to avoid armchair reasoning, though some of Malinowski's suggestions with regard to participant observation (1929) were unrealistic in his own days and a even more so in the post-colonial epoch. During any research effort, contingencies are important or the major reason for success or failure, as I hope to demonstrate in the following.

In the days of *pax britannica* researchers could choose a people from one of the many colonies and engage in the unrestricted study of "Primitive Society", then the object of the discipline. Local conditions might be uncomfortable or even dangerous, if the 'natives' were non-cooperative, but certain privileges could outbalance some of these hardships. In the 'remote' Koraput district of Odisha, for example, Verrier Elwin, the most prominent authority on tribal India, was protected by policemen during his fieldwork among the local Bondo (Elwin, 1950). Another leading ethnographer of this 'field' during the 1940s, Christoph von Fürer-Haimendorf, recalls in his autobiography (1990), that he had the blessings of several leading executives of British India, among them the viceroy. He also mentions "His Most Exalted Highness", the Nizam of semi-independent Hyderabad, who financed the ethnographic publications of the Austrian, the latter being his 'special advisor'. Occasionally both Elwin and von Fürer-Haimendorf mention their servants who seem to have facilitated life during the respective field-excursions of these dedicated anthropologists and their wives.

By December 1980 conditions had changed. The bus service that was to take me on the serpentines of the steep mountain barrier from coastal Andhra Pradesh up to the plateau was on strike, so, the cockpit of a truck, filled with six or seven passengers, served as a substitute carrier to Jeypur, the small but major town of Koraput. The twelve-hour journey witnessed the rather unusual accommodation of a confident young businesswoman on my lap and this proximity had a certain side effect. Her only luggage was a fresh fish measuring about a metre. On the next day each one of the passengers smelled like a member of the coastal fishing caste, though my scent was perhaps the most noticeable.

To continue the journey for another five hours, an ancient bus took me from Jeypur across the holes of a so-called road to the Lamptaput crossing on the very top of the plateau. On any day, the advent of the two scheduled buses was the major attraction of this place[1], though three or four brick buildings appeared in the background. In the self-made tent of an immigrant shop-keeper one could expect a meal, if one turned-up around seven p.m. to sit on bare ground and harbour modest expectations. My research assistant from coastal Odisha, in a concentrated effort to find a place to sleep for us, was finally successful in the new primary school which was one of the brick buildings, the others being assigned to the Block Development Officer. By a stroke of luck this BDO happened to be a benevolent outsider, so the two newcomers received an unexpectedly warm welcome. As a tribal Santal from northern Odisha, this representative of the Indian state had fallen in love with a Gadaba woman, abducted and married her as is customary in all tribal communities, and become a respected associate of the indigenous people. The family of Mrs. BDO had not been displeased by developments and was keen to take us to a first extended chat with palm-wine and friendly people around the evening fire in the centre of a Gadaba village.

As we had hoped, these hosts had relatives everywhere, so the next two weeks were spent hiking to several Gadaba and Parenga villages, where delightful inhabitants welcomed the two outsiders, as we happened to arrive in the season of little work and frequent festivities. Some of the dignified elder men covered their upper bodies with second-hand blazers of German origin while keeping the traditional loin-cloths on the lower parts. Having worked as indentured labourers in the tea gardens of Assam, they took charge of affairs and saluted me in the military style due to a 'Sahib' (European director) of these tea plantations. However, their ways of communicating, like those of all other Gadaba, were far from submissive. Compared to *homo hierarchicus* in the lowlands, such a self-assured personal conduct remained as my major impression of the entire excursion. One could remain at ease. Before more extended ethnographic endeavours my aim had been to get a preliminary idea of local conditions, and they turned out to be attractive.

The second excursion to Koraput was less strenuous. A ten-seat aircraft of a newly founded airline took me from Odisha's coastal capital to Jeypur by flying just above the treetops of the extended forest with a bird's view upon many different but uniformly structured settlements of the tribal Kond. The flight was a marvelous experience. During the only stop en route, the pilot carefully checked the engine while servicing the entire plane. Six months later, I read about its crash and the death of all passengers, resulting in the termination of the air line. On my tour, I could take advantage of quasi-colonial privileges, since a leading administrative officer of the province happened to be a personal friend. His message to the Collector[2] of the district had the effect that a jeep took me from the airport to the Collectorate and further to a Governmental 'Inspection Bungalow' (IB)[3] at a small housing colony called Machkund right in the centre of Gadaba country.

All officers, including my personal friend, were obviously astonished to find a senior female student as my only[4] company on this tour and all were obviously trying to hide their profound amazement, having learnt by innumerable tales that 'the West' was ruled by moral disorder. The local policemen, on the other hand, were highly irritated, when the two Westerners, on arriving at the IB, chose to settle separately in the two rooms that made up the building. On one of the subsequent days, however, the Germans had to sleep (or attempt to) in the same chamber, as the other one was required for an official meeting of several officers who apparently had good reasons to celebrate.

On the day after our arrival, a local policeman dutifully informed us about a grand secondary funeral to be celebrated in a certain Gadaba village. All of these ritual events must be supervised by at least two constables, since homicide cases are not very unusual on such occasions. Moving to the site in a police jeep certainly worried me, because I did not want to be identified with the representatives of the government, but the issue remained insignificant. Whenever they wanted, the two constables were provided with a chicken or two along with sufficient hard liquor to put them to sleep. During the subsequent three days, they did not appear on the scene. Of the many assembled Gadaba, most married males and females were either tipsy or drunk. They had more than sufficient music, food and drink and communicated in a spirit called 'effervescence' since the classic work of Emile Durkheim (1912/2001). On the third day, a crowd of about a thousand people, all in an exalted mood, made it necessary for the two German anthropologists to retreat into the bushes of a nearby hill. Any close-up observation, leave alone participation, would have been impossible.

The assembled youngsters had not indulged in drinking. From the distance we watched them dancing day and night on the circular threshing floor. As a long line of females and males with interlocked shoulders they continued as a whole while displaying beautifully concerted snake-like movements, or so it seemed. Without interrupting the dance, individuals constantly joined and left the line in motion, while musicians of the client category[5] performed as drummers and pipers. After some time, Klaudia, my senior student, repeatedly remarked "look at this clumsy policeman making a fool of himself among the graceful dancers".

The only non-tribal dancer was not a policeman. On the third day this man in an odd uniform made a shy introductory effort. Hussain was the name and he was employed as a local aid of the police, a 'village guard' of the government, on 15 days of a month for a miserable salary that included the official *kaki* clothes. In fact, good-looking Hussain was not a bad dancer, though he certainly could not compete with the easy stride of the Gadaba youths. To my knowledge, this man was the only non-tribal in the region who communicated decently and sympathetically with any of his tribal counterparts. In the following week he invited us to his house.

II

At this point, reference to the history of this southernmost district of Odisha is required. In the days of Elwin and von Fürer-Haimendorf, the entire Gadaba country was without either roads or lowlanders. Wheelcarts were unknown. as oxen could carry the grain in sacks on their backs.[6] However, a year before Indian independence, a dam began to be constructed to close the valley of the river Machkund at the major cañon for a huge hydro-electric project that filled vast artificial lakes[7] in later decades and provided electricity for coastal towns and cities. Due to this venture, a connecting road of some 40 km was built from Lamptaput to the construction site in the wilderness, just as workers, engineers, technicians, administrative officers, policemen and an IB entered the scene. A settlement of about 500 miscellaneous lowlanders[8] arose next to the huge new barrier of the river. Hussain lived in this place which, following Strümpell (2006), I shall call Chatamput.

Like all new settlements raised by the government, this one contained houses of four or five different 'classes' with Hussain's of the lowest category or, in material terms, as a room built of tin sheets on bare earth without a processed floor. A small kitchen section was added on its side. For ten identical houses of this kind the common tin-walled latrine with an open drain made-up the centre. Receiving us at this home, Hussain displayed a natural kind of dignity that he always retained in conversations with neighbours and relatives, women and children, officers and *kulis*. Base language or false compliments never passed his lips. His wife fixed some rice and vegetable curry which we consumed in customary style by sitting on a piece of linen on the floor without a glance at the rats crossing the room now and then. Somewhere in the building, in the sole bed or below it, Hussain also housed four sons of different characters. The eldest of 14 years was shy and responsible, while the next one was the rebel and Ghulam as number three had to look after Salim, the youngest, who was spoilt by all.

In the course of this dinner, Klaudia and I learnt that our host was also a watch-maker and a radio mechanic to earn a few Rupees on occasions. Any kind of technical job was his domain. His father had driven trucks for the project until the day, when—in a state of advanced drunkenness—he crushed against a tree and died. They belonged to a caste of lowland Telugu craftsmen, also involved in petty business, and they are derogatively known as 'Pathan' in the region, though all they have in common with the leading ethnic unit of Afghanistan, called by this name in colonial English, is their Muslim faith. Probably their religion is not of the most profound kind. Hussain observed the annual Islamic festivals but, at the same time, took us to the shrine to inform us of his passionate devotion to Batamangala, the goddess of the roads. Indeed, he paid great respect to any kind of sacred site, tribal or not, and celebrated together with Hindus, Christians and Buddhists among Chatamput's workers, who came from all regions and communities of the subcontinent.

Cynics would also note two other observations. One referred to Hussain's addiction to alcohol which did not agree with his miserable wage and his duty to feed a family. If, however, he hiked to a tribal village, as he liked to do, he was sure to receive a welcoming drink on every veranda he approached, because ordinary visitors are always offered hospitality among the Gadaba, the Rona and most others. The second point concerned tribal crimes. Policemen were frequently transferred and the writ of the state had only recently become a relevant factor on the plateau. None of these lowlanders really liked the idea of looking into affairs of the despised indigenous population, or of visiting a village once in a while. By hiking to and reporting on the tribal homes of the neighbourhood, Hussain was a known asset of the officers and had an opportunity to receive the meager 'daily allowance' for such trips.

Among the proletarian population of lowland workers and the assembly of grocers, liquor vendors and pimps of Chatamput, Hussain had less delicate duties. My regular obligation to report at the lone police station of Machkund every week forced me to observe once, how my new acquaintance beat up a suspect, thereby following the detailed orders of the commanding sub-inspector. In the 'civilized' districts all-over India police-stations witness such actions as a matter of daily routine, just as policemen are taught these practices in regular police training courses. Usually, the tribesmen of the plateau are not manhandled, since in such cases[9] their 'brothers' are known to retaliate. Also, tribal crimes are of a different kind.

Hussain was our chief informer in this matter. He insisted that theft and rape, blackmail and robbery were unknown among the many indigenous people of southern Odisha. Among the Gadaba insults or physical controversies were neither reported to nor persecuted by the police. Privately he had occasionally come to know of a manslaughter case among members of this particular tribe, but all involved parties, be they police, culprits, or victims, did their best to hush up such incidents. By contrast the neighbouring Bondo are given official attention. Their homicide rate is ranking among the highest in the world (*see* Pfeffer, 2008) causing the number of their female population to be twice as high as that of their males. Any of these rather short-grown hillmen would, after killing a man[10], send word to Hussain who would hike to the culprit's village; have a drink with him, allow him to bid farewell to the family and escort him to Chatamput, where the Bondo would be provided with an evening meal and a corner to sleep on the floor in Hussain's house. On the following morning, the village guard would take the killer by bus[11] to Koraput jail, where the culprit would normally serve a term of five years, if the deed had been committed without extraordinary cruelties.

After listening to these accounts during our initial contacts we concluded that Hussain was personally familiar with Gadaba country and also a respected man with numerous contacts. Furthermore, he belonged to the few people in India who enjoyed walking long distances off the beaten track. Thus for expenses and an additional monthly salary, he could introduce Klaudia and me, or other students of later excursions, to the tribal people of the Koraput plateau.

Soon after we concluded this contract, we wanted to shift from the IB to a Gadaba village, so our guide right away took us to one and introduced us to his friend, a newly wedded young man. The latter had just personally built and decorated his colourful one-room house. He volunteered to take us to the girls' dormitory and ask its three inhabitants to shift into the home of widow so-and-so. For a moderate rent they would let their little mud-construction to the two tall-grown foreigners. With night approaching, it soon became clear that my physical size—along with someone else—would not fit into that house built for a few Gadaba girls, but the veranda was long enough for the rucksack and me in the sleeping-bag on the aluminium-mat. Hussain, as usual on his tours, covered himself with his pseudo-police overcoat. For that night, Klaudia and he arranged themselves in the interior without major problems. Our guide had been too polite to question the two Europeans about their relative status, but a few weeks later, when taking them to his sister's family he introduced them as brother and sister. The information was greeted with respect and accepted by everyone else during our subsequent stay, though anthropology students of the 'kinship' sub-discipline would need time to understand such a classificatory construction.

Hussain's brother-in-law, who himself did not touch alcohol, had the job to provide the higher officers of the hydro-electric project with 'foreign'[12] liquor or beer at night and probably other disreputable services for the representatives of modernization. Our guide was also blessed with an identically looking twin-brother named Hassan, also a non-drinker. Whenever the latter rode along with us on the same bus, he would remain in the rear, whereas Hussain would stay with us in the front. The two brothers hardly spoke to each other and never exchanged a word in the company of non-relatives. In my German anthropology classes, they figured as the standard example of what is known as "avoidance relationship" in the discipline. Occasionally, I ran into Hassan on my own on roads and markets and then the conversation moved directly to the ordinary topics of an alert young man meeting a rich European. I was asked whether I had and would sell cameras, binoculars, tape-recorders or the like.

Hussain never touched such themes. In Chatamput he made it a point to introduce me to M.N. Rao[13], a veteran Congress trade-unionist, for whom he officially served as a security man, though in practice the two met several times on a day at a liquor din behind the front row of the bazaar. Rao threw a three-person dinner for me to recount the Congress luminaries he had known. At times he gave an account of his competition with the other two trade-unions of Chatamput and their joint struggle with the project officials. Hussain also knew, when someone had died in the region, or a bear had attacked a person, or the Maoist army of the so-called Naxalites had passed through a village.

In the subsequent years, I spent mid-February to mid-April on the plateau in Hussain's company, each time taking along one or two students, among them clever young Markus who was stationed in a Didaye village of Andhra Pradesh just across the provincial border. His host was an old shaman whose sons, after a day's hike, would occasionally visit the weekly market of Chatamput to sleep in Hussain's house. In another state and beyond police control[14], Markus had a good time harvesting, hunting and dancing with his hosts, or participating in shamanic sessions as well as elopements and marriages. For the farewell party at the end of his stay, I bought two goats in Chatamput. For the whole day they hobbled along with us downhill all the way to Andhra, crossing the border-river in a dugout canoe, before being slaughtered for the feast. When this event was about to take place, a new problem had to be solved. Hussain had carried along the butcher's kit borrowed from an elder brother and made it clear that he was the one to cut the necks of the goats in Muslim style (*ziba*), to let all blood of the animals ooze out, before the meat could be consumed. The villagers, on the other hand, thought this method of slaughtering to be a frivolous waste of food. After about an hour's debate I suggested that, while Hussain would be executing the butchery, the blood could directly flow into a pot, so that the Didaye might boil and consume it with rice in their usual fashion, whereas the Muslim would not taste the forbidden substance. By that time everyone was hungry enough to agree to these terms and the farewell feast turned into a delightful event.

In spring 1996, the students brought two bicycles from the coast, fastened along with the luggage on top of the bus for the three-day journey. We wanted to be independent of the only two daily buses commuting in Gadaba country and also to increase speed and range of the many cross-country excursions to the numerous village festivities of the season. On the narrow road cutting through the mountains a jeep driven by young lowlanders would sometimes—for the sake of their amusement—deliberately press the two pedalling Europeans to the brink with only a few centimetres remaining before the steep gorge of the river Machkund opened. When we mentioned these incidents to Hussain or his police superintendent, the two were duly disgusted but unable to act, since the young men who used and owned a jeep in the region were its real political leaders[15] or the sons of such 'big men'.[16]

With the new millennium our work in Koraput and our relationship to Hussain changed considerably. In a major research project several young anthropologists were to conduct long-term fieldwork in the region rather than, as had been the earlier routine, appear in the spring months to leave when temperatures ran high. Instead of the meager internal means of a university institute, we now had a special budget to be spent on studying the tribal complex in Koraput for six years. Given these new obligations, we needed a field-office, but renting a house in Chatamput proved to be extremely difficult, in spite of the fact that many people were known and well-disposed to us. But they were not the proprietors of buildings. The huge hydro-electric project of two provinces owned the houses. Its officers were in no position to sign rental agreements. The alternative idea of constructing a meeting-point of several Europeans in a tribal village was too absurd to be considered. After an extended search and under considerable stress we finally did manage to rent a large but very modest one-room building with a tin roof, which earlier had served as a store and was one of the few private constructions in town. Only through Hussain's good services we obtained this depot that could be used for an occasional night-halt.

After difficult transport operations, we could also bring a lockable metal cupboard, called 'almira' in colonial English[17], in which valuables such as camera equipment could be deposited. Each one of the German doctoral researchers would usually live in a different village and occasionally join the others at Chatamput for a conference or the writing up of field-notes. Since Hussain had retained the habit of inviting any outsider for a meal, the expatriates would at times stay for supper at his house. Very soon, however, they noticed a certain coincidence. Whenever they had rice and vegetable curry at Hussain's, burglars broke into their building, stole a few things and vainly tried to open the steel almira by force. Though the foreign residents improved the quality of the locks on doors and windows after each one of these experiences, the unknown miscreants[18] were always clever enough to find an entry.

Initially, the coincidence was too embarrassing to be mentioned to Hussain, the generous host, but after its regular repetitions the topic could no longer be avoided. Living at the end of the only road in the wilderness, we did not want to start playing thief-and-cop on our own. Irrespective of the result, such a venture was bound to lead to more embarrassment. In the vicinity of mostly single men who had moved in from all corners of the subcontinent, village guard Hussain was rather familiar with petty crime, especially with theft and burglary. He knew that any person on the adjacent bazaar road was in a position to observe, how the conspicuous Germans left the house for a visit. Accordingly, Hussain's skills as a detective were challenged and proved immediately. In next to no time, he identified his older sons and their cronies as culprits which of course led to extended thrashings in public, even though non-violence had been the urgent request of the European visitors. In case the material damage had been worth mentioning, their own negligence should have been taken into account as well.

The major change of our activities, i.e. substituting regular annual excursions by an official long-term research project, had to have its effect upon Hussain's status. As a poor man he had been most helpful in several essential measures of our work. A considerable raise in pay appeared to be only just as well as a matter of enlightened self-interest. However, German bureaucracy was to be taken into account. Any kind of regular employment needed a proper job description. Being a Telugu speaker, Hussain's minimal English and simplistic Oriya ruled out any formal job as interpreter or the like and the position of 'man for all seasons' would not be recognized by the German Research Foundation. Thus, we concluded that driving our new jeep would be the most adequate work for him, even though our friend did not possess a driving-licence, whereas each one of the German researchers carried one along, though only some of the—otherwise confident—young anthropologists were willing to expose their skills to the vagaries of Indian traffic on the so-called roads or cross-country on the plateau. Hussain's best qualities were those of creating contacts and communicating with local people of any kind, but we also needed someone to keep an eye on our posh new jeep, when we ourselves were involved in participating and observing.

As expected, Hussain produced a new driving-licence within a few days and since any kind of machinery was his daily bread, nobody had to teach him, how to operate the vehicle. The problem was his style of driving. As was usual, the beginner who mastered the technicalities of an automobile had to test his skills as a racer. Whatever may have caused our man's craving for speed, all of his European passengers felt that sharing a ride implied mortal dangers. As the senior spokesman, I had to complain day after day. Such a routine in the course of a few weeks caused Hussain to become aware of the problem. He chose a more moderate pace during the first twenty minutes of a drive, though in due course of time, or when he had had a drink too many, the old instincts returned. The only way to solve the dilemma was to relegate our motoring expert to the passenger bench on most of our rides, even though this meant that some of the less adventurous German licence-holders had to shiver through the feat of taking over the wheel.

In 2003, an extended drive witnessed a somewhat dramatic interlude. Tina Otten, her Indian assistant Ruby, and I were to take the jeep and its official driver from the southern to the northern tribal area of Odisha, or travel some 500 kilometers on what was euphemistically known as 'highway'. About half the distance, with most of us dozing and delighted by the view of the high Kond hills with waterfalls breaking through lush green forest, a big bang interrupted our peaceful progress. Involuntarily and disorderly we came to a halt. The petrol tank and several other mechanical members of the jeep family had decided to proceed on their own. Minutes later, two Kond tribesmen in loin-cloths appeared from the bushes uttering nothing but the international password "oh!" to depart swiftly.

In those olden days, mobile phones were unknown in rural India and the next auto-repair station would in any case be found only beyond a radius of a hundred kilometers or two, so we had to solve the problem on our own. As the first major task, a cloth was spread at the road-side where the ladies, by then calming down, could rest with the senior researcher for a picnic. Then our official driver took a good look at the damage and, collecting the smaller bits and pieces that had been dispersed, told us that outside help was required. About every 20 minutes a huge truck touring through India would bring life into the loneliness of the jungle highway and perhaps Hussain knew the secret code of the truck-men or displayed the unique symbols of the drivers' tribe, since the first one of these dinosaurs took him along after a very short verbal exchange. The weather was fine and the picnic unit could discuss much of anthropology, before we first heard, and then saw, an approaching moped with Hussain on its rear saddle. The cheerful owner ran a two-wheeler repair station in Bissamcuttuck, a small town at a distance of 30 km. Soon the two men descended under the remains of our jeep and after yet another hour or two, I noticed that our friend and colleague was now inversely positioned with shoulders on the ground and the soles of his feet facing the sky. The load lifted by his legs was the petrol tank. They had raised the heavy container and Hussain balanced it in the air, while Mr. Moped was reuniting the big box with the vehicle by fitting most of the screws, nuts, bolts, hooks, and clamps earlier lost in operation. Only as a boy had I seen such a spectacular athletic feat and only in the comics of our newspaper. A permanently masked character known as "Phantom" had been my childhood hero, who used to remove big rocks from the openings of caves in such an upside-down position. In the Kond hills of Odisha, for the first and only time in my life, I could admire a live performance of such a task. Not so much later we could continue our journey. I asked the local mechanic for his fee and added a tip to the 30 Rupees (or some 50 cents) he had demanded. After about two hundred metres back on the road, his moped overtook us with a laughing driver waving his goodbye. He too had the heart of a racer.

In 2005, our project in Koraput came to an end and we had to leave Hussain and his family. About a year later, a letter informed us of his demise. His liver had ceased to function. The strong, good-looking man of about forty years had for ever left his many friends. A deep sense of remorse overcame me, because his relatively high income during the last years of his life had not improved the conditions of his family but had certainly raised his daily intake of liquor. Before we parted for good, Hussain had given me a small green plastic piece in the shape of a heart, to be tied to my key-bundle. On it was written in Arabic script the name of the most compassionate and merciful. Sometimes I look at it.

Notes

1. Meanwhile, the crossing has grown into a bustling bazaar town of lowlanders. Peter Berger (2014) enumerates the different schools and colleges, just as he found an excellent new road during his visit of 2016. Within an hour many buses arrive and depart.
2. Since the early British days the Deputy Commissioner (or "Collector") is the little king of a district. He combines executive, judicial and legislative powers with those of "collecting" taxes and is responsible for economic development. In a 'remote' rural district, his position is even more exalted than in an easily accessible one. According to Peter Berger (*pers. comm.*) he takes over the role of the king in the royal ritual of Jagdalpur (in the neighbouring district of Bastar) and elsewhere.
3. The word 'IB', like innumerable other administrative abbreviations, is a standard term in rural India.
4. No Indian research assistant accompanied us then.
5. Everywhere in middle India the so-called weavers work for the tribal cultivators as craftsmen and petty commercial agents. They also play some, or all, musical instruments during the ritual performances (*see* Guzy, 2013).
6. The site of these load-carrying animals, still customary in the 1980s, is very much in my memory.
7. The flooding of the land brought disaster to many tribal owners who remained without compensation. I cannot touch this subject here.
8. A detailed ethnography of the industrial settlement is provided by Strümpell (2006).
9. I have described such individual occurrences (*see* Pfeffer, 2008).
10. Non-Bondo tribesmen are in the habit of avoiding any kind of contact with these 'fierce people'. Bondo are not known to hurt females.
11. All bus drivers knew Hussain who got a free ride on any occasion.
12. All-over India the expression 'foreign' stands for the bottled drink rather than the self-made brew of the locals.
13. I have forgotten the exact initials. Innumerable Telugu Mr. Raos decorate their name with two or three capital letters without ever revealing the full identification.
14. These Didaye live just across the river Machkund that separates Odisha from Andhra Pradesh, though a high mountain range segregates their villages from the rest of their province. Accordingly, the police of either state are unconcerned about them.
15. In these "reserved constituencies" tribesmen compete in elections as "dummy candidates" of the businessmen hailing from the lowlands. These politicians do not have the best reputation, though it is not as foul as that of their respective sons.
16. A Bondo woman usually marries a man who is her junior of five or more years.
17. The Arabic word is perhaps loaned from Spanish. I do not know how it reached India.
18. This term is frequently used by Indian journalists, but I have never read it in a British or American newspaper.

References

Berger, Peter, 2014. "Dimensions of Indignity in Highland Odisha, India." *Asian Ethnology,* 73 (1): 19-38.

Durkheim, Émile, 2001. (*French org.* 1912). *The Elementary Forms of Religious Life.* (Translated by Carol Cosman and Mark Sydney Cladis) London: Oxford University Press.

Elwin, Verrier, 1950. *Bondo Highlander.* Bombay: Oxford University Press.

Fürer-Haimendorf, Christoph von, 1990. *Life among Indian Tribes: the Autobiography of an Anthropologist.* Delhi: Oxford University Press.

Guzy, Lidia, 2013. *Marginalised Music: Music, Religion and Politics from The Bora Sambar Region/Western Orissa.* Bern Berlin: Lit Verlag.

Malinowski, Bronislaw, 1929. *The Sexual Life of Savages in North-western Melanesia: An Ethnographic Account of Courtship, Marriage and Family Life among the Natives of the Trobriand Islands, British New Guinea.* New York: Halcyon House.

Pfeffer, Georg, 2008. "Bondo Violence", (pp. 69-92). In: Carrin, Marine and Harald Tambs-Lyche (eds.), *People of the Jangal. Reformulating Identities and Adaptations in Crisis.* New Delhi: Manohar Publishers.

Strümpell, Christian, 2006. *Wir arbeiten zusammen, wir essen zusammen "Konvivium und soziale Peripherie in einer indischen Werkssiedlung*". Berlin, LIT.

INDEX